The complete book of

HOME DESIGN

The complete book of

HOME DESIGN

MARY GILLIATT

LITTLE, BROWN AND COMPANY
BOSTON   TORONTO

LIBRARY OF CONGRESS CATALOG CARD
NO. 84-81171

FIRST AMERICAN EDITION

Original room designs created by Mary Gilliatt and illustrated
by Ross Wardle/Tudor Art Studios

Special photography by Jon Bouchier and Jessica Strang

Published simultaneously in Canada
by Little, Brown & Company (Canada) Limited

Printed in Italy

CONTENTS

Every other room in the house—kitchen, bathroom, bedroom, dining room—has its own fixed function that to a certain extent dictates the arrangements within it. The living room is the only one that does not at least partly arrange itself, which makes it, of course, the most taxing on the imagination. It's the one room that has in some way to accommodate the changing interests of all members of the family; it's also the room that is most on show, the room where your guests stay the longest.

Since a living room is literally the room for general living it often has to serve as a study, playroom and dining room as well and still manage to reflect your tastes and be a comfortable extension of your personality—or personalities. Everybody, including the family pets, should be able to stake a claim in the living room and feel thoroughly at home there. So how do you set about decorating it for all its possible different uses? How do you make it a room that is as pleasant to live in as it is to look at? Should comfort come first, or practical considerations, or style? Or can all three be happily reconciled?

Any decorator asked to help design a room for a client would start by asking certain obvious questions. You must do the same. Ask yourself: What sort of life do you lead? Do you entertain much? What are you going to use the room for—sitting, talking, reading, listening to music, tv, parties, cards, hobbies? Will there be people of different ages all doing separate things or do you go in for family activities or both? Do you possess any furniture, furnishings or equipment already that will need taking into consideration? If so, do they need altering, adapting or re-vamping? Re-covering perhaps, or re-painting to fit in with their new circumstances? Are you starting from scratch or just hoping to re-style an existing room?

The answers should help you to keep a realistic grip on your decorating ideas and these should be as flexible as possible. An idea isn't wonderful if it doesn't work. If you've set your heart on some specific feature—say, white carpet—and find it's not feasible or practical or that it's too expensive, then look sensibly at the alternatives and find a less impossible compromise. Furniture should be versatile enough to suit different needs and situations which might well change over the years. Surfaces—floors, walls, upholstery, table tops—should be practical so that you're not constantly worried about spoiling them. The arrangement of the room should be as efficient and convenient for several people moving about as for one person sitting reading. Above all, it should be as physically comfortable and relaxing as it is easy on the eye. So try not to be too rigid or too carried away; a happy balance will help the general feel and atmosphere of the room in the end.

Any room is easier to plan, decorate and arrange if you imagine it divided into three basic parts: *the background*—walls, ceiling, floor, windows and lighting; *the furniture and furnishings*; and *the accessories* —the personal possessions that will give it personality and character. The background provides the framework; get this right and the rest will follow. And take comfort from these two decorating truths, confirmed by much experience: that too perfect rooms are as boring as too perfect people, and that most successful decoration is the result of successful elimination.

A comfortable, relaxed and stylish room in which shape, colour and texture all play their part. The accessories, lamps, ornaments, tablecloths, cushions, echo the colour and pattern of the walls, curtains and chairs.

7

Faced with an empty room what do you do first? You have a long, hard think about it, because it's a great mistake to simply accept or adapt to whatever space you have, however cramped or awkward it is, without questioning whether it's right for you. So, long before you rush into the basic decoration and furnishings you must first of all make a proper plan of the room and its needs and then work out how best to spend what money you have.

Think, plan, budget

Obviously there are certain key factors to any sort of reasonable living space: walls and ceiling will have to be decorated along with all the woodwork; windows and floors have to be treated in some way; there must be light both to see by and to enhance the space; there should be something to sit on and probably to eat from and almost certainly somewhere to work at times. Finally there are the decorative accessories like pictures and ornaments and the entertainment equipment—books, stereo, tv, records, tapes—for which there must be storage space.

So the next step is to write down everything that you consider ab-

solutely essential to an ideal furnishing/decorating or renovating scheme. Not the frills; they can come later. Then cost it all out and work backwards from there seeing what you really can afford—and can afford to be without. The total sum might give you a shock but will also help you to be more ruthless at the start and put changes into effect.

Work out a budget

A realistic budget will do three things for you: it will sort out the urgent essentials from the details which can wait; make you feel good if you manage any or all of it at a lower price than your original estimate; and inspire you to improvise, to consider if you could achieve an equally good effect and still fit in with what you can comfortably afford. This way you'll not only get more personality into the room but you'll also go more slowly, giving yourself more time to think around problems.

Problems of size and shape determined the look of these rooms. Right, mirror, wicker and old pine give a casual feel to a smallish space, while left, low shelves and cool colours smooth out an awkward angle.

STARTING FROM SCRATCH

Learn to make lists

Once you are sure of your priorities start to make lists. Write down any repairs that are needed and/or any alterations you think desirable. Transfer to paper any thoughts or suggestions on how to treat the walls, the floor, the windows. Think about what sort of lighting you're going to need and how you can achieve it. If the space is very small and you want to enlarge it, put down all the possibilities. Can your furniture be made to serve several purposes? How is the room going to be heated? How much or how little storage do you need?

Start off with a basic check list along these lines; then you won't leave out anything important.

Fill in details about the present state of the room in the first column; then what you would like or propose to do about it in the second, and finally, in the last column, what it's going to cost you. Date the list and keep it in a file. If you have to compromise, change your mind or adapt an idea, make a new list, date it and file it so that you end up with a master check list that is a complete record of the whole procedure. With everything committed to paper you're less likely to forget details and it will help you tackle the situation in a very or-

ganised way. You'll also see how ideas progressed and developed as well as how much they cost.

When to spend, where to save

Once you have a clear idea of the essentials you can decide where to compromise and where you must make an investment. Again, make haste slowly because you won't get everything right first go off. Some things are going to have to last you a very long time and withstand a great deal of wear so these must be the best of their kind that you can possibly afford.

Comfortable seating is essential. You can do without carpet but you've got to have somewhere to sit and the least you can make do with is one sofa or two good chairs. If you're young you might think that cushions or even a thick rug will be fine for sitting on but not everybody would be happy—or able—to put up with this and certainly older people would prefer something more comfortable.

You don't have to have curtains; blinds are a good alternative or if the room has a marvellous view you might want to do without any form of window dressing. Lighting, however, you can't do without for obvious reasons and also because it adds a great deal of extra interest to a room (see *Lighting is important*, page 39).

You can easily make your own coffee table and improvise on dining and side tables (see *Improvise with flair*, page 80) until you can afford better, but generous storage and some large healthy plants will make all the difference between a comfortable, comforting room and a stiff, conventional one. Better to eat off an orange box and get pleasure from a plant than to spend the money on a cheap and nasty table which is going to be an un-satisfactory stopgap. Save money and effort right at the start by sorting out priorities—which should include enjoying the room you live in—and try not to stray too far from your original objectives.

DATE:	PRESENT STATE	REPAIRS/ALTERATIONS	DECORATIVE TREATMENT	£
LIGHTING	Central light only	Replace with recessed down-lights on dimmer switch	Add uplights and table lamps	
ELECTRICITY	One wall socket	Put new sockets in each corner. Add TV socket	Check out hardware - brass, brushed steel or white?	
HEATING	Gas heater in fireplace	Restore fireplace, add two radiators under windows	Add coal-flame effect fire	
WALLS	Shabby paper	Strip and line	Stipple and add border below ceiling	
CEILING	Cracked	Line with paper	Paint white emulsion	
FLOOR	Floor boards - fair condition	Strip, sand and polish	Buy rugs	
WINDOWS	Peeling paint	Strip and repaint	Roman blinds initially later add curtains	
DOORS	Undistinguished	Strip to original pine	Replace hardware	
ACCESSORIES	No storage facilities or pictures	Fit glass shelves in recesses	Remount old prints	

uplight makes
interesting tracery

wall-mounted reading lamp
takes no floor space

skirted table
for working/dining

aquamarine
rag-rubbed
walls

blinds are
economical
with space
and fabric

a mass of
cushions in
the colours
of the blind

old sleep-sofa
recovered

perspex
fold-up
chairs

affordable coir
matting provides
attractive texture

glass-topped table takes up
less visual space and
provides storage

inexpensive wicker
sofa blends with
coir matting

This room was planned on a tiny budget but looks fresh, comfortable and interesting. Candy-striped Roman blinds, wall lamps, glass-topped table and pale coir matting all help to visually enlarge the rather small space. The wicker sofa, palm and blue/green rag-rubbed walls help the freshness, while cushions piled on the sofa-bed spell comfort. The table (above) is both pretty and practical; folding chairs save space but can accommodate four diners.

STARTING FROM SCRATCH

The three-stage plan

When money is tight it's a good idea to plan the room in such a way that it can progress in stages and still look furnished at each point. Say you have, for example, a fairly commonplace sort of living room, rectangular, featureless, with one or at the most two, undistinguished windows. You'll need seating, table space, wall and window treatments, flooring, shelving and good lighting as an absolute minimum. How, and in what sort of order, should you tackle it so that it never appears either unfinished or unfurnished?

The first stage

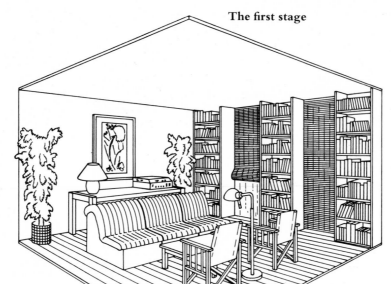

Right: This long, narrow room with its several windows and high sloping roof could have been awkward to furnish. Instead it has the air of a graceful sunroom-cum-living room with its comfortable, inexpensive wicker furniture, match-stick blinds, dhurrie rug, garden hammock and lavish use of green plants.

Left: Three-stage room treatment showing how one room can be progressively better furnished over the years as and when improvements can be afforded. At no stage, however, does the room look sparsely furnished.

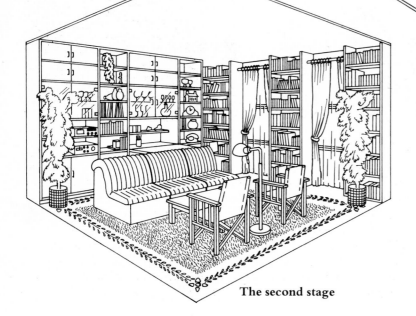

The second stage

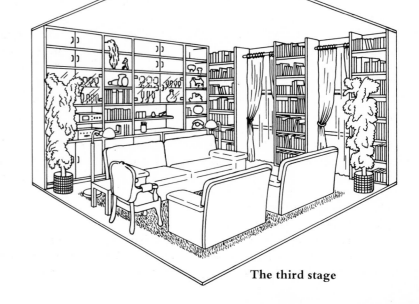

The third stage

12

The first stage Two things immediately make an emptyish room seem warmer and more furnished than it actually is: richly coloured walls and an interesting floor treatment. So it makes sense to spend money first of all on, say, a glossy chestnut paint for the walls and natural-coloured coir matting or sisal or wool cord wall-to-wall carpet. You could even just paint the floorboards if they are in good condition.

Windows can be made to look infinitely longer and more graceful by lining them either side with strips of wood trim (see *Good alternatives*, pages 69–70). These would be then fixed from ceiling to floor at right angles to the walls and then painted to match. If you like, the strips could also act as a framework for simple bookshelves. All you will then need to complete the illusion of elegant French windows is the addition of roller blinds in inexpensive cotton or matchstick blinds long enough to hang all the way down to the floor with perhaps a long voile curtain behind for privacy if needed. You'll have achieved a very impressive and luxurious effect at very small cost.

For comfortable seating you could use modular upholstered seats which could also double as a spare bed from time to time and add a couple of inexpensive wicker chairs or wood and canvas director's chairs. Add also a console or Parsons table to take drinks, books, radio or record player and to act as a desk; a low coffee table, a floor lamp or table lamps for reading with two uplights in the corners for general lighting. Finally put up some posters or secondhand prints or frame a good-looking piece of fabric and indulge in one or two spectacular plants in deep rush baskets. Now you're in business. You have a warm, inviting room for the minimum outlay.

The second stage When you feel richer you could add some wall units which might include a desk, a bar, space for stereo and tv and more sophisticated shelving. Replace the strips of wood at the windows (if you haven't put in bookshelves) with long curtains, or folding shutters or narrow folding screens. These could be covered each side in a different fabric or painted a different colour or even mirrored one side, to make them reversible for summer and winter. The floor could be stencilled, bleached, painted or given some other treatment at this stage (see *Old floors*, page 49). If it needs extra softness and colour add a sheepskin or dhurrie rug.

The third stage Replace your cheaper occasional chairs with two good comfortable armchairs; move

the other ones to a bedroom or playroom. By this time you can probably afford a large, squashy sofa instead of the modular units. A good antique chair could supplement the seating, and a couple of side tables would look well on either side of the sofa. More luxurious flooring would be in order: either very good carpet or oriental rugs. Splash out on better floor lamps, maybe brass ones, good prints or paintings and more or better quality accessories.

The point is that at no time will the room look under- or half-furnished or unpleasant to live in and yet at any stage it is capable of being improved on without wasting precious money or effort.

Airs on a shoestring

The great secret about starting from scratch, and on a limited budget, is to leave room for improvements over the years without the room looking as if there is any need for improvement. This is not so hard as it seems since there are all sorts of good-looking short cuts that can be taken from using deck chairs as seating, to making your own coffee and dining tables, plus the clever use of plants, cushions and ready-made blinds. In this room the major financial splurge was in the quarry-tiled floor which immediately gives a clean-cut, spacious air. The major visual splurge was in the choice of colours: luxurious pale yellows, greens and white, which both expand and freshen the space, making it look airy and sunny at all times. Another great secret is knowing when to save and when to spend when you only have very limited funds; the case, alas, with most of us. Here, the expense of buying two sofas is offset by the fact that they can also be used as guest beds, and the fact that they look and are so comfortable. Other seating can be provided by low-priced canvas stools and a deck chair. The sideboard down one wall holds an enormous quantity of stuff as well as providing good shelf space, and the low table is a sheet of plate glass on an old crate. Details of the materials used are shown right.

STARTING FROM SCRATCH

Be creative with colour

Colour can transform a room—or wreck it. Just by changing the colour of the walls and soft furnishings you can provide a completely new background that may have a profound effect on the existing furniture, making it look entirely different.

Some people have very firm ideas on colour schemes. They decide they want a mainly blue or green or apricot room and know just how to set about achieving it. This sort of assurance is very rare and really only

Different shades of one colour

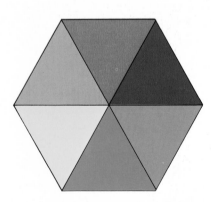

Colour wheel

comes with experience. But because mistakes are expensive and we have to live with them for a long time we tend to play safe and go for rather bland schemes. This is a mistake in itself because the result is often uninspired and therefore uninviting. How can we overcome this?

Be confident with colour

Should I put green or purple against that dark blue? Can I live with all those reds? Would I find a brown background restful or depressing? If you are not sure what goes with what or even which colours you feel comfortable with there are several things you can do to improve your confidence.

Start by noticing colour all around you. Then try to look at it as an artist would look at it, really *analysing* it. Look out of the window; which colours look particularly good next to each other? Those red-tiled roofs against the blue-grey sky; do they please you more than the slatey-purple ones? Which shades of green blend best with each other, with pale colours, with vivid colours? Look no further than your own garden to see the most interesting and often surprising colour combinations.

Train yourself to be conscious of colour wherever you go: in hotels, shops, restaurants, theatres, stately homes. Which schemes make you feel excited, relaxed, on edge? Go

and look at paintings in art galleries just to see what effect the artist is trying to achieve. Look at the marvellous build-up of colours in oriental rugs or tapestries and embroidery. It all helps to get your eye in and is far better than trying to rely on memory. You'll soon find yourself developing a pretty sure grasp of what colour is all about.

It's a good idea to buy as many magazines and books on interior decoration and home-making as you can afford and study their colour pages carefully. Pull out the magazine schemes that appeal most to you and stick them in a file; mark the pages you like in books. Then take time to look at them all together and see what they tell you. Is there a definite theme running through them all? Do the illustrations you have chosen have certain colours and styles in common? Be guided by them because they're obviously the ones you feel most comfortable with and they'll provide a reliable starting point.

The colour wheel

The primary colours are red, yellow and blue. Equal amounts of these mixed together produce secondary colours eg red+yellow=orange. All other colours are formed by mixing together various amounts of these colours and by adding black or white to make lighter or darker versions.

The secrets of colour schemes

When you have decided on the main background colour for floor or walls or both, you can set about building up the scheme throughout the room. A very simple but effective way is to stick to one major colour livened up with accent colours in cushions, rugs, the odd chair, blinds, borders, prints, paintings, books and plants. A fairly neutral background will make any small splash of colour sing out with particular vibrance and significance.

One very exciting and yet subtle way to treat the subject is to keep to one main colour but to introduce it in all its different shades and tones. Learn how to do this by taking one colour, say yellow, and thinking of all the objects that come within that category.

This should remind of you of the infinite varieties in any one colour and also set you thinking about texture. It will help you when it comes to choosing upholstery, blinds, curtains, rugs, carpets and general accessories. Varying the textures within this sort of monochromatic colour scheme can be just as interesting and lively as a scheme full of more obvious contrasts. At the same time it's worth remembering that at least one contrast colour, even if only a large plant or a mass of flowers or cushions, will help to emphasize the clever harmony of the background colour scheme.

Above: The burnt orange predominant in the inexpensive seating (two foam mattresses), is picked up in the cushions and walls.

Far right: Although the emphasis in this room is on blue, the colours of the wall-hanging have been cleverly reflected in the piping on the chair and in the dhurrie.

Right: The harmonious range of creams and yellows, toned with white and green, was inspired by the colours in the large painting.

STARTING FROM SCRATCH

Make a floor plan

Taking time to plan your space to its best advantage is essential when you are starting from scratch. This way you'll make quite sure that anything you buy in the way of furniture, equipment and accessories will be the right shape, scale and style to suit the room and your lifestyle. It's perhaps the one time you'll bless starting with a completely clean slate; at least there are no existing possessions that might perhaps prove difficult to accommodate.

So the most helpful thing to do before you start shopping is to draw up a scale plan of the room. It's quite easy. All you have to do is measure the length and width of the room and draw it lightly out in pencil on a sheet of graph paper allowing say, 1 cm ($\frac{1}{4}$ in) to represent 25 cm (1 ft) in reality.

Long narrow rooms are a difficult shape to furnish if you want to avoid a corridor feeling. This room gets over the problem with see-through occasional tables and pale colours for walls and seating. The squared dhurrie rug (washed to pale the colours) effectively makes the room seem wider, as does the fact that its colouring is picked out by the cushions or pillows. Huge plants soften the angles of the walls. Note the simplicity of the single stem glass specimen vases.

Now measure and mark in door openings with their clearance, windows, radiators, electrical points, fireplace, alcoves and any fixtures, again making sure that everything is completely accurate; the slightest inaccuracy can ruin the brightest idea. Correct measurement of doors and windows is particularly important as far as the moving of furniture is concerned. Many a large sofa, armchair or piano has had to be sent back at unnecessary cost because it wouldn't go through the door. Make sure to measure the ceiling height as well because if you multiply this by the wall measurements (see *Calculating quantities* on page 61) it will give you an idea of the amount of paint or wallpaper you will need.

Take your plan and a tape measure with you whenever you shop and always make sure you measure whatever you are thinking of buying. Try to avoid making instant decisions; instead, go home and draw the proposed piece to scale on some card. Cut it out, mark it with 'armchair' or whatever and juggle it around on your plan together with any other pieces you're planning to buy until you're sure it fits in. If quick decisions are needed, say during the sales, then at least work out the approximate size of the spaces you have in mind and look out for pieces of furniture that will best fit into them.

How to take measurements

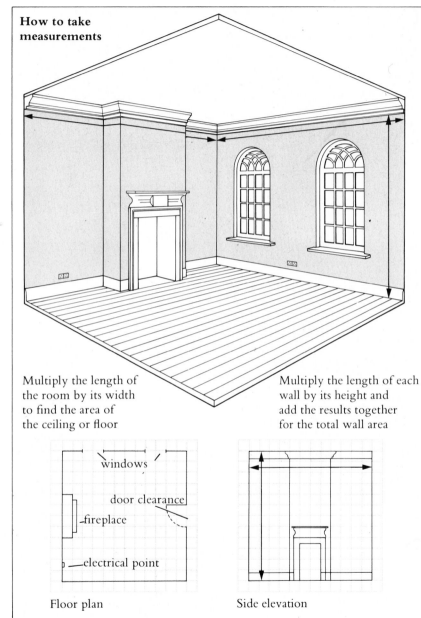

Multiply the length of the room by its width to find the area of the ceiling or floor

Multiply the length of each wall by its height and add the results together for the total wall area

Floor plan

Side elevation

How to draw up a plan
First make a sketch of the room or rooms. Then measure the length of walls, the width of doors and openings, the thickness of partitions, as well as the position of electrical outlets, radiators, telephone attachments and any other permanent fixtures like pipes and ducts. Mark them all out clearly on your rough sketch. This is the preliminary step.

Now decide on a scale. A quarter of an inch to a foot or 1 in 50 cm is fairly general, but half an inch to a foot or 1 in 25 cm is usually better for kitchens, bathrooms and utility or laundry rooms which have to take a lot of equipment and where every fraction of space counts. If working in inches, use graph paper with the inch square divided into eights and then take two (a quarter of an inch) for a foot.

Take a sharp pencil and an eraser and draw the perimeter of the space to the chosen scale. Erase door openings to the exact widths, and mark in windows, radiators, outlets, fixtures and the thickness of current partition walls, *making sure that everything is completely accurate* (many a bulky piece of furniture has proved impossible to get in because it wouldn't go through a door or window).

Very few people have the luxury of starting completely from scratch although those who do seldom see it as an advantage. Most of us have possessions we want, or have to go on using, so the best thing to do is to take a very positive attitude and use them as jumping-off points. Let a rug or painting suggest or inspire the colour scheme; if you can't re-vamp old curtains (though beware! re-making can sometimes be just as expensive as starting afresh) turn them into cushions; cut down carpets which no longer fit but are too good to be thrown out, and make them into small rugs.

Existing rooms which need a face-lift or which you would like to have a completely new image are much more of a prob-lem. Here we have to work around not only a collection of possessions which have become part of our lives, but also carpets or curtains or wall coverings we feel we can't afford to replace. How can we achieve a new look when some things are going to stay exactly the same?

'Use it up, wear it out; make it do or do without!' the old New England maxim goes. But if we have a conscience about our familiar old things what can we do?

Make the best of it

The best solution is to analyse each item in the room. If the existing carpet is in reasonable condition but you're sick to death of it you could add rugs to cheer it up. If it is in very bad condition but you really can't afford to buy new carpet then see what the floor is like underneath. If there are boards that seem in good shape they could be stripped, sanded and polished. If they are rather the worse for wear you could always just paint and perhaps stencil them.

New-look curtains

If there's nothing wrong with your curtains except that you've grown rather bored with them there's quite a lot you can do to give them a new lease of life. Consider adding a border to the leading edges and making tie-backs to match; or having tie-backs where none existed before. Another solution would be to keep the curtain tied back and to add

Different cushions, massed plants, and new curtains all help refresh the room to the left, injecting colour and pattern, while the room on the right owes its crispness to vertically striped cotton blinds over a horizontally striped sofa bed.

Tailored tie-backs

Even if you feel you are not up to making curtains you can improve the looks of existing adequate but dull ones by looping them back with tie-backs. You can use cord or special metal fitments, but it is really quite easy to make your own tailored variety.

You will need per pair:
Some fabric to match or contrast with the existing curtains
Iron-on or fusible interfacing
11.5 cm (4$\frac{1}{2}$ in) diameter plastic rings
2 largish cup hooks
Plenty of pins
Sharp shears or scissors

Find out the best size by experimenting with a spare piece of material to make a rough model. Do this by cutting a strip 5–10 cm (2–4 in) wide, and about half as long as the width of the curtain. Loop it around the curtain and move it up and down, tucking in the edges and folding it until you see what looks like the best position and the best width. When you have decided these, mark the right size on the fabric with pins, and pencil a mark on the wall where the cup hooks should go. Repeat the mark in the same position on the opposite side. Screw in the cup hooks.

Fold the fabric in two and lay the rough pattern on it. Double the width, leave a 1.25 cm ($\frac{1}{2}$ in) seam allowance and cut out the two tie-backs. Cut out two interfacings the same size but without the seam allowance.

Centre each interfacing on the wrong side of each of the strips and iron in place according to the manufacturer's instructions.

Next, fold the tie-backs in half lengthwise with the right sides together. Stitch along the strips 1.25 cm ($\frac{1}{2}$ in) in from the cut edges and leave the ends open.

Fold them right side out and press with the seam running down the centre (this will be the back). Turn the cut edges inside, press again and stitch up neatly.

At this stage you can sew on the plastic rings to the back of the tie-backs (the seamed side), centring them about 0.6 cm ($\frac{1}{4}$ in) from each end, avoiding sewing through the front of the fabric. All you have to do now is loop them round the curtains again and attach each ring to the cup hook, gently pulling out the curtain fabric to its best advantage.

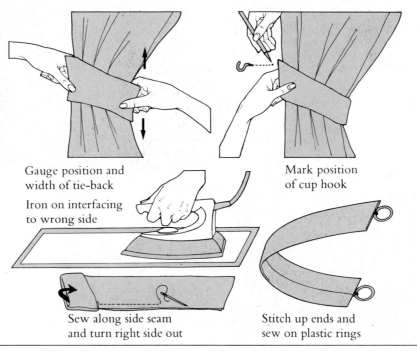

Gauge position and width of tie-back

Iron on interfacing to wrong side

Mark position of cup hook

Sew along side seam and turn right side out

Stitch up ends and sew on plastic rings

Roman or roller or Austrian blinds underneath. Or you could make under-curtains in a lighter, toning or contrasting fabric to pull back-wards and forwards while the original curtains remain stationary.

Upholstery

If the upholstery is still in too good a condition to change, add plain col-oured cushions in one of the colours taken from a patterned fabric or patterned ones if the upholstery is plain. Either of these could match the new borders or blinds or under-curtains, perhaps bringing out a colour that had not been empha-sized before. Pale *plain* loose covers could be dyed a different, darker colour and occasional chairs changed round with old ones rele-gated to another room in the house. Old close or tight-covered sofas and chairs can be utterly transformed by giving them new loose covers.

Don't make the mistake of think-ing that any changes must be major ones, on a smaller scale it's amazing what a few new accessories will achieve—paintings and prints, plants, perhaps a new round table with a floor-length cloth on it, a small but eye-catching rug, some concealed uplights in the corners (see pages 41 and 43). You'll find that quite often this sort of selective improvement will give a room the new look it needs for far less money than a drastic change-around.

Top left: Partition walls were knocked down in this small terraced house to make room for larger furniture from a previous home. The long coffee table cut down from an old school table, is exactly the right shape for the space.

Above: Dual-purpose library-dining table widens a narrow room.

Left: Matching sofas, side tables and vases give an air of graceful symmetry to this room, freshened by contrasting loose covers and a profusion of plants and dried and fresh flowers. Overmantel mirror and long, low glass coffee table placed unconventionally in front of the fireplace add extra sparkle and a sense of added space.

23

Left: A deep paper border gives an interesting distinction to these plain walls. Note also the painted stripe between ceiling moulding and cornice which further helps to delineate the space, as does the mirror, carefully chosen to repeat almost exactly the width of the fireplace surround.

Above: Added moulding around the architrave of this doorway turns what was a very plain opening into a most distinguished feature.

Details that make a difference

You have only to look through one or two stately homes to see what a great difference the architectural details—the cornices, mouldings, hardware on doors and windows, doors themselves—make to a room. If your house doesn't possess them already, there's nothing to stop you adding your own.

You can buy one of the many reproduction plaster or fibre-glass cornices by the foot and have it added to your room just under the ceiling or, if you cannot afford this luxury, go for a stylish compromise with a paper border. There are some good-looking ones on the market. Choose one that contrasts with the current wall colour or wallpaper and see how it totally changes its character. If you can't find a pleasing paper border, there are other alternatives: look amongst the fabric borders in soft furnishing departments. You could even run a contrast border of webbing around the walls just under the ceiling, and around doors, windows and skirting board as well if you like.

Another way to transform walls is to form false panels on them. Do this by making squares or rectangles (or both, one above the other, depending on ceiling height and proportion) either with the same sort of webbing or with lengths of picture frame edging, or plain wood moulding from DIY shops.

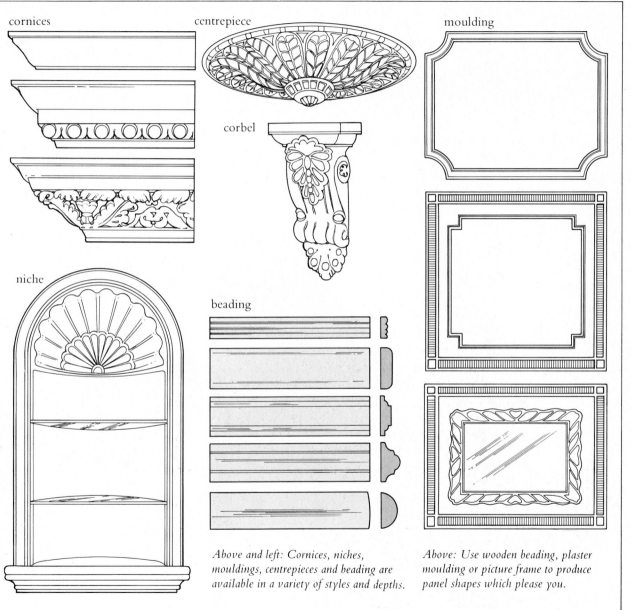

cornices

centrepiece

moulding

corbel

niche

beading

Above and left: Cornices, niches, mouldings, centrepieces and beading are available in a variety of styles and depths.

Above: Use wooden beading, plaster moulding or picture frame to produce panel shapes which please you.

superimposed panels make
the best of plain walls

matchstick blinds add textural
contrast for little cost

top line of
panels aligns
exactly with
top of window

Edwardian milky-
glass wall lamp
adds to charm –
as does converted
blue glass oil lamp

hardboard floor
decorated with
green paint
'combed' into
squares

inexpensive sofa allows
money to be spent on
good-looking accessories

green and white diamond pattern
on planter intensifies colour
and pattern of floor

*Painted panelling over
sponged walls combined
with a combed and painted
hardboard floor (left) cheer
up a rather plain room.
While the subtly-coloured
bird panels add a charming
touch to the door of the
room above. Paper would
achieve a similar effect.*

If your doors have rather ugly or undistinguished knobs and finger plates change them. Handsome new brass ones—or modern anodized steel if they suit the room better—look very impressive and if you can afford it you could have matching light and dimmer switches. Again, for remarkably small outlay, you will have added new interest and improved the quality of the room.

Changing the style and/or structure of the doors will have an immediate effect on the feel of a room. Unattractive old doors might look better stripped; they are very often a handsome pine underneath. Really ugly doors can be replaced or left off altogether and the space widened to form an archway, although this will inevitably increase draughts and the demands on your heating system.

Rather ordinary plain hardboard doors can look quite special if they are 'panelled out'—that is, given false panels with picture framing or beading.

The main thing is to try to reassess all those long familiar features in a room that are taken completely for granted because you are so used to them. Look at them long and hard with a fresh eye, question their presence and their use; there are very few that don't lend themselves to ingenious transformations.

In these rooms, mirror has been used to create an illusion of space. Right: Mirror panels either side of the fireplace, and light festoon blinds made this formerly square room look totally different and larger for very little cost. Below left: This door was first stripped down to its original golden pine and then panelled with mirror. It had the happy effect of adding light as well as interest to an undistinguished corner. The palm looks good next to the light walls. Below right: Mirror is also a very good way of both disguising and brightening an ugly fireplace surround.

The treatment of space is what good design is all about but far too many people think that if they cannot afford to change a room *structurally* nothing else is going to alter the look and feel. Yet it is quite possible to change the feeling of space *cosmetically*, that is by the clever use of colour, pattern, texture and arrangement, all of which can make space *seem* much larger as well as unifying and simplifying it. It might sound dull to advise using the same pale colour for walls, floors and larger pieces of furniture but this treatment will make the most confined area seem lighter and airier and will make bulky objects like sofas, armchairs and beds recede into the background. And you can avoid monotony to a quite remarkable degree by using the same colours in different textures against which any extra added colours like plants, scatter cushions, pictures or books will stand out with dramatic intensity.

Diagonal designs, whether painted on bare floor boards or woven into carpets, will always seem to push space out. Any wallcovering design that produces a sense of perspective like some geometrics, trellis patterns or inexpensive garden trellis itself fixed on top of walls, will seem to give extra depth. Shiny or reflective walls, ceilings and floors will also make space seem much bigger because they throw out extra light. And light itself has a blurring, softening effect on the hard edges of a room, making them seem further away and less constricting.

Make space with mirror

Mirror can work magic on a room. Cleverly used it will double, treble, even quadruple the size. Mirror panels are expensive of course and you must always be careful to ensure that large slabs of it can be got through doors and onto lifts and so on. There is no way it will bend and it can break en route only too easily. But once safely in position it will be worth its weight in gold for the extra light and space it will create. You can always save on something else.

This brilliant platformed solution to a small space (left) was made entirely from hollow core doors. The angular table has a twin panel which hangs on the wall like sculpture. Mirror and geometric carpet double the space to the right.

DEALING WITH PROBLEM SPACES

If you use mirror from floor to ceiling and at right angles to a window or opposite a window it will give you twice the light and twice the view. If you use it from floor to ceiling in a recess—say the recesses either side of a chimney breast—it will look as if you can walk into a whole extra room next door. Mirror tiles on a ceiling will gain height for the room and a miraculous sense of spaciousness.

Mirror tiles are also a good substitute for panels and are very much cheaper if you don't mind the obvious break in reflection caused by the lines. Plastic mirror is another possible substitute and has the advantage that it won't steam over; on the other hand it can crack very easily when it is being fixed into place and it does seem to give a more distorted reflection.

Pre-cut panels of mirrors sold for hanging on wardrobe or cupboard doors are often surprisingly cheap compared to custom-cut pieces and they can be hung side by side or used in certain places to look like slit windows in a wall. Strips stuck on skirting boards or used instead of a cornice between ceiling and walls can greatly expand the sense of space for very little cost.

More space by arrangement

Built-in furniture—window seats, wall units all down one wall—will always take up less space than free

'floating' pieces and if you can manage good storage space under a window seat or built-in seating around a wall so much the better. All you need do is have a lift-up lid instead of a solid base or shelves added under the actual seat part and you have immediately doubled the usefulness of the piece as well as gained some footage.

If you have a small room use as much transparent and fold-up-and-put-away furniture as possible. See-through desks and small tables of glass and metal, or plexiglass, or perspex will appear to take up much less space. Fold-up furniture can either be stacked neatly in one place, hung from a large hook on a wall or stashed away out of sight when it isn't in use. Cane and wicker will look lighter than wood; white-painted pieces will look less conspicuous and therefore less space-consuming than dark. The most common advice is to place large pieces of furniture around the sides of a room but there are exceptions. Two sofas placed back to back in the centre of a space can often define the divisions of space very well. And in a one-roomed flat or apartment a large bed placed in the middle of the room can be used as an island lounging unit. By positioning a bolster in the middle of the bed instead of at the end the mattress will look as if it is divided into two separate areas.

Top left: Built-in seating around the corner of this narrow space gives extra seats for half the price — and room — of two sofas. Geometric fabric on a white ground and pole-hung back cushions help the sense of space.

Bottom left: Diagonally-striped cotton blinds, matching fabric on the low window seat and a similarly-patterned carpet and carpet-covered stool are all clever space stretchers.

Above: Arched mirrored corners make this room appear spacious.

Right: More mirror at right angles to the window seems to double the space and increase the light.

Surface distraction

If you have an awkwardly-shaped room, one with sloping ceilings perhaps on a top floor, the great thing is to go with the room, not to fight it. In other words fill up difficult spaces like odd corners and alcoves with custom-built shelves or units, keep the framework of the room – the walls, windows, ceiling, floor – as simple as possible, and keep to a limited palette of colours.

Vary the pace as it were, with complementary patterns and plains (not difficult to do these days with the many ranges of co-ordinated papers and fabrics to be bought), interesting textures and accessories. In this room, sand-coloured walls are teamed with sisal matting and creamy white blinds bordered with a double stripe of the chair and chair cushion fabrics. These mini-fabrics are offset by a multi-coloured bird and floral print with predominant blue tracery pepped up with red, which stands out wonderfully against the more sombre sands and blues. The blending pattern of the rug also works well against the herringbone of the matting, which in turn compliments the collection of baskets on the end wall and the weave of the plant baskets. Specially-fitted bookshelf units have glass shelves for lightness and tie in with the curved perspex sidetable. Plenty of green foliage and blue glass complete the scheme. Details of fabrics and carpets used are shown on the right.

Left: Here are several excellent space-cheating ideas combined in what is, but does not look, a very small room. Various shades of the same colour, mushroom, add to the effect of space. A desk top suspended across a corner between recessed window and mantelpiece effectively disguises an awkward space as well as taking advantage of every square inch, and a slim platform built on the diagonal gives relaxation and tv space while at the same time providing an area behind for plants and lighting.

Above: Banquette seating is recessed into bookshelves and across this narrow room.

Clever ways to win space

Useful tips for stretching a room without changing the structure.

Use very light colours and limit the colours of accessories. Or stick to one basic colour but vary the textures.

Give ceilings, walls, floors and furniture the same light colour to increase the illusion of space. Use light or natural coloured wall-to-wall flooring. No rugs.

Achieve a three-dimensional effect with pattern by using a colour against white.

Create perspectives as much as possible so that the eye is always drawn along. Go for geometric, directional or diagonal lines on a floor or wall, especially dark colours on a light ground which will give depth as well; stand objects in front of a mirror; set a table and lamp or plant in front of the hinges of a screen; use blinds in conjunction with curtains; have vertical louvres half open.

Expand space by mounting mirrors on wall, doors or storage cupboards; on ceilings; in the reveals of deep-set windows; across corners; in recesses. Economise with mirror tiles, pre-cut mirror or mirrored laminate.

Use a minimum of furniture at the lowest level; have it custom-built along the walls as much as possible. Keep all the surfaces as uncluttered as possible.

Gain extra storage space over and around doorways, under banquettes and window seats, under and around beds.

Make short walls look longer with strong horizontal lines like bookshelves or countertops.

Divide space without constricting it with a pair of screens, or trellis or even large plants.

Use fold-up, stack-away furniture.

Have occasional furniture in glass, perspex or plexiglass or surfaced in mirror; it will look lighter than wood, marble, chrome or plastic.

Cane, wicker and open-work furniture is better than anything with more solid lines.

Use spotlights to highlight details, objects and plants for a three-dimensional effect. Soften hard lines and make them recede by washing walls with light using wall-washers or uplights (see *Lighting*, pages 40–43).

Use reflective surfaces to make space seem larger.

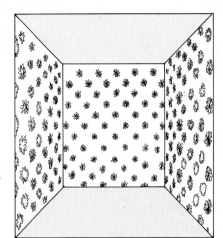

Any patterned paper with a white or pale ground will give the illusion of more depth to a smallish room.

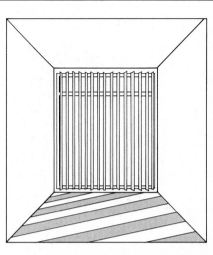

A diagonally-striped floor and vertical louvered blinds will both lengthen and widen any room.

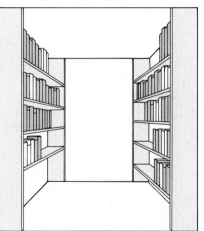

Short walls can be made to look longer by the strong horizontal lines of shelving.

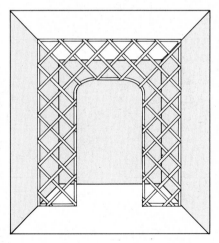

An archway formed from garden trellis divides this space without in any way constricting it.

35

room enlarged by taking down corridor wall
leaving book–lined passage (detail left)

philodendron
trained to make
a charming
natural border

large mirror,
airy side table
visually enlarge
space

black shades
on lamps match
paintwork

floor and ceiling
are slightly darker
tones of the walls
to enlarge space

*A corridor wall was
taken down in this classic
thirties flat to increase
living space. Black has
been used to define the
skirting and door frames
and is repeated in the
lampshades. A
foreshortened corridor
leads to the bedroom
(detail, above).*

portrait colours
are repeated
in cushions

rugs repeat colours
of walls, upholstery
and portrait

Some structural solutions

If cosmetic changes are not enough there are some fairly obvious and simple ways of altering the structure of a room to gain extra space. If you own your house or flat you can take down partition walls, improvise new ones, block up old doors and make new openings in more convenient places to improve on the space. Compared to the visual and practical differences these sort of changes make, the cost is small.

It pays, first of all, to get hold of a plan of the place (managing agents of blocks of flats should be able to provide one) or draw a rough one up yourself as described on page 19 and see on paper where more space looks possible. For example, if you have a large hall or corridor you might be able to slice off bits to add to your living room.

Walls can be cut half-way down or at either side to form dividing slabs rather than solid masses. Or once the partition walls are down, you can create your own flexible dividers, with bookcases, shelving units, screens or screen-like structures like trellis, or even Murphy beds that let down at night from what looks like a panelled screen.

You could consider making internal windows or openings in a dividing wall to get more light and airiness. They could be conventionally square or round or in the shape of long slits so that the adjoining room shows through and gives extra perspective.

In a very small studio or one-roomed flat where space is at an absolute premium it would pay to build in multi-purpose furniture that would solve the problems of sleeping/working/eating and sitting all in one area.

Above left: Every inch is used in this long narrow room. Shutters make the window seem wider, an effect which is reinforced by the horizontal lines of the sofa placed directly underneath. Spotlights define different areas at night, bulkier seating is kept the same colour as the walls, the rest is kept light.

Above: A cut-away stair wall makes an effective backing for a sofa covered with multicoloured pillows backed by plants and a painting. What could have been an area of blackness has become an interesting useful corner.

37

EFFECTIVE LIGHT AND HEAT

Lighting is important

Lighting is one of the most important elements to get right in any room, but particularly in the living room with its many different functions, all of which need to be appropriately lit. It is also the quickest way to change atmosphere and mood, to exaggerate space or diminish faults, to bring out texture, pattern and colour, and to highlight special possessions and achieve particular effects.

Yet when people think of lighting they mostly think of lights or lamps—the actual fittings—rather than of a flexible medium, just like heat, which can be manipulated by the flick of a switch or the turn of a dimmer. When they buy fittings they buy them mainly for their shape or colour or looks, but neglect to find out what sort of light they will give.

Ideally lighting should be planned and installed before the walls and ceiling are decorated in case any re-wiring is necessary. All too often, lighting is an afterthought superimposed on the final decoration instead of being planned from the start. In most housing a centre light fitting, for example, goes unquestioned, although people would find even daylight very harsh and glaring if it poured from the centre of the sky all day. Plugs or outlets too, are often fitted in a haphazard way around the room, with the result that when a lamp is placed where it seems most needed, it frequently has to trail a dangerous mess of flex or wire with it. If spots or downlights are bought, they're often used without benefit of a dimmer switch.

Light where you need it

So how do you plan an efficient lighting system? Before you start it helps to understand the differing functions of the various types of fixtures available. Remember you are aiming for not one lighting effect but several. All living rooms need a mixture of light: background lighting; local light for working by; and decorative accent lighting.

Lighting should be both atmospheric and practical. Left, concealed light illuminates both the ceiling and floor and a spotlight provides light for working by. Table lamps, bottom right, and a wall-washer give dramatic illumination while, top right, track and wall lights provide accent and work light.

EFFECTIVE LIGHT AND HEAT

From firelight to fluorescent

There are basically four main groups of domestic lighting – five if you count candlelight and firelight. These are:

Conventional pendant and ceiling lights, wall lights, table lamps, floor lamps and strip lights.

Fluorescent lighting

Downlights, wall-washers and up-lights, spotlights, track lights.

The more ambitious kinds of 'effect' lighting, like neon and rotating lenses.

Conventional lights

These come in a huge choice of shapes, colours, materials and prices. The pendant or hanging variety give good overall light but tend to flatten shadows and do not provide enough light by which to read or work comfortably. The amount of actual light they throw out depends on the type of shade used and the height at which they are hung. Ceiling mounted lights also give good general light, but the effect is flat unless used in conjuction with other types of light.

Wall lights are best if they are directional and used to bounce light off a ceiling or floor, or to light a picture or piece of wall. Table lamps should provide concentrated areas of light. They will bounce light up or down or spread it horizontally,

depending on the type of shade. Directional desk or table lamps for working by should be adjustable to let light shine down on the work in question. Floor lamps can give general or directional light depending on the type and shade: some are fitted with spot lights and can be used to light objects or to highlight. Hooded brass or chrome floor lamps make especially good reading lamps since they can be moved around to various chairs or sofas, and set to shine on books, or they can be directed on to a wall or ceiling. If you prefer shades, the translucent silk variety are the best light diffusers followed by linen, card or paper.

Incandescent strip lights (as opposed to fluorescent tubes) are good for concealed lighting behind pelmets or baffles, or down the sides of cupboards.

Fluorescent lights

Fluorescent tubes give about three times as much light as a tungsten or incandescent (normal everyday) bulb. They come in straight or circular shapes and are best concealed behind a baffle of some sort. They have an average life of 5,000 hours and are, therefore, much more economical to use in places where high levels of light are needed for long hours at a time.

Fluorescent lighting, however, can look cold; the best colour to go

An adjustable brass floor lamp with a coolie shade is useful for reading. An inset downlight gives general or accent light.

for is 'de luxe warm white' (not just 'warm white' – which is neither warm nor white) as this is nearest to warmer incandescent light.

Downlights

These are round or square, natural or painted metal canisters that can be recessed or semi-recessed into a ceiling, or ceiling mounted to cast pools of light on the ground or any other surface below them. The kind of pool of light depends on whether the bulb fitted inside is a spot, flood or an ordinary bulb.

A spot will throw a concentrated circle of light and is therefore best

directed down on to, say, a bowl of flowers or a plant. A floodlight will give a wider, less intense, cone-shaped light. An ordinary bulb will provide soft, all-over light. Downlights can also be used for wall-washing. This means literally washing a wall with light. Several downlights angled close to a wall of paintings (say 60 cm [2 ft] out from the wall and 60–90 cm [2–3 ft] apart) will give a dramatic overall effect by

Small lamps with big effects.
Top left: An uplight contrasts with a
reading lamp opposite. Top centre:
Articulated clip-on desk lamp. Top
right and bottom left: Brass wall
lamp and noguchi wall light provide
gentle down light. Bottom centre and
right: Lights used for accent.

splashing light on to various surfaces with contrasting shadows in between. They won't light individual paintings unless they can be manoeuvred to direct light to a specific place. Downlights should be, if possible, fitted with some sort of anti-glare device or any unfortunate standing underneath could feel that he or she is in an interrogation chamber.

Uplights
Uplights are simply downlights in reverse and meant to stand on the floor. Of all lights in the room these make the biggest difference and are a blessing since you can plug them in and put them behind plants, or in corners, or behind large pieces of furniture to give a beautiful, dramatic accent light, creating mood and interest that could never be imagined by day. A good mixture of uplights and downlights supplemented by spot and reading lights will give a particularly warm and interesting atmosphere to a room.

Spotlights
These are used for accent lighting, to pin-point objects and give a strong punch of light whenever and wherever needed. They come in a great many varieties and can be mounted straight on to a ceiling, on to walls or on to tracks, and then pointed towards whatever needs special lighting. Miniature free-

standing spots can be stood amongst objects and collections on a table, or amongst books and ornaments on a shelf.

Some spotlights have a magnetic backplate so that they can be attached to any surface and pointed in any direction or can be set to swivel around inside a container.

Track lights

Track systems make it possible for one electric source to supply a number of separate fittings without extra expensive electrical work and all the making good, or restoration work, afterwards that this entails. Mount them on or recess them into a ceiling or down the side of a wall. Arrange them in lines or rectangles and fit them with spots or floods or downlights or a mixture, depending on your needs.

Dimmers

These are absolutely essential for any sort of lighting scheme that involves spot or floorlights. They save energy, prolong the life of the bulbs and mean that you can control the intensity of your light at will.

Good lighting needs planning

When you are still in the planning stage of a room but with the furnishings decided upon, work out what type of light you want where; should it be direct, indirect, concealed, background, very bright?

Decide too, what style of lighting fixture would be best for each area and whether you're going to need any more electrical outlets, switches or dimmers, and where they should go. If spots or downlights are to be inset into a very high ceiling, make sure you have the longest-lasting bulbs possible and that they are very easy to change; otherwise you'll be for ever climbing ladders to deal with them.

Are they safe?

Many electrical accidents are caused by ignoring common safety rules; for example, failing to replace old and faulty wiring; by loading too few outlets or points with too many appliances; and with the thoughtless placing of wires or cords leading from outlets to table or floor lamps. Always check the recommended wattage on any light shade purchased and do not fit bulbs which exceed it. And never try to do any sort of re-wiring yourself unless you are absolutely sure you know what you're doing; have it done and tested professionally.

Improving what you have

How do you improve the lighting in existing houses, flats or apartments when the electrical lay-out is far from ideal and far from flexible? You can either add new points or outlets to existing circuits, if they can take the increased load (which is

good but expensive) or install lengths of track to the odd ceiling outlets that are there already. If there are no ceiling outlets, make do with the kind of floor lamps that have adjustable spots or, if there are wall points, get wall-mounted spots. Buy uplights and put them anywhere you think would make a difference—in corners, behind sofas, on mantelpieces, behind plants, in deep bowls or vases.

The colour of bulbs will change the feeling of room colours. White

Track lighting and adjustable downlights light window, plants and seating area. Adjustable floor lamps in foreground are right for reading.

bulbs cast a yellowish light; pink ones give a mellow effect. Plain white walls can be radically changed at night by using coloured filters over downlight, uplight, spot or wall-washer fixtures. Most reds will be emphasized by artificial light; blues and greens tend to be diminished by it.

How to create special effects

Light and shade should be balanced. An evenly lit room can be boring and often curiously depressing, whereas areas of strong light where it's needed, with dark shadows between, can be dramatic and interesting and still comfortable to live with.

Washing walls with light using wall-washers will make a space seem much larger.

Uplights set into corners will draw attention to the limits of a room. Uplights set under glass shelves or glass side tables will add sparkle. Uplights behind big plants will cast intricate shadows on the ceiling and upper part of walls as well as highlighting the leaves.

Low lamps and lamps placed at a low level with the light coming from underneath an opaque shade will make a room seem more intimate and a high ceiling much lower.

Spotlights and downlights carefully positioned will flatter the textures in a room. A downlight mounted close to the wall will show off a textured wall covering by just grazing it with light, while a spotlight fully trained on to it would cancel it out completely.

The lighter and whiter the surfaces in a room, the more they will reflect light, but a dark-walled room with a light carpet and ceiling will still look surprisingly light.

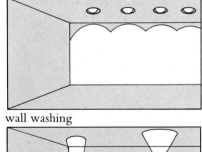
wall washing

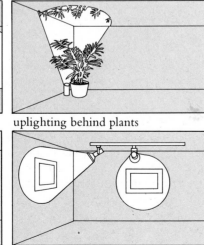
uplighting behind plants

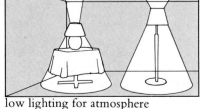
low lighting for atmosphere

spots used to highlight prints etc

uplight

angled uplight

sandbag uplight

recessed downlight

semi-recessed downlight

exposed downlight

shuttered wallwasher

angled wallwasher

spotlight on track

moveable eyeball spot on track

clip-on spotlight

parabolic spot

low voltage spot

box spotlight

high framing projector

43

Radiators

single convector radiator

convector radiator panel

compact steel column radiator

steel column radiator

electric low level radiator

electrically-heated skirting panel

flat-fronted convector radiator

A variety of radiator shapes is available to fit in with most heating systems.

Heating

Central heating is actually fairly easy to sort out right at the beginning provided you are clear about certain facts. To get some idea of the best system for your particular way of life you should ask yourself the sort of questions a heating contractor would ask:

Who goes out during the day and who stays in?

If you are out all day what time do you get back in the evening?

What sort of temperatures do you prefer?

Do you want different temperatures in the living room and the bedroom?

Does your living room face north or south?

How old is your home?

How big are the rooms and how high?

How compact is your home and how well insulated?

Do you have room to store oil or solid fuel or wood?

Would you prefer a wood-burning stove, conventional radiators, skirting or baseboard heaters, warm air ducts, underfloor or ceiling heating (given a choice in a new house) or, if you can't have a central heating system, storage heaters?

With the uncertainty about oil prices and the expense of both gas and electricity, many people are opting for wood-burning stoves that have long been a favourite in Northern Europe and America. These can be amazingly efficient in heating most of the house as well, quite apart from being decorative.

Living room heat

The living room needs to be a warm room. Generally speaking, people in this room are sitting around relaxing; they aren't bustling about generating their own heat so the atmosphere around them needs to be kept at a comfortable temperature. The average would seem to be about 70 degrees Fahrenheit/21 degrees Centigrade. On the other hand, a lot of bodies could make it too hot for comfort, so you need to be able to control the temperature with a room thermostat. You must also consider where to put heaters and radiators, and whether you still need a fireplace as a focal point in the room. Many people who took out their fireplaces several years ago now find they want to restore them to have a real open fire or some acceptable substitute like gas logs or a gas coal effect. If you're in rented accommodation some sort of portable heating is necessary and there's quite a lot to choose from: electric fan-assisted or convector heaters, free-standing stoves, oil heaters, calor gas fires, electric storage radiators.

Different types of heat source produce different levels of humidity.

The 1980s have seen a great revival of the woodburning stove in many guises and forms. New stoves have the advantage of being airtight and thermostatically controlled, older ones, as the model above, are coveted for their looks and fine detail. All should be set on some sort of tiled or cast iron surround which is usually raised a few inches from the floor all round. They are ideal for energy conservation as well as for their cosy good looks and can often be used to heat water as well as provide warmth for a large area.

*How to exploit unlit fireplaces:
with painted panels (top left),
a shirred fireguard (top right);
a black frame to a stunning
sculpture (above) and as a home
for wine crates (right).*

Electricity, for example, is a drying heat which produces a slight condensation. Do check before installation as too dry an atmosphere may affect furniture adversely.

You need insulation

However efficient the method of heating, it will be of no use if the room (and of course, the house) is not well insulated. It has been calculated that in an average semi-detached house only twenty-five per cent of the heat generated actually warms the house: twenty per cent may be lost through unlagged upstairs ceilings and the roof; twenty per cent through windows, doors and flues; twenty-five per cent through external walls and ten per cent through the ground floor. An atrocious waste. On the other hand, don't attempt to stop up every opening. The room will get muggy, the fire won't draw properly, the boiler, if you have one, won't work to its full capacity and the doors may warp. You need a healthy amount of ventilation.

Walls are generally the greatest source of heat loss and correspondingly expensive to tackle. If the home has cavity walls, they can be filled with an injected cellular compound. Dry walls can be covered with polystyrene sheeting and lined, then painted or papered. Or walls can be battened and covered with another layer of plasterboard with more insulating material. Damp walls can be given a damp-excluding lining as well as being insulated. If the plaster is in bad shape, get it ripped off, line the walls with corrugated bitumastic building paper and then re-plaster with plaster containing insulating vermiculite. If the plaster is still in reasonable condition, have the walls lined with bitumin paper or brush them with a waterproofing liquid, adding battens treated with a preservative, and hang with plasterboard to make a new surface in front of the old one.

Doors with gaps underneath could have a draught-proofing strip fixed. The best kind is the flexible bronze variety.

Windows can have their heat loss cut down by double glazing and, in the US by storm windows, but it is expensive. If you have large draughty windows on the east- and north-facing walls, it might be worth the expense for the resulting extra comfort. A cheaper alternative to glass is to double glaze them yourself with plastic sheeting, but this will obviously affect their appearance. Otherwise you can only tuck insulating tape in the cracks or fit draught-proofing strips as for doors.

Heat loss through any window can be substantially reduced by using curtains which are lined. The quality of the lining is irrelevant.

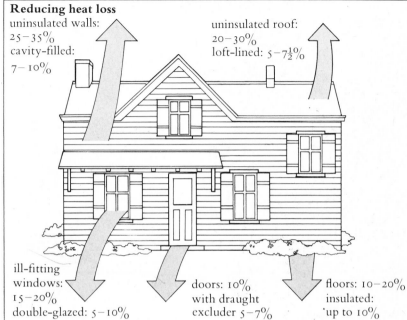

Reducing heat loss

uninsulated walls: 25–35%
cavity-filled: 7–10%

uninsulated roof: 20–30%
loft-lined: 5–7½%

ill-fitting windows: 15–20%
double-glazed: 5–10%

doors: 10%
with draught excluder 5–7%

floors: 10–20%
insulated: up to 10%

Above: Typical heat loss from an uninsulated house with figures reduced by insulation below.

Below: A polystyrene panel fits neatly into the window frame to give both privacy and effective insulation.

Above: The welcoming and cheerful look of a traditional beamed open fireplace. This one, with its handsome brick surround, old grate and gleaming warming pan, is thoroughly in keeping and proportion with the character of the room.

Left: Radiator covers come in all sorts of guises and can be chosen or treated so that they are absorbed into the general decoration of the room. This one, made from bamboo panels, affords useful shelf space.

Clearly, the largest surfaces to be covered in any room are the walls and the floor, and there are invariably two schools of thought about which should have preference in the budget. I usually start at the walls because I find it easier to think up the general colour scheme first, but many people prefer to start with the floor because they automatically think of carpet and presume that this will be the most expensive item. But flooring need not cost the earth; nor is carpeting the only solution. In fact, floors are not necessarily improved by having a cover at all.

Old floors

Wood floors in reasonable condition – that is to say, without gaps, splits and frayed or splintered ends – can be made to look like new with some sanding and polishing. Sanding can be done yourself as long as you wear a medical mask (from chemists or drug stores) and are prepared for a lot of noise. Look in your area trade directory to see where you can hire a machine with a dustbag attachment, or ask at your local hardware or DIY store.

When the surface is completely free from all dust you can seal it with clear polyurethane in an eggshell finish if you want a good

gleam, or matt if you prefer. Apply it with a roller in a thin, even coat and let it dry without disturbing it for a good 24 hours. After this time, apply a second coat and repeat the drying procedure. Finally, you should hire an electric floor polisher, rub on two coats of floor wax and buff it all up.

Another quick improvement can be achieved by dyeing or staining the boards or parquet. If the floor does not need sanding, at least give it a good scrub and a final wash of white spirits, or a mixture of two parts water to one of ordinary vinegar. If it does need sanding, get this done and then give the scrub and wash treatment. This will leave the wood immaculately clean, dry, smooth and receptive to the stain or dye. You can either use a water-based or an oil-based stain. The water-based ones are quite easy to apply and dry quickly but they often look patchy afterwards unless

A bordered carpet of 'body and border' looks well in a large living room (left). Borders can be chosen from a range or can be specially designed. Stripped and sanded floors like the one on the right can look exceptionally elegant left bare.

you finish off with a water-based varnish instead of the usual oil-based polyurethane. A range of oil-based stains in a reasonable choice of shades have recently appeared on the market; these give a more even colour, but they do dry more slowly. Again, let the surface dry and finish off with two coats of polyurethane and wax as for the straight sanding process.

Try bleaching Bleached boards can look quite spectacular provided the surface has been well prepared. Sometimes it is enough to scrub with ordinary bleach and rinse off, sealing with polyurethane afterwards as usual. Or, you could try a stronger chemical bleach, taking good care to follow the instructions on the packet. More professionally, you can lighten them to that bleached-bone look by staining them with a white stain, thinned down with fifty per cent white spirit. Apply it over the boards with a roller, wait a few seconds, then wipe it up with a clean cloth. Let the surface dry, then apply another coat of white stain mixed with matt polyurethane on a five per cent stain/ninety-five per cent polyurethane ratio. Let this dry for 24 hours, then apply a second coat of unadulterated polyurethane. When dry, rub on two coats of white floor wax and finish off by polishing it well.

Paint to the rescue If boards are in too bad a condition to be revived by any of the preceding methods they can almost certainly be retrieved by paint topped up with several coats of polyurethane. Boards can be painted all over in one colour, or individually to form a formal or striped or variegated pattern; they can be stencilled, given a border, or topped with all sorts of imaginative *trompe-l'oeil* effects. You do not need to use expensive gloss or enamel paints, because you have to finish off the surface with polyurethane anyway. Eggshell paint will be fine—or deck paint, although this often looks rather dense. The important thing to remember when painting is that boards should first be given a couple of coats of undercoat and left to dry properly. Tint the undercoat with whatever you are using for the final colour and you will get a good, even finish.

Stencils can be bought from art and craft shops and come complete with instructions for use. There are also a number of excellent books on specialist painting and decorating techniques which will provide you with inspiration as well as practical help.

New hard floors

If your existing floor is beyond improving and needs a fresh start in life, there are several solutions. If it's

Above: Black and white floor tiles set on the diagonal make this room look very cool and large – a feeling helped by the white wicker furniture.

Right: Terracotta floors are a good foil for rugs like this stunning zebra.

a concrete floor you could either put down a new wood floor or tile it with some sort of composition tile or sheeting like vinyl or linoleum which is showing quite a revival. You can cheer up an expanse of plain flooring by setting in borders and designs which can look very handsome, or make two-tone squares: black and white; brown and white; brown and cream; or two shades of the same colour, like two blues or two greens.

Top left: Cream/grey/white painted tiles look elegant contrasted with the grey background and matt fireplace tiles. Top centre: The stencilled border on this stripped, sanded and polished floor matches wall frieze. Above: White painted floor stencilled with diamonds in a leaf design, matches frieze. Far left: Simple, bold and stunning – white painted floor, black chairs, red lamps. Left: Strong colours of chairs, rug and plant stand out from white painted floor.

Cool colours, calm grace

You obviously need a starting point for a colour scheme and once you have found the right one you are away. In this case, one of the new paint effect wallpapers in the subtle pinks and greys of pinky marble was teamed with an equally subtly-coloured printed cotton and the rest was easy: the palette was right there for the choosing; we could hardly go wrong. Graceful curtains between the long bookcases were made from the print which was used again for an underskirt on the table in the corner and for two cushions on one of the armchairs. The pale fresh green in the fabric was repeated again and again: as an overcloth on the table, as piping on the quilted cotton of the upholstered armchairs and stool, in the dhurrie rug and in the pale green beading used for mouldings on the white-painted dado running all around the room. The gentle quality of the colouring was kept with the glass-topped dining table, perspex coffee table and light bamboo dining chairs. Flowers and plants spring up everywhere and the whole is based on a thickly luxurious carpet of porridge-like texture and colour. Even this sense of quiet luxury is repeated again in the soft quilted upholstery. Note too, how the height of bookshelves and window at one end of the room is repeated in the tall plant at the opposite end. Details of materials used are on the right.

Soft floors

If you still decide on carpet for comfort, warmth and quiet, it should be as expensive as you can afford. It is one item you should never skimp or compromise on, and you should make sure you buy the right quality and the right grade. Since a much-used living room has to stand up to a lot of traffic, it needs a superior quality, heavy duty carpet of either 100 per cent wool or 80 per cent wool/20 per cent nylon. They don't come cheap but they do offer the sort of value, wear, sound and heat insulation and dirt-resistance that you're going to expect. They'll also look very good and have great durability giving you years and years of good wear for your money. Then too some of the new man-made fibres are improving; they are losing their old harshness of touch and are being produced in a better range of colours. They're worth considering because they are less expensive and have strong wearing qualities.

Axminster

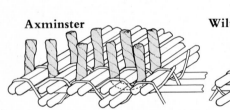

Cut pile tufts are put in position as the backing is woven and are not visible underneath. Any number of colours may be used and any pile effect produced.

Wilton

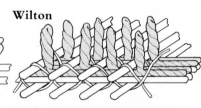

Surface pile is woven in a continuous thread with the backing for added strength, and taken to the base when a new colour is introduced.

Tufted

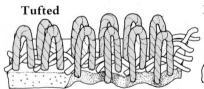

Made by needling tufts into a woven backing and securing on the reverse side with a latex coating.

Bonded

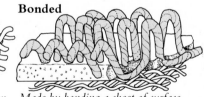

Made by bonding a sheet of surface yarn directly onto backing and cutting pile afterwards.

Taking care of carpets Good carpet needs a good underlay. Sometimes this is built-in to the carpet in the form of a heavy foam backing which only needs layers of newspaper underneath it. Otherwise you'll have to buy it separately. There are many kinds of underlay –felt, foam rubber, pvc, latex. Some have a secondary woven-type backing to give added strength. Felts come in various thicknesses, the thicker they are the more they cost and the better protection they'll give your carpet. Felts are best for 'bedding-down' seams and joins. Rubber or foam backings provide resilience and firmness underfoot but tend to push carpet joins up making them prone to wear. When choosing either foam or felt remember that the more resilient the underlay the more it will improve and therefore prolong the life of your carpet. Underlay forms a necessary cushion between carpet and floor which helps to even the wear, absorb sound and cut down on heat loss. It should be laid with care, preferably by an expert, so that there are no gaps, creases or folds which will cause the carpet to wear quickly in those places as well as making it look unsightly. Before you make your final purchase, do shop around and check whether or not fitting is included in the price. Having bought the best you can afford and laid it properly, you should keep it clean. Vacuum at least once a week and shampoo whenever it starts to look grubby– probably once or twice a year. If you can afford to have it shampooed professionally it'll need doing less often. Old dirt is obstinate and also begins to destroy the fibres if left.

Good alternatives

Other cheaper and very hard-wearing forms of floor covering well worth considering are sisal, coir or coconut matting or hair and woolcord. Although rougher and hairier in texture than wool and man-made carpet and not so soft or luxurious, they come in good colours–the natural shades are particularly attractive–and are tough enough to withstand the most active family on its feet. You won't sink into this sort of flooring but it has a neat appearance and will pull together a disparate collection of furniture and styles and make a roomful of old things look firmly set in the twentieth century. Again, it is especially important to keep matting regularly cleaned to avoid a build-up of dirt and stains. Carpet tiles are marvellously practical because they can be moved around stress areas–under chairs, in front of sofas–and worn ones replaced as necessary. They are particularly useful for temporary and rented accommodation because they can be so easily taken up and put down.

Top left: Coir matting looks neat, and works perfectly with a mixture of styles as well as being an excellent contrast to rugs.

Above: Wall to wall Berber carpet, can also be a good link between the traditional and the modern; its neutral shades and chunky texture makes it an interesting contrast for different colours.

Far left and left: Geometric carpets and rugs look fresh and modern.

FLOOR AND WALL TREATMENTS

What to put on the wall

There must be countless ways to cover a wall but let's narrow it down to the three basic choices: paint, paper or fabric. Of these, painting is generally the easiest and least expensive. Clever painting can disguise faults in a room, lose unsightly features like too many doors, ugly pipes or angles, emphasize good proportions and minimize bad ones. And these days, it can do more than this: it can introduce all sorts of excitements in design, colour and texture. Up till recently, ceilings, walls and woodwork were either done in gloss, eggshell or flat paint, with perhaps the odd contrast border or super graphic thrown in as an added bonus. Now the increasing sophistication in most paint ranges, plus a new interest in the purely decorative aspect, has resulted in the revival of old traditional crafts and techniques such as stippling, rag-rolling, colour-washing, dragging and lacquering which can all be learnt and practised without too much difficulty. If you've never tackled these techniques before you should experiment off the wall first, using lining paper.

Simple tricks with paint

● You can make a ceiling seem much higher by painting it a lighter colour than the walls and keeping the floor a light tone as well. Lower a too-high ceiling by painting it darker.

● Liven up dull-looking spaces with bands or outlines of colour. Keep a simple, light background and paint skirting or baseboards and mouldings in a contrasting shade. You could paint two or three bands of different colours in different widths, starting from the baseboard or skirting. If there isn't a false cornice or cove, form one by painting a stripe or two immediately under the ceiling. This could be continued down corners to the skirting and around doors. Draw the stripes lightly in pencil first and take great care to get them precise.

● Create impressive graphic designs on your walls; all it takes is courage and a little sleight of hand. If not graphics, then try freeflowing bands of colour in varying shapes. Sometimes the shape of a bedhead or a mirror or storage unit can be echoed over the object proper in 1920's or 1930's style and then exaggerated with a contrasting edge of another colour. Have a little fun with it and let shapes drawn down a wall spill over a dresser or chest of drawers.

● Get the feeling of panelling by sticking rectangles of contrasting tape on a plain painted wall; or by drawing rectangular stripes in panel

shapes and carefully painting them in contrasting colours.

● Disguise eyesores—a confusion of unboxed pipes, off-centre doors or windows, breaks in ceiling levels, awkward angles and unsightly radiators—by painting the area in a dark colour. This makes everything melt away into the background. Alternatively, a messy jumble of pipes could actually be picked out to look like an interesting feature in its own right.

Paint is obviously very versatile and adaptable but wall coverings of paper or fabric can cheer up a dull room, obliterate uneven, cracked walls, help to even up proportions and generally soften the look of a room, and needn't cost the earth.

Left: Lengths of picture framing are used here to create false panelling on what otherwise might have been a bland-looking wall. Panels like this make an excellent background for prints. Similarly, a dado can be added to a wall to give additional interest, as here, painted in the same shade as the panelling border; the wall beneath it is given a different treatment.

Bottom left: Red glossy walls diffuse angles in this room and make it look much larger. Note too, the bentwood chair which has been given a smartener coat of shiny black lacquer.

white-painted brick gently contrasts with floor but harmonizes with furnishings

downlights cast pools of light on floor

exposed beams add interest

dried flowers provide pleasing texture with tonal integration

wood-burning stove adds shape and warmth

old chest complements modern furniture

wool rug and brick floor tone in with colour scheme and provide contrasts of texture

Above: Tongue and groove wood bleached to a weather-worn shade contrasts well with the white-painted brickwork of the end wall and the darker bricks of the floor. Walls like this are a decoration in their own right with their pleasing textures.

57

FLOOR AND WALL TREATMENTS

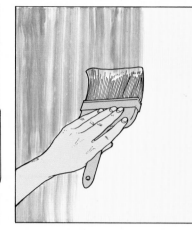

Rag-rolling
Paint background coats of oil-based eggshell paint. Measure and mix equal quantities of white spirit and tinted eggshell for glaze.

Paint a thin glazing coat onto the dry background with a 10 cm (4 in) brush, in even vertical strokes, to cover the base coat.

While glaze is still wet, roll up a clean cotton rag into a sausage shape and roll upwards until saturated. Change rag frequently.

A pale blue-grey tinted glaze has been rag-rolled over an oil-based ivory eggshell base to produce a distinctive tafetta-like pattern.

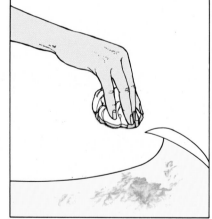

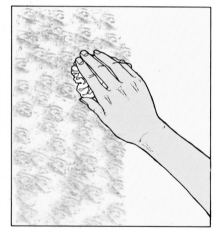

Ragging on
Take cans of oil-based eggshell paint for background; bowl for tinted glaze; fine cotton rag, spoon for mixing, and brush.

Experiment on lining paper. Brush on background paint and let dry. Soak rag in glaze, bunch it up and press onto paper.

Dab off excess paint and when satisfied, *gently* press rag onto wall using same pressure as for testing; change angles at intervals.

Here a dusty pink has been ragged on a paler pink ground for a delicate look. The random method produces a hand-printed effect.

Sponge stippling
Spoon 1 tablespoon of chosen sponged colour into a bowl, and spread with back of spoon. Moisten natural sea sponge.

Squeeze sponge so that it is damp but not wet; hold the round edge of sponge and press flat side into paint. Test impression on paper.

Now place, but don't press, the sponge onto the prepared wall. Lift and repeat, replenishing and testing paint as necessary.

An interesting speckled effect has been achieved here by sponging on deep yellow and warm orange tones over a creamy matt vinyl background.

Dragging and swirling
Paint on base coat of matt emulsion. Slowly dilute a slightly darker or contrasting colour with water and stir well to mix.

Drag on the graining colour thinly in even strokes from the top downwards, covering about a 60 cm (2 ft) square.

While still wet, take clean brush and swirl paint at random so that base coat underneath is subtly revealed. The technique is simple.

This particular finish gives a pleasantly hazy effect and because emulsion can be used it is quicker drying and less messy than oil.

59

FLOOR AND WALL TREATMENTS

Achieving expensive effects

The choice of wallpapers is enormous, with prices to match at every stage up and down the scale, but you don't have to pay the earth to achieve a very luxurious look. Fairly inexpensive papers can be made to seem—and last—like very expensive versions if you know some of the tricks:

● Use a heavy lining paper to hide any defects in the wall. Hang it horizontally and be careful to stick it precisely edge to edge so that no bulge will show through the paper proper.

● Paint over inexpensive non-vinyl paper when it is hung, with a coat or two of either matt or eggshell polyurethane. Test the varnish out on a small piece of leftover paper first to make sure that the colours don't run. The varnish will deepen or 'yellow' the paper slightly but this generally makes it look richer and more interesting. It will last longer and you'll also be able to sponge it gently to clean it.

If you want to use a good quality wallpaper like the one in this room, you can save money by learning how to put it up yourself. A professional tip to getting a good finish is to lay the lining paper horizontally. A final coat of matt polyurethane will protect it and increase its life.

How to afford the best

It's easy to make one very expensive roll of wallpaper stretch all round a room which, if you could ever afford it, would normally take 10 or 12 rolls. The trick is to paint the walls the colour of the background of the paper, using a matt latex paint, then cut the paper into equal rectangles or squares and stick them on the walls in regularly spaced 'panels'. If the paper has a border, use it as a finishing edging. Again, you can make it more durable and cleanable by giving a coat or two of poly-urethane. Test the paper first for colour fastness.

You are better able to afford good wallpaper if you hang it yourself. The pre-pasted range is a boon to the DIY expert. Being self-adhesive it only needs wetting and sticking on. It takes about 20 minutes to adhere—time enough to correct mistakes.

Fabrics look fabulous

Wall fabrics are generally more expensive than papers but can often make the walls look so luxurious that you can get away with minimal furnishings. They will also com-pletely cover up imperfections, have good sound and heat insu-lation properties and, if they've been treated with protective spray, will last for years and years – long after paint has become chipped and discoloured, and paper faded.

Calculating quantities

Paint To work out the area, multiply the perimeter of the room by the height from skirting board to ceiling.

Quantity	Gloss		Emulsion	
	sq yds	(sq m)	sq yds	(sq m)
1 pt (0.568 l)	10	(8½)	12	(10)
1 qt (1.135 l)	20	(17)	24	(20)
1 gal (4.54 l)	80	(67)	96	(80)

Wallcoverings Check the size and origin of rolls of wallpaper before ordering. English papers generally have different measurements from American varieties. For example: English papers are more or less 10.98 m (12 yd) long and 0.64 m (21 in) wide when trimmed or 7.03 sq m (7 sq yd) in area; most European papers are 8.25 m (9 yd) long and 0.46 m (18 in) wide when trimmed or 12.35 sq m (40.5 sq ft) in area; most American papers are 7.32 m (8 yd) long and 0.46 m (18 in) wide when trimmed or 3.34 sq m (4 sq yd) in area. Check if paper is trimmed before buying; allow extra to match pattern drops. Order more paint and wallpaper than you think you'll need.

English wallpapers Table for calculating number of rolls required

Height of wall		Measurement around the walls in feet (metres)					
Feet	Metres	28 (8.53)	32 (9.76)	40 (12.19)	44 (13.41)	52 (15.08)	56 (17.01)
7–7½	2.13–2.29	4	4	5	6	7	7
7½–8	2.29–2.44	4	4	5	6	7	8
8–8½	2.44–2.59	4	5	6	7	8	8
8½–9	2.59–2.74	4	5	6	7	8	9
9½–10	2.94–3.05	5	6	7	7	9	9
10–10½	3.05–3.24	5	6	7	8	9	10
10½–11½	3.24–3.39	5	6	7	8	9	10
Feet	Metres	60 (18.29)	64 (19.50)	68 (20.73)	72 (21.95)	80 (24.38)	84 (25.60)
7–7½	2.13–2.29	8	8	9	9	10	10
7½–8	2.29–2.44	8	9	9	10	11	11
8–8½	2.44–2.59	9	9	10	11	12	12
8½–9	2.59–2.74	9	10	10	11	12	13
9½–10	2.94–3.05	10	10	11	12	13	14
10–10½	3.05–3.24	10	11	12	12	14	14
10½–11½	3.24–3.39	11	11	12	13	14	15

American wallpapers Table for calculating rolls required

Feet (metres) around room	Height of wall					
	8 ft (2.44 m)	9 ft (2.74 m)	10 ft (3.05 m)	11 ft (3.35 m)	12 ft (3.65 m)	14 ft (4.27 m)
28 (8.53)	7	8	9	10	11	12
36 (10.98)	9	10	11	12	13	16
44 (13.41)	11	12	14	15	16	19
52 (16.08)	13	15	16	18	19	22
60 (18.29)	15	17	19	20	22	26
68 (20.96)	17	19	21	23	25	29
72 (22.18)	18	20	22	24	27	31
80 (23.38)	20	22	25	27	30	34
88 (25.84)	22	24	27	30	32	38
92 (27.06)	23	26	28	31	34	39
96 (28.28)	24	27	30	32	35	41

Making it stick Some fabric wall coverings—ranging from hessians or burlaps, felts and flannels to suedes, wool, silk and moiré—come with a paper backing which makes it easy to stick them to the walls. However, if you use the correct adhesive and somebody with the right sort of skill, almost any fabric of reasonable weight and texture can be stuck to walls. You can then choose from a very wide range indeed, from lengths of artists' or sail canvas (available quite cheaply from art supply stores or marine goods suppliers) to upholstery fabrics and velvets. It is best to go for fabrics which are stretch- and fade-resistant as well as stain- and mildew-resistant.

When sticking fabric up apply the paste to the walls and not to the fabric. Cover any frayed edges with braid, or a thin painted beading, or lengths of narrow picture-framing wood, polished, silvered, gilded or lacquered. (This can often be bought by the foot from the picture framers.) As well as being practical, the end result will look as if it cost many times as much.

Fixing fabric There are special wall-track systems for attaching materials of all weights to the wall. The fabric stays neat and taut without the need for adhesive. These track systems are comprised of long plastic strips with 'jaws' to hide ragged edges and an adhesive strip to hold the fabric tight. You simply screw the strips to the walls just under the ceiling and just above the skirting or baseboards to make a kind of frame, and use the special tool provided to push the fabric into the frame and secure it in position. Although it is obviously more expensive than sticking with applied adhesive, this method means that you can change fabrics if you like to achieve a fresh effect, and also clean the fabric as necessary. Do check therefore that you use fabric that will not shrink. This makes it a good bet for rented accommodation as you can take both the material and the wall-track with you when you leave.

Upholster the wall Pre-cut fabric can actually be stapled to the wall and any raw edges covered with braid or trim, but you can get a much softer, more professionally upholstered look if you batten the fabric. This means nailing or stapling (with a proper staple gun) lathes or thin strips of wood (about 5 cm [2 in wide]) horizontally, just below the ceiling or moulding and just above the skirting. Similar strips of wood are then fixed vertically at 1.8 m (6 ft) intervals. If paintings or prints are to be hung on the walls it is important to work out beforehand where they are going to go, and to make sure that battens are

Left: In this room, material has been used on a lavish scale to create a very expensive look at relatively little cost. Metres and metres of fabric have been gathered on to a pole that runs around the perimeter, then left to hang free in generous folds. It's easy to put up and take down, making it ideal for rented rooms.

Above: In this more tailored room, fabric is attached to the wall just below the cornice and caught up at intervals in graceful folds like elaborate curtains, and, like curtains, left to sweep the floor. The effect is both graceful and original.

fixed in these particular areas. This applies equally to light switches and electric sockets. When the fabric is up, these battens can be felt through the fabric, making it easy to fix nails and picture hooks to them.

When all the strips of wood are fixed, staple lengths of synthetic fibre padding between them. You are now ready to attach the fabric which should have been cut in panels to fit the wall measurements and seamed where necessary to join the lengths.

Attach the first fabric panel by centring it between the outside edge of the first vertical batten and the

middle of the second one. When the top of the fabric is level with the top horizontal batten, lightly tack it—with thumb tacks—in the middle. Stretch it to either side, tack it, then staple into position.

You can keep the whole thing very neat by using 5 cm (2 in) wide cardboard strips cut to the height of the walls. Place the second panel, right side down, on to the edge of the first panel so that their two cut edges line up. Lay one of the long strips of cardboard over this join and staple through card and fabric on to the batten. Continue all round the room, remembering that any staple marks and rough edges can be covered with lengths of matching or contrasting braid. Braid should also be used around the top and bottom of the fabric and around doors and windows.

Wall fabrics that hang If you have rented accommodation and can't or don't want to put fabric up permanently—or are not allowed to paint, for that matter—then you can hang fabric instead.

Inexpensive cottons can be hung from rods or poles and left to hang free at the bottom, although they should be caught back over doors and windows with tie-backs.

Lightweight inexpensive fabrics like cheesecloth and muslin can be shirred and hung between rods, wires or traverse poles attached

below the ceiling and above the skirting or baseboards, and either caught back at doors and windows or fixed around them (with rods or wires attached to the top of the frames). If you use this method you will need a generous amount of fabric, about three times the width of the wall. You can then either hem and gather it with shirring tape before it is fixed to the walls; or let it gather itself naturally as you push the rods through the turned-over hems at top and bottom. Make the casing only just large enough for the rods, so that they fit tightly.

Fabric you can afford
Wall fabric always sounds like the last word in luxury but in fact need not cost much. For instance:
Cheesecloth muslin
Painters' dust sheets or drop cloths in clear colours and simple patterns such as checks and stripes
Indian cotton quilts
Removers' quilts in plain or printed cotton or satin
Artists' canvas
Sail canvas
Book-binding cloth
Khaki and navy suiting cloth from Army and Navy surplus stores
Reject fabric of any sort
Rolls of embroidery canvas.

Safety factor
To avoid any fire risk, you can treat fabric with a flame retardant spray.

63

Windows are like eyes: they are looked *at* as much as they are looked *out of*. They also provide light. ventilation, protection and, very often, a focus. But they usually have to be covered, which means yet another thing to budget for in a room. For even when the proportions are beautiful or unusual, the view stupendous, the privacy assured, a window covering is still the most practical way of shutting out the depressing sight of rain, avoiding too much heat loss, preventing draughts in winter and the discomforts of too much sun in summer. The sort of windows that need little or nothing in the way of treatment are usually narrow slits of glass, small ovals, round, arched, stained and etched glass windows that only show a glimpse of the outside and are often unopenable anyway. In cases like this, a decorative object on the sill, like a plant, a single flower in a vase, a piece of old glass or china, a sculpture, a small lamp or candle, even a beautiful book, is often far better than attempting any sort of curtain. However, most of us have very ordinary windows and want to know how to treat them well and interestingly for the least possible expense.

Curtains

The variety of curtains is enormous. They can be as simple or as elaborate as you like, depending on the fabric, the heading, the pelmet, whether they hang free or are tied back and, of course, on your taste and what suits the room. Headings range from simple gathers to complicated arrangements of pleats and include the popular French heads— groups of three pleats—single goblet pleats, pinch pleats, pencil pleats, double pleats, gathers and smocks. If you're making them yourself use the appropriate heading tape. Swags and tails, done by draping and folding, are another fairly elaborate form of heading and can look enormously impressive. Pelmets can be hard or soft. Hard ones are usually of wood in straight or fancy shapes, painted or fabric covered. Soft pelmets, in the same material as the curtains are lined, gathered or ruched.

If windows are a handsome shape and not overlooked just leave them be. The triple set to the left is complemented by an array of healthy plants. The graceful curtains on the right are gathered high to show off arched panes.

Bringing the garden indoors

Windows, they say, are beginning to be the new status symbol. Certainly there has never been a better choice of fabrics on the market, and, more useful still, a better choice of ready-made curtains and window accessories like poles, tie-backs, tracks and so on. Many of these curtains and a wide range of fabrics have their own matching papers which make it hard to make a mistake in a room, thus giving an instant injection of confidence to home decorators. In this fresh and garden-like room, willow green moiré wallpaper is matched to ready-made curtains in heavy cotton with an interesting carnation-pattern border in greens and rust. Matching green cord has been cut to form separate tie-backs and the same cotton fabric has been used for a round tablecloth. Wicker furniture is upholstered in a mixture of green and apricot cotton and scattered with cushions in co-ordinating colours and fabrics. The generally sunny atmosphere of the room is sustained with the white-painted floor boards, the airy dhurrie rug, the mass of plants in various sizes and stages, and the visual pun of the huge fern painting on the back wall. Much the same atmosphere can be duplicated at night with the well-thought out lighting: a mixture of strip light behind a pelmet running all round the room and uplights on the floor behind plants. Close-up of details on right.

WHAT TO DO WITH WINDOWS

How long is a curtain?

Short windows don't necessarily have to have short curtains which only really look good in small cottagey or attic windows. Short, neat café curtains that cover half the window can sometimes be the answer to shut out an ugly view. If you have short windows and don't want long curtains, use blinds.

Generous, full-length curtains look rich, graceful and generally room-enhancing. They should either just touch the floor–no gap between hem and floor–or be allowed to fall down to it in folds, Thirties style. Give long curtains good hems to allow for shrinkage.

Fabric

Whatever you buy, don't skimp on the amount. Curtains should look full so it's better to have yards and yards of a cheaper material than meagre amounts of an expensive one. It won't even look expensive if you've been mean about it. Bound, edged, or bordered curtains, or all three, look sophisticated and beautifully finished off. Lining is a must– except for sheers–and interlining recommended for insulating–both keeping in the heat and keeping out any cold air–cutting down noise and dirt absorption. Properly lined curtains hang nicely; unlined ones just droop.

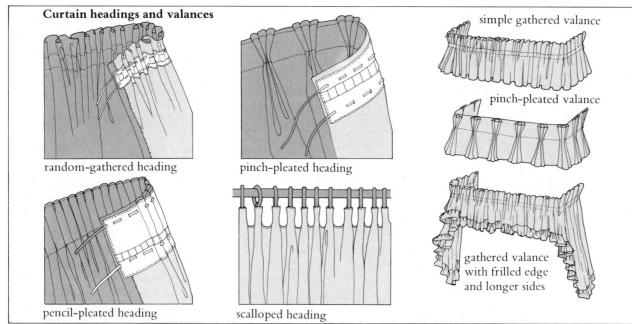

Curtain headings and valances

random-gathered heading

pinch-pleated heading

simple gathered valance

pinch-pleated valance

pencil-pleated heading

scalloped heading

gathered valance with frilled edge and longer sides

Above left: Double café curtains are made specially interesting with their frame of stencilled flowers. The smaller pattern seems to be repeated by the leaves trailing from the hanging basket, and the larger pattern by the tulips on the table.

Above: In this room elaborately painted shutters, which are more like decorated panels, give a better effect than curtains. The table, with its patchwork overcloth in front of the window adds to the picturesqueness.

Right: Loose cream linen weave curtains on this bay fall gracefully to the floor over Holland blinds. False panels of wood beading give distinction to the wood below.

Blinds

These have now become as popular as curtains and, like them, range from the plain and simple roller fabric blinds to elaborately frilled and ruched varieties. Then there are the wood and metal blinds, including Venetian and louvred. See the *Glossary* (page 342) and Blind identikit (page 265) for description of available blinds.

Good alternatives

If your insulation is reasonable, and heat loss and energy conservation not therefore serious considerations, or if the window is more useful for its light than its view, or the view needs disguising, then see what you can do with the frames. These can often be very imaginatively treated. Short windows can be given extra height by fixing wood trim to the frame from floor to ceiling and perpendicular to the wall. It will also give the window more depth. Add a blind or shade to drop from the ceiling level as well and you will suddenly have long graceful windows, or what will pass for them very well. The frames can be painted, papered or covered in with the walls or painted a contrasting colour or white.

Another possibility is to have double-hinged solid wooden shutters or panels made for each side of the window, again from ceiling to floor. Were you to feel particularly

WHAT TO DO WITH WINDOWS

extravagant you could have the room-facing side mirrored – worth it for the wonderful effect of light and space. Alternatively, you could make the screens or shutters easily detachable and have one surface painted or covered in fabric so that you could ring the changes when you felt like it or have different ones for summer and winter. Other good ideas are to fill the window with plants hung from the ceiling; to fit glass shelves for a collection of coloured glass or masses of pretty pot plants. (Always check first that the plants are suited to a position where they will be subjected to extremes of light and heat, like some hardy ivies.) Or surround the window with shelves for books and interesting collections of objects.

Cheerful improvements

It is quite possible to cheer up existing curtains, blinds or shades that are perfectly adequate but tired and boring. And what's more, it needn't cost very much.

● Long curtains or drapes hanging loose will look better–and different–immediately if you loop them back with tie-backs made from lengths of cord and attached to hooks fixed to the window frame. Or make your own fabric tie-backs (see instructions on page 22).

● Add a border or binding down the leading and bottom edges of curtains for a real interior designer touch. Choose a colour from the existing design or a contrast colour if the fabric is plain. Make fabric tie-backs to match.

● If you are handy with a needle you could sew in another lining or backing in a contrasting or toning fabric to the existing one. Add a print lining to a plain material; a small scale design in the same colours to a large scale design; a geometric in the same colours to a mini-flower pattern; an abstract pattern to a more clear-cut one. If you then loop the curtains back you will get glimpses of the new lining, which will give it fresh interest.

Top left: Tied-back print curtains (which match the table-cloth) allow plain under curtains to be drawn underneath. Note the cleverly concealed radiator below the window, and the attention to detail shown by the blue edging to the green cloth.

Top far right: A Roman blind with its tailored folds fits this window neatly and has an unfussy look.

Right: Elaborate festoon blinds behind rather tailored curtains add an air of depth and perspective to this room. This is reinforced by the use of mirror on the wall, and glass to support the unicorn head and act as a coffee table.

Above: The colour scheme of pale yellow with turquoise blue trim used to decorate this charming Regency period room, was based on that used in the drawing room of the Sir John Soane Museum in London. In keeping with that period, the window treatment has been confined to shutters with Holland blinds for privacy. The small table, which like the rest of the furniture is contemporary with the house, was originally backed with mirror. New distressed mirror has been cleverly used between the long windows to continue the effect of enhanced space. The faux bois treatment used on the skirting board and the Greek key pattern of the border are also period features which have been added.

Know your window terms

Here is a brief guide, in alphabetical order, to the names you're most likely to come across once you start thinking about window treatments.

Austrian blind Arched blind or shade more commonly known as a festoon blind or pull-up curtain. It has rows of vertical shirring and can be raised and lowered by cords threaded through rings concealed at the back of the blind.

Backing This is the special material laminated to roller shade fabric to act as a lining, a stiffener and a blocker-out of unwelcome light.

Balloon blind A shade or blind with deep inverted pleats which create a billowing balloon-like effect.

Blind A vertical window covering which can be rolled up on a spring-roller attachment, or drawn up by cords threaded through rings.

Café curtain A short half-curtain hung from a rod going across a window, as in French cafés. This sort of curtaining is sometimes hung in a double tier, and is a useful treatment for windows that open inwards, or face the street. The tier system gives both light and privacy.

Casement window A window that opens on vertical hinges.

Cornice A wooden frame or pelmet mounted over a window treatment to hide the hardware.

Festoon blind See Austrian blind.

Finials The decorative ends of a curtain rod, either wood or brass.

Heading The top of curtains or drapes. Different varieties include gathered headings, pencil pleats, pinch pleats, box pleats, scalloped headings and smocked or shirred headings.

Leading edge The inner edge of a curtain or blind which is often bound or bordered.

Mullions The vertical, narrow wood members that separate panes of glass.

Muntins US term for mullion.

Pattern repeat A design term for one or more motifs repeated either vertically or horizontally on a fabric. It is useful to quote the size of the repeat when ordering fabric for curtains or blinds so that you do not cut off in the middle of a formalized pattern. Large repeats in fabric make curtains very expensive

Pelmet: See cornice and valance.

Pull-up curtain See Austrian blind.

Ring-shirr tape Fabric strip with regular rings and two enclosed cords used for shirring blinds like the Austrian or Festoon variety.

Ring tape Fabric strip with rings used for Roman and Balloon blinds.

Rod pocket The open-ended casing at the bottom hem of a Roman or Roller blind through which a rod, batten or wooden slat is passed to add extra weight.

Roller blind A flat blind that is controlled by a spring-mechanism.

Roman blind A shade or blind that draws up into neat horizontal folds by means of cords threaded through rings attached at regular intervals to the back of the fabric. You can either use rings alone or, on heavier fabrics, you can attach light battens to keep the folds crisp.

Sash curtains A flat piece of fabric or curtain panel with rod pockets sewn at top and bottom. Ordinary brass or tension rods are then threaded through and mounted at top and bottom of the window to stretch the curtain between them.

Shirring A permanent gathering of fabric achieved by drawing up material along two or more parallel lines of stitching, or over cords or thin rods threaded through casings or rod pockets.

Tie-back A piece of fabric, cord or chain attached to the window frame and used to loop back curtains.

Valance Or pelmet. A decorative, horizontal panel of fabric usually attached to the top of the window frame, or just above, to hide rods and provide added interest.

WHAT TO DO WITH WINDOWS

Measuring curtains

Accurate measurement is essential. Don't guess—looks are deceptive. Measure every window with a steel tape (fabric ones stretch). Double check each measurement and write it down immediately, identifying each window if you are measuring several at once.

Once you have measured the window, decide where the hardware—the tracks and screws and so on—is going to go (above the frame; overlapping the sides; tucked neatly inside a recess); buy what you have decided upon and install it before you start calculating the fabric. If you are going to replace existing hardware, make pencil marks to show the new position. This is important because hardware measurements will affect your calculations as you will see from the more detailed instructions for measuring curtains which are given on page 73 opposite.

Above left: Venetian blinds are used both for window and room divider in this large Hi-Tech living space.

Above: Clear blue shades are fitted to draw up from the bottom on these overlooked windows. Fixed like this they ensure maximum privacy with the benefit of maximum light as well.

Right: Cheap rattan or matchstick blinds allied to massed plants introduce sunny conservatory quality.

How to measure curtains

Before you can estimate how much material you are going to need, you must first decide what style of curtain you want, whether a heading is required, what sort of fabric you want to use and what length they should be. The appropriate curtain track or rod should also either be in position or its precise location and dimensions marked with a pencil.

The first thing you need to establish is the final length and width of the area the finished curtains are to cover when drawn.

The width To find the width of the curtain area (**AA**), you only need measure the length of the supporting track or rod, or the combined length of both tracks where two overlap.

The total width of the curtains is this measurement multiplied by the fullness required by the type of heading you have chosen, plus 7.5 cm (3 in) for each side hem. Curtains look mean when they don't have sufficient fabric to hang in luxurious folds, so don't skimp. Multiply the width by two for a standard gathered heading, by two and a quarter for a pencil pleat heading, two and a half for pinch pleats and three for sheer and lightweight fabrics.

The length To find the finished length of curtains you must know where they are to start and finish. Measure from the top of the curtain track or rod (or pencilled position) for headed curtains, and from the bottom of the rings where the curtains are to be suspended below a rod.

Measure from there to the point where you want the curtain to finish. This is usually the sill (**AB**) or floor (**AC**).

Add 15–25 cm (6–10 ins) to this length for hems and heading (15 cm [6 in] for lightweight and sheer fabrics and 25 cm [10 in] for heavy ones).

How much fabric to buy To find out how many fabric widths you will need, divide the total width of the curtain by the width of the fabric you want to use, always rounding up the total (i.e. $6\frac{1}{2}$ widths should be seven widths).

If you are using a plain fabric, multiply the number of fabric widths by the length in centimetres and divide by 100 to get the number of metres. Do the same for yards but divide the inches by 36.

Matching patterns If you are using a patterned fabric you will have to allow for repeats of design

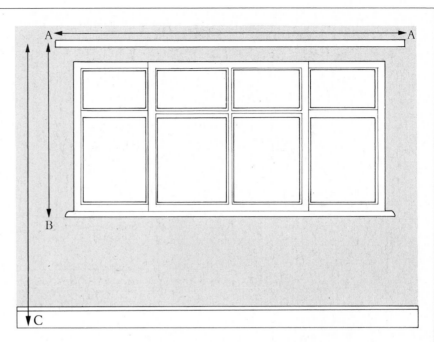

in the length. With floor length curtains or drapes you usually start off with a full repeat just below the heading; short curtains and blinds have the repeat at the bottom. Repeats on each width must match exactly; so should every window in the room.

This applies not just to large designs; even tiny all-over patterns jar if they are out of true. To test this in a store, simply unroll enough fabric for you to see two pattern sections side by side. If, when you shift one section slightly, you can't see any

difference in the pattern, you won't need to bother about measuring the repeat. If it looks odd, you must measure.

You do this by measuring the length of a complete pattern before it repeats again. Make a note of it along with all the other measurements. Then measure lengthwise from the dominant motif within a repeat to the next identical one. Since you want to keep the repeats even and not cut off in mid-air as it were, you usually have to buy more patterned fabric than plain.

People often get very guilty about choosing furniture. They feel that they should know what they want in a room from the very beginning, and feel incompetent if they cannot make up their minds right away. But any truly individual room has to evolve slowly; this is half the fun and certainly half the charm.

If you have existing furniture and are merely re-doing a room, you will almost certainly know what you want to keep and what to replace—or re-upholster, re-cover, re-finish or re-paint. If you are starting from scratch, make a list of all the pieces you think absolutely essential, with a note of what they are likely to cost. If you get into the habit of always checking the prices of furniture you like in shops, sales or auction rooms, you will soon have a pretty clear idea of most values whether antique, second hand, reproduction or modern. Make a second list of other pieces you think you would like when you can afford them, say over the next five years or so. This will be a more flexible list because prices tend to creep upwards (except when you want to sell anything) and your tastes and finances might well change a little or a lot along the way.

Choosing a style
The style of a room is what gives it its own particular character. Style often becomes as big a bugbear as colour schemes and for the same reason; it means laying what passes for your taste on the table for all to judge. But I cannot emphasize too strongly that you should only choose furniture and furnishings that make you feel comfortable. If they don't, they won't make other people feel comfortable either. Once again it boils down to confidence, and the small test I recommended on page 16 for finding out the colours that make you feel secure, can apply just as well to style.

The most usual styles to see around today could include what pass for country, city-sophisticated, improvised junk, garden room, Italian modern, French (Louis Le-whatever) uncompromisingly antique of whatever period is chosen (Georgian, Jacobean) art deco, art nouveau and eclectic mix.

Different styles for different tastes. City sophistication is achieved in the room on the left by cool colours and sleek furniture. Thirties furnishings contribute comfort to the room on the right.

Far left: The combination of streamlined chairs, abstract art, steel and glass furniture and clear colours, gives this room an International style.

Top left: A Country or Cottage style is achieved here by the presence of comfortable upholstered furniture, soft furnishings and wallcovering, all in complementary floral prints. This is reinforced by the use of cane, wicker and an abundance of fresh flowers.

Bottom left: The predominant style here is Art Nouveau, reflected in the cushions and light fittings, with an unobtrusive assortment of additional pieces for practicality.

Above: Garden style is brought into this living room through the massed display of plants in front of the lattice-effect windows and in other parts of the room. Rattan cane chairs and floral and leaf chintz fabrics set against a light background are equally appropriate.

They all have a sort of recognisable shorthand: *Country*, for example, would include mini flower prints and fresh stripes, comfortable sofas, and perhaps a lot of wicker or cane as well as stripped pine furniture. *Junk* would pride itself on a collection of re-vamped, painted-up old pieces and found objects. *City* would conjure up sophisticated leather and chrome, glass, marble and wall-to-wall carpet. *Modern Italian* would be bright, primary coloured, or 'dolly-mixture' lacquered furniture or plastic, white floor and walls, with, perhaps a strong dash of the new Memphis daring. 'Memphis' is the name of the design partnership set up by the Italian designer Ettore Sottsass in 1981 when he exhibited the furniture which has now become pseudonymous with this name at the Italian Furniture Fair. *Antique*, relates to any room which is consistently furnished in the style of one period, such as Victorian, Georgian, Art Deco. Art Nouveau would relate to furnishings of the 1890's, typified by the use of images of plants, hair and the sea reflected in sinuous curves in pale and subtle colours. Art Deco has come to mean brilliant oriental colours, all things Persian and elaborate curtains. *Garden* would be lattice, cane, plants and flowery chintzes. And the *Eclectic mix* is what most of us are probably happiest with; a little bit of every-thing, old and new, treasures, heirlooms and favourite things collected from all over.

Sitting comfortably

If you are starting from scratch, or just about, decide what has to be bought and what improvised in the way of seating. Whatever you buy, make it the best you can afford. If comfort is important to you—and if it isn't now, it almost certainly will be at a later date—anchor pieces like sofas and large armchairs should be the best looking and most comfortable you can pay for and find. Second best is not good enough. In upholstery you really do get what you pay for and you usually have to take the quality on trust since you cannot see all the underpinnings of frames, filling and springs unless you are shown a sample cross section and have it all explained to you in the shop.

Most good stores display a whole section of upholstered pieces from traditional to modern in a range of different shapes and sizes, but most pieces come in a far greater variety of sizes, covers and colourings than those on show. So, if you like the shape of something but not the size and colour, do not give up on it. For instance, you may like the look of a sofa but think it too small; it may well come in other lengths from 137 cm to 229 cm (54 to 90 in). Arm and back heights too, can be varied since they have to be built separately in the first place, and there is almost always a large range of covers available for the choosing within the price range. If you are willing to pay the difference in price there is usually even more choice. It pays to inquire. Living-room seating should be as adaptable as your life-style demands and able to cope with crowded parties as well as quiet evenings if need be. Try to plan to seat at least six comfortably, and also have some really occasional chairs that can be stashed away in a cupboard somewhere or brought in from the hall or a bedroom. If they can fit in with the room's general style, or at least colour, they will look so much the better.

Other furniture

Most other furniture—tables, desks, storage and occasional pieces—will either be made of wood, glass and some sort of metal or perspex or plexiglass or even marble. Whether you choose antique, modern, repro-duction or a mixture of all three is purely a question of personal taste, combined with the sort of style you're aiming at. Some people are ardent collectors of 20s, 30s and 50s furniture, or even the 40s utility pieces which are now enjoying a new vogue. If you are far from rich but hanker after earlier furniture, scour the second-hand shops, junk yards, charity shops and Oxfam

Far left: Comfortable and flexible modular seating units in toning coloured upholstery, which is removable for easy cleaning.

Above: Regency drawing room with real candle candelabra, and genuine period furniture. Original window surrounds have been painted then combed to look like grained oak.

Left: Stylish simplicity is produced by the framing of a classic black Corbusier chaise longue against the unexpected combination of vivid green stippled walls and pink carpet. Note the empty frame.

centres as well as any sort of sale.

Most good modern furniture is expensive and if you have set your heart on a piece you can't afford it is better to improvise for the moment than try and compromise.

Flexi-furniture

If you plan to eat in the living room, try to buy as generous a table as possible but one which will look quite in keeping with the room when it is not laid for a meal. Round tables are best for this because when they aren't being used for dining they can be piled with books, magazines and plants, and have the look and feel of a library table. You can make up round tables from cheap wood and cover them with long cloths and changeable overcloths. Alternatively, try to find the sort of rectangular table that can also double as a long desk or work table when required. Chairs should look just as good for occasional seating as for dining. If you feel more comfortable having at least a visual dividing line between sitting and dining areas you could make a dividing 'wall' with a low storage unit. This could act as a bar and serving area as well. Even a large sofa with its back to the table can make an effective divider.

Small space seating

If a room is tiny, don't despair. Try to work out the best solution to your background problem (see pages 29–37), then forget altogether about conventional seating (one or two sofas, armchairs, two occasional chairs). Plan on using instead, a set of very comfortable chairs spaced round a lowish round table. This will create a seating island which is probably all you need in a confined space. It will work for most occasions, especially if it is properly lit.

Get the scale right

The size of a piece of furniture can look amazingly different when placed in different surroundings— lost in a vast, tall room, overpowering in a small one. You can prepare for this by having a scale plan of your room as described on page 19, and drawing your furniture on it to scale too. There is also the question of height: getting some height into a room can make all the difference between a monotonous and an interesting space. Most furniture today is fairly low which means that a good deal of the furniture in your room is going to be exactly the same height. So, if you can get the occasional high point in to vary the scale, the difference will be as important as an interesting flash of colour or pattern. Even if you can't find or afford tall elegant pieces of furniture much the same effect can be produced with a tall plant or lamp, wall-fixed shelving, mirrors and, of course, pictures.

CHOOSING THE RIGHT FURNITURE

Improvise with flair

Since most of us have very limited budgets for furnishing it is essential to know when to spend, when to save and how to improvise. For example, comfortable anchor pieces like large upholstery and capacious storage should, and will, certainly have first call on your money. This leaves the smaller pieces like coffee tables, ordinary tables, work tables, side tables and occasional chairs and low storage to make demands on your ingenuity and imagination. Most of them can be put together quite cheaply but without ruining the style or atmosphere of the room; on the contrary it's often these that add most of the character to a room and reflect your personality better than the bought pieces which can look like everyone else's.

Style on a shoe-string

● Find black tin trunks to act as coffee tables or side tables. Or use oriental packing cases—or occidental ones come to that, if they are waxed or painted—topped with a rectangle of glass cut to size.

● Ready-cut slabs of thick glass on top of painted, lacquered or carpeted wooden cubes make stunning tables and provide storage space.

● The same cubes, padded with foam and covered are fine for occasional seating. Add semi-concealed castors for easy manoeuvrability.

● Old flush doors (or new flush doors) set on painted or natural wooden trestles; or on 60 cm × 60 cm (2 ft × 2 ft) steel supports, make good-looking desks.

● Shabby [not valuable] old oriental rugs can be used to cover large floor cushions.

● Forget about conventional sofas and seating. Build a plywood platform at one end of the room, cover it with a carpet and pile it with floor cushions. If storage space and seating are both at a premium, try building in boxes around the perimeter of the room. Give them hinged lids for storage and add foam pads covered with fabric for comfortable seating.

● Old kitchen or office chairs—there are always some in second-hand and junk shops—look fine stripped and painted in a variety of colours, some red, some pink or purple, for example, or all white with perhaps a coloured strut or leg, or all black.

● Dreary reproduction chairs can be given a thoroughly modern look, smartened up with paint and the seats covered with a strongly textured fabric like tweed or corduroy. Paint plain wooden chairs a dark or vivid colour and try your hand at painting a scene, birds, flowers, a ship, on the seat. Old dressers and chests of drawers, if you

can still find them, can be stripped and polished or painted and decorated. Have fun with them—paint each drawer a different colour or do a small 'mural', perhaps of clouds or trees, across the front. Or stencil or lacquer them.

Once you have got into an improvising state of mind almost any piece of furniture will begin to develop potential.

Above: This bed-sitting room has been furnished to great effect at minimum expense. The floor is simply polished, sheeting-covered floor cushions serve for seats, while the bedhead bookshelves are made from planks balanced on bricks.

Right: Elegant bookshelves either side of a mirror-lined opening form a dividing wall between two rooms.

Everything in its place

Books, records or tapes, cassettes, stereo, tv, video, papers, files, stationery, typewriter, decorative objects, sewing-machine, sewing things, magazines, telephone directories, drinks, glasses, ice bucket. . . . The living room has to house some or all of these things and if it's used for eating has to come up with storage for china, glass and cutlery too. Where do you put it all? Obviously good, well planned and ample living room storage is a must.

Highly sophisticated storage

A wall of storage units will make provision for most of the paraphernalia you own and might either incorporate a bar and a desk flap to let down, or a permanent table set at right angles to shelves and cupboards for work, games, sewing and hobbies. There are many versions and permutations to choose from in all price ranges and many finishes, so again it boils down to a question of taste, style and pocket, although here, unlike upholstery, expense does not necessarily indicate worth. Some of the German, Scandinavian and Italian built-in units are particularly smooth and luxurious with inbuilt fridges and mirror-lined bars but cheaper versions can look just as good, if not better, depending on finish and the final arrangement of possessions on shelves.

    You can build in your own

Civilized comfort

Cool, calm colours, nice, comfortable
seating, sensible lighting and well-
organized storage units are all
attributes of this spacious country
living room. Each piece of furniture
has been carefully chosen to both
blend and balance well with the next:
soft is off-set by hard; fine by
chunky; solidity by openness. The
scale too, has been well-thought out.
The storage units under the windows,
which hold books, logs, stereo,
speakers, records and discs with equal
ease, are perfectly proportionate with
the windows above. The large
sophisticated chaise and more rustic
coffee table one side of the room are
balanced by the chair, upholstered
stool, cane and glass desk and
Windsor chair on the other. The
golden hues of the wood and cane
are repeated in the generous basket at
the end of the chaise which holds
newspapers and magazines, and
echoed again in the camel throw
folded on the uphostered stool. A
thick and nubbly berber carpet makes
a good base for the natural coloured
ribbed fabric on the upholstered
pieces, and the camel-grey and rose
of the cotton print used for the
blinds is picked up by cushions
matched by a pink, camel and grey
tweed. Swing-arm brass wall lamps
give a pleasant light and are matched
by a desk version. Walls and
woodwork are kept white to keep
the room as light and serene as
possible. Details of fabric and carpet
are on the right.

bookshelves. The breakfront version is useful; this has cupboards below and a deep shelf at waist height to hold drink trays, stereo turntable and so on. The cupboards could be deep enough to hold filing cabinets and a tv set which would be concealed when the doors were shut. You would then need a separate desk or work table.

You would get a different sort of feel again by installing a big armoire or bureau bookcase if you could afford one or the other. Both pieces of furniture would be handsome additions to any room and would provide necessary height as well as being very capacious. A good substitute might be one of those huge Victorian or Edwardian wardrobes which you can often find cheaply in second-hand shops or junk yards, because they are too big for most bedrooms. These can be stripped, re-polished, painted, lacquered, decorated or mirrored to form decorative and useful pieces.

Or something simple

A little lateral thinking pays dividends here. Simpler storage items could include a drinks trolley by the side of a sofa to hold glasses, trays, ice buckets and so on. Industrial or hospital steel trolleys could just as well store stereo, files, tv, video, sewing or hobby equipment. Even good-looking baskets set side by side on the floor can hold a good

Above: Glass shelves are lit from above by concealed downlighters, which focus subdued attention on the books and ornaments.

Above right: More glass shelves look light and elegant in an equally pale, elegant and well-proportioned room.

Right: Lid of carpet-covered wood seating unit around the perimeter of this room lifts up to reveal neatly arranged drinks storage. ,

Far right: Both tv and stereo are cleverly concealed in this cupboard with its trellis-effect mirrored panels and white framework.

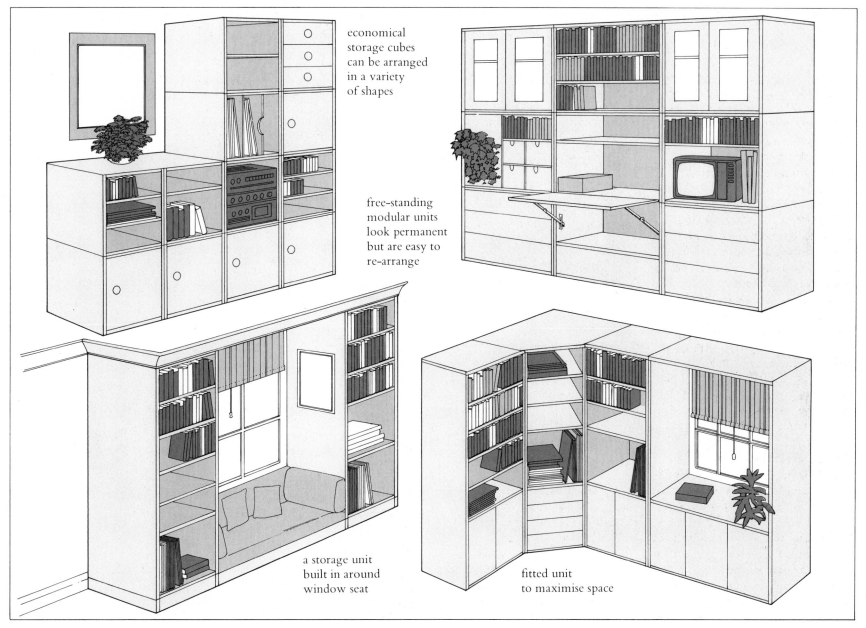

economical
storage cubes
can be arranged
in a variety
of shapes

free-standing
modular units
look permanent
but are easy to
re-arrange

a storage unit
built in around
window seat

fitted unit
to maximise space

Far left: A low dividing wall in this luxuriously large space acts as housing for magazines, stereo system, tapes and records.

Above left: A modular storage system all down one wall holds tv, drinks, stereo system, books and objects.

Above: The space under the stairs in this house provides room for a meticulously stacked wine crates.

Left: Vertical panels between shelves in this crowded book wall are faced in mirror to give an illusion of space. Note the door which has been painted to look like walnut.

deal of paraphernalia—including bottles or books—with a certain panache.

Don't always think in terms of hiding things away. Some hobbies and interests use equipment or materials that are fascinating or colourful in their own right and these can often lend character to a room if they're left out on display. Skeins of wool and silk used for tapestry work or embroidery, lace-making pillows and bobbins, can look highly decorative. Plans and drawings or maps can be stored in neat rolls in large baskets or drums or laid flat in thin drawers set into a wall of storage; these can look interesting in themselves with their severe and narrow horizontal lines.

Living rooms that also have to act as office or work room by day (and more and more people elect to work at home if they can these days) can still perform both functions with comparative ease. If a modern desk seems too business-like for the room, try to find an old bureau or pedestal desk with as many drawers as possible so that papers and work can be put out of sight; conceal filing cabinets in cupboards or keep files in drawers and in a storage wall. A slab of wood or an old door, or a thick glass top, placed on two neat white or coloured filing cabinets acting as supports could double as a work table by day and carving or service table at night.

Once people have got the framework of a room together–the walls, floor, ceiling, windows, lighting and furnishings–they often run out of ideas for what to do with smaller objects and any family treasures they possess. Good arrangements and an eye for detail can only be achieved with practice, so it may help to have a few guidelines to follow in the first place, if only to act as a springboard for producing interesting and unusual ideas of your own.

Whether you are starting to decorate a first home, have just moved into a new place or are redecorating an existing room, the problem is often much the same: not so much how to arrange things as how to fill up big blank walls and table or shelf surfaces when you don't seem to have very much to use and certainly very little to spend. If it is any consolation, the whole question of arrangement seems just as much a problem for people with enviably rare and valuable collections as it is for those with hardly enough to call a collection of anything. And the same thing applies to people who have collections of quite valueless things: baskets, keys, hats or whatever. How do you display what you

have to its best advantage? And where is the best place to display these objects?

All kinds of things look good on walls. It doesn't have to be artwork like paintings, drawings, etchings, prints or even posters. Consider any of the following: pieces of framed fabric or even beautiful wrapping paper, particularly if they accent the background colours or furnishing themes in the room; framed arrangements of dried flowers or grasses or corn on a dark background; collections of framed cigarette cards (from old cigarette packets still available in many antique markets), or postcards; rugs, of course, and any sort of interesting quilt whether old or new.

Then too, any flat decorative thing–a fragment of embroidery or lace or part of an oriental rug – can be clamped between thin glass and hung up. You can buy corner pieces or special flat screws at most art shops.

Finishing touches: a miscellany of objects (left) makes a charming still-life in front of stained glass, while (top right) rugs decorate a plain wall and a mantel-top (right) acts as a gallery to some well grouped and balanced photographs.

DEVELOP AN EYE FOR DETAIL

Make your own *bas reliefs* by buying a good-sized piece of wood from a local timber or lumber yard, and sticking on it a series of related objects, for example, egg boxes, old pocket watches, Coke tins, bicycle reflectors, geometry instruments or small kitchen utensils. When you have made an arrangement to your satisfaction and secured it firmly to its background, spray the whole thing with the paint colour of your choice, silver, black, white, terracotta, blue, a vivid grass green or yellow. You could do much the same thing with a collection of book covers. Stick them a few inches apart on a white painted board and varnish over with polyurethane.

You can make handsome still-lifes on walls with arrangements of old tools, or chains or even bits of metal or plastic construction kits. One effective wall decoration I have seen was simply made from a multi-coloured collection of felt squares stuck straight on to the wall in checkerboard fashion. Another was a whole series of small foil freezer containers mounted in a large square with the backs facing toward the room like a silver *bas relief*. Weird but very impressive.

Another bold idea is to fix long coloured fluorescent tubes to the wall in a pattern of diagonals or V shapes. Lit up in their various colours against a white wall they can look spectacular; unlit they take on an almost sculptural quality.

Arranging pictures and prints

On the whole, people are divided into those who want to make room for a serious collection and those who want to use wall space to its most decorative advantage. The first school thinks of a wall as a means to an end, a support, a mere background. The second thinks of it as a canvas to be made the most of; yet another surface to decorate or ornament. The big problem with this latter group is to find some sort of unifying factor that will make sense or give a theme to a miscellany of oddments that are less than distinguished.

A collection of nondescript prints, for example, can be given a sense of unity if each is mounted with the same distinctive colour: camel or chrome yellow or red, whichever fits in best with the room, and then edged all in the same way with a thin strip of wood or chrome or brass.

Try not to hang things too close, too high, or too far apart. Do not fix anything so low over a sofa that people can knock their heads on it when getting up or even leaning back; all the same, try to place everything at a reasonably flexible eye level. Obviously vertical arrangements will make walls look taller; horizontal will make them

Above: The soft, subdued shades of blue, grey and white in this pretty composition of objects is complemented by green foliage

Right: A pleasing arrangement of different sized paintings on the wall beyond this centrally placed sofa, looks particularly effective against the plain light walls.

Above right: This painting has been enclosed in a painted frame of its own for individual emphasis.

Far right: A snake-like articulated lamp rears over an artist's palette forming a still life in the process.

look longer. Most paintings look good against dark walls but if a wall is strongly patterned, try mounting prints against a deep matt or ground of the same background colour. In this way, a subject is becalmed in an area of its own and does not get lost in the richness of the surrounding background.

In order to avoid making nasty marks on the wall when you are experimenting with the hanging, it is best to decide on the overall shape of the arrangement first—a square, oblong, diamond or triangle—and on a painted wall mark out the area with light pencil which can easily be rubbed off, or with chalk on a paper wallcovering. Mark out the same sized area on the floor, then lay out the various items, juggling them around until you are satisfied with the positions. Draw a rough sketch and then translate them all in a permanent fashion to the wall.

Table-top inspiration

Still-lifes on tables, dresser tops, window sills and mantelpieces can be improvised just as successfully as those on walls. Old bottles, mugs, (new and old) minerals, stones, shells, tiny baskets, old paper boxes (relics of the nineteenth century which are still very cheap if you manage to find them) miniature bottles in different shapes, an assortment of small vases stuck with single-stem flowers or leaves. . . .

Once you start, all sorts of possibilities will present themselves and you'll find real inspiration in some of the unlikeliest looking things.

Gather and group

Collections of small objects should always be gathered together and arranged in a group rather than being thinly spread around the house. Very small things like pebbles, marbles, polished beach stones, old buttons and so on, can be put into large glass goblets or jars and displayed on window ledges (against the light) or on shelves. Slightly larger objects, however different and unrelated, should be grouped so that they have something in common like colour or

national origin. Or if they're placed significantly with larger things, the impact and interest of the contrast will give harmony to the group.

If the arrangement is on a table, add a plant or dried grasses or flowers and perhaps one taller object to give balance. Since most tables are also used for dumping, leave space so that the arrangements aren't continually being disturbed.

If an arrangement is on a glass table try lighting it from underneath with an uplight. If it's on a solid surface you could light it from above with a downlight or spot.

Cheerful little odds and ends arranged with flair can often make a room seem far more interesting than much grander collections.

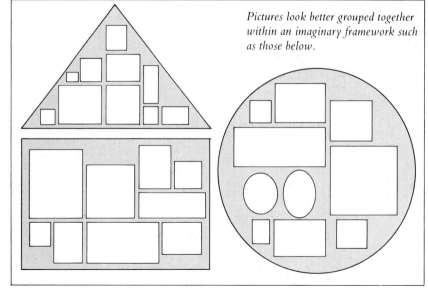

Pictures look better grouped together within an imaginary framework such as those below.

Subtle memorability

An eye for detail means giving a room the finishing touches that make it memorable. But the details do not necessarily hit the eye first off and are often as much in the fit and finish and quality as in the juxtaposition of colours, choice of accessories and the subtle repetition of a theme. In this interesting room it is difficult to know which element came first, the beige carpet with its tan and dark blue border or the checked beige, tan and dark blue fabric on the *chaise longue*. Either way, the rest of the room melds in beautifully with its repetition of colours used in different ways: warm beige painted walls and ceiling, creamy beige Roman blinds with their edging and inset border of dark blue upholstery webbing, dark blue table-cloth with creamy beige underskirt and chairs in tan and yellowy-cream. More dark blue webbing is stuck on the walls to give a pannelled effect and neat built-in bookshelves are lit from above by inset downlights which just graze the front of the shelves with light. The look is comfortable, warm, prosperous and interesting all at the same time: a far cry from the 'safe beige' that can be so monotonous, although it is certainly unexceptionally elegant. Freshness is injected with plants, flowers and foliage; sparkle and warmth by the fire. Details of fabrics and carpet are shown on the right.

DEVELOP AN EYE FOR DETAIL

Plants furnish a room

Plants are wonderful accessories. They are the quickest injectors of liveliness and freshness to a room, can add height, variety, colour and drama all at once and are generally worth every penny you pay for them. There is almost no gap in a room that a plant cannot fill and improve, no piece of furniture that cannot be balanced by a spread of foliage. I really would not feel happy in a plantless room.

The right setting

All the same, it is important to choose plants well, to make sure that light, position and treatment are right, or your investment, far from bearing fruit will become a mass of sad, browning leaves. If the setting is not right no amount of cossetting, fertilizing, spraying and careful watering will stop the rot. I find that you can usually begin to tell after a week if there is something wrong. There is an unmistakable air of malaise, a faint sense of lethargy. After that, the end comes fast. If, on the other hand, the plant settles, it will often thrive willy-nilly in spite of neglect and may only need the occasional re-potting. Almost all plants are now sold with labels detailing the sort of position they thrive in and the attention they should get in terms of temperature and water. Do examine these carefully before you make a purchase.

contrasting leaves provide variety of texture and colour

white venetian blinds consistent with colour scheme

white lamp shades reflect green of leaves

cane furniture maintains light and airy feeling

sofa bed useful for guests

textural contrasts between planters

Above: Green and white can hardly be beaten for a fresh colour combination and these massed plants of varying sizes and types look well against the white walls and floor.

white floor visually enlarges space and makes a good background

Above left: A group of plants in identical Michelin-man-like china bowls looks interestingly dramatic, expecially against the positive/negative effect of the fabric.

Above: A Philodendron laciniatum has been used to fill the space left vacant when the fire is not in use. Its leaves contrast well against the brick and bark.

Left: Tree-like plants cannot help but be dramatic in a domestic setting and this large and willowy variety looks particularly effective set against the general cool of the room and the pellucid quality of the coffee table and tall étagère.

How to arrange them

On the whole, I think plants look best grouped in twos or threes or left single (in the case of tree-like plants) rather than mixed up with different species. Different heights of the same plants like *Dracaenae* can look sculptural. Large or spreading plants like *Ficus benjamina* or palms can make splendid room dividers or window treatments. A good way of masking curtainless windows is to hang plants in baskets in front of the glass, but remember to check the light and draught requirements of the plants first. Fix a brass or wood pole across the top of the frame and hang the baskets from various lengths of chain so that the effect is staggered. If you want large plants that can be moved easily from position to position it's sensible to buy planters with wheels.

How to care for them

Plants need as much rapport with their owners as do people: you must be sensitive to their needs and prepared to give them a lot of attention, until you see that they thrive very well on their own.

For healthy growth most plants need light, warmth and humidity in varying degrees. Work out what direction each window faces and from that how much daylight the room receives. Find out the lowest temperature the room drops to in winter, usually at night, and what the average temperature is. If you have central heating or air conditioning, which tend to dehydrate plants, you may need to correct this by using a humidifier or, more cheaply, bowls of water.

Good natural light, but not direct sunlight, is what most plants need. Plants with variegated or pale green leaves generally require more light than those with dark green leaves.

Most plants will thrive in temperatures between 10–21°C (50–70°F), and will be far healthier if you remember that in nature nights are cooler, and allow your plants the same facility. Some hardy ones, ivy, aspidistra, tolerate temperatures as low as 4.4°C (40°F); others, ferns, begonias, won't thrive if it's below 10°C (50°F). Remember too, to spray plants much more in the winter when the central heating is on, and water them more frequently, using tepid water.

Generally speaking, you are more likely to kill a plant by over- rather than underwatering. Certain plants do need to be kept constantly moist while others need to dry out completely between waterings. Labels should tell you this, but very often you have to learn by trial and error, which means you have to be alert to their needs and sense when they are not happy with their conditions or treatment. The kind of watering guide that you stick in the soil is usually a help.

One-room living has come a long way from the old bed-sitter image with its general note of poverty and desperation. Today, some people actually prefer to live in one room: they even choose to take down partition walls in two- or three-roomed flats or apartments to make one big open-plan space.

But most one-roomed flats or studio apartments are box-like spaces with little to commend them in the way of interesting detail or character. And generally they are small. Since they are going to be not just living room but bedroom, dining room, and very often office as well, this means that every inch of space has to play its part, every piece of furniture has to be dual-purpose if not multi-functional, and every activity has to be properly catered for and duly compartmented. To work efficiently this sort of room needs discipline, neatness and, above all, imagination. Successful one-room living is more an attitude of mind than anything else.

Everything is something else

The sofa bed or studio couch has made a great difference to one-room living. Beds that fold down from the wall when they are needed have lost their makeshift image and have been updated to a new smooth efficiency and now come complete with a wall of closets or wardrobes. Even double beds can be piled and piled with cushions to make an inviting couch for yourself and guests by day.

Tables can be used as desks; end tables can be used for dining; chairs can fold up and be hung from large colourful hooks, or be stacked up into a tiny space; armchairs can become spare single beds; well thought-out storage will take care of clothing, books, files and china. Manufacturers are now geared to one-room flexible living as never before. But if the room is not to look a complete jumble you have to try to create distinct areas for relaxing, sleeping, eating and work. Since you very often cannot physically divide the space, you have to divide the 'look' with different lighting or rugs or colour to make separate visual areas.

In the crisp red and white space on the left, cooking, eating and sitting areas are all neatly defined by the furniture itself, while the area on the right relies upon changes in level.

Living at different levels

One of the most impressive examples of one-room living that I have ever seen was in a long, narrow space approximately 7.5 m by 3 m (24 ft by 10 ft). Sleeping, sitting, eating and working areas had been divided into 2.4 m (8 ft) steps, each 23 cm (9 in) higher than the other. Colours had been kept to a minimal dark grey and white with black and the occasional flash of green in plants and cushions. Storage was behind flush doors concealed all down one wall. The table did for working and eating; the mattress (put straight on the floor and covered in black tweed) did for sleeping and lounging; and the steps made extra seating areas as well, with the help of large flat black or white cushions which stacked like striped playbricks when not in use. Transparent fold-up perspex chairs were at the table.

Another successful room had a large floor to ceiling panel about 2.4 m (8 ft) wide set in the centre of the room. On one side was a desk/dining area; on the other, a sofa and easy chairs. At night, part of the panel was let down, revealing a bed with concealed lighting behind. Cupboards and shelves were built all round the room and concealed behind neat panels of canvas-covered wood, with touch-opening mechanisms so as not to break the continuity of the limited space.

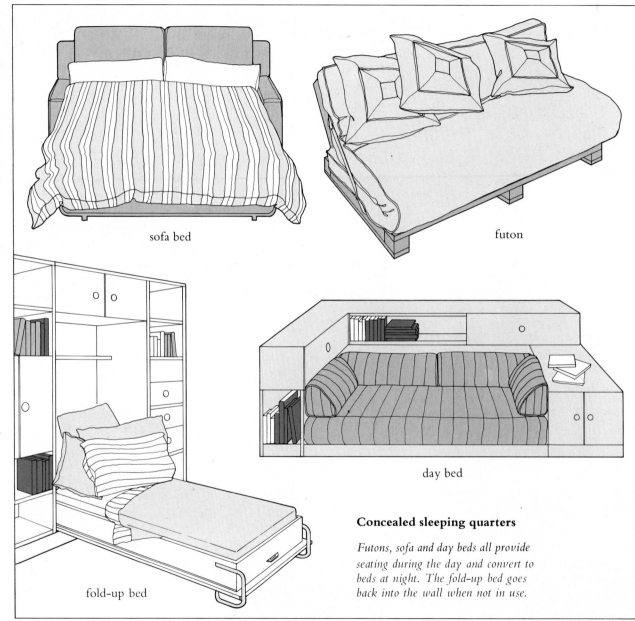

sofa bed

futon

fold-up bed

day bed

Concealed sleeping quarters

Futons, sofa and day beds all provide seating during the day and convert to beds at night. The fold-up bed goes back into the wall when not in use.

Above left: Strong horizontal lines of tables and seating bound by bookshelves and the kitchen counter sort out the various functions in this spacious area.

Above: An off-the-floor bed frees the floor space. Clothes are stashed away behind curtains.

Far left: Yellow and green stencil border on floor covering, matching border on bed and tablecloth, pale blinds and louvred screen make this room look fresh and sunny.

Left: Another very neat idea for one-room living is this mattress folded up under a glass and chrome coffee table.

Dual (and treble) personality

Getting the maximum amount of function out of the minimum amount of space when you live in one room is obviously an exercise in dual-function and discipline. Here, colours taken from the fresh-looking curtains are kept to a limited palette repeated in different permutations in cushions, rug and furniture. Sisal matting makes a good uniting background for both colours and different styles of furniture. The comfy-looking chesterfield is also a bed. The slatted table is as useful for working at as for dining and, like the matching chairs, can fold-up to allow more floor room when necessary. It has the added plus that it can be lowered to make a coffee table. The platform built along the fireplace wall makes space for seating, TV and log storage. Alcoves either side are mirrored to make space and topped with glass bookshelves. The capacious cupboard stores china, glass, linen, and clothes and the side table has a lift-up top for extra storage. Details of fabrics and matting are on right.

Disguising the bed

Nowadays, it is more a question of fitting in adequate storage as well as a good size sofa bed, than trying to disguise a bedstead. Almost every shape of sofa can now conceal a full-size mattress, and many ordinary beds can be bought with space-saving drawers underneath and be disguised with fitted covers and back cushions. One way of fitting in closet and sleeping space together, apart from the fold-up bed idea, is to build wardrobes or shelves around a bed-size area to form a bed alcove. The back of the recess can then be mirrored to enlarge the sense of space or covered with art or fabric according to taste.

An interesting room I saw in New York made ingenious use of its space. It measured 4.9 m by 4.3 m (16 ft by 14 ft), and had full length storage at one end, and low level storage—for files, journals and papers—under a window at the other end. Floor to ceiling book-shelves and low level cupboards were built about 1.6 m (5–6 ft) in front of the full-length storage to form a kind of corridor or ante-room, and a large double bed was placed in the middle of the room, tight covered like a sofa. In the middle of the bed, across its width, two substantial bolsters were set next to each other. In this way the bed became two back to back sofas by day and reverted to its original function at night. A round table served for working and dining, and there was still room for various arm chairs, occasional chairs and side tables.

How to decorate it

Much the same ideas about decoration apply to one-room living as to small spaces (see pages 29–37). Mirrored walls are obviously useful; so is good lighting—particularly up-lights in corners—and anything that takes the eye out and along like diagonal patterns, trellis, pale colours, to add a sense of perspective.

Right: In this extremely clever arrangement of a long and minutely narrow space, the owner has managed to squeeze in a double bed, storage, seating and dining table. Note how the bed is set on a stepped platform, carpeted to match the floor, which serves both to provide extra seating and to make room for storage drawers below. The bed itself can be cut off from view for extra privacy by matchstick blinds which match those on the window. The simplicity of the objects within the room and the light colours prevent any feelings of claustrophobia.

blinds pull down
as room divider

versatile suspended platform
provides additional storage

diagonally positioned
sofa increases
feeling of space

wrap-around
storage unit
doubles as
wall and
desk support

*Small white ceramic tiles
form the demarcation area
for the kitchen-dining
area and well-organized
office (right). A short
suspended platform holds
plans as well as plants to
liven up the prevailing
white. Note the white
shelf running along the
room at sill level and the
diagonal sofa.*

note wine stored
under shelf

zig-zag table
is practical
and decorative

step reinforces
break between working
and eating areas

Many people are stuck, at one time or another in their lives, with dreary furnished rented accommodation that they cannot change because of the landlord's stringent regulations; or could change but think it would all cost more than their budget would allow. Alternatively, they might be allowed to make changes in an unfurnished rental and have the money to do it but, understandably, don't want to invest in something they'll only have to leave behind for the benefit of their landlord and his future tenants.

Nurses, medical students or young interns living in hospital accommodation, armed forces and their families living in service quarters, students in college rooms, all have much the same problem. How can their rooms be made comfortable, efficient, easy to work and live in, quick to dismantle and in addition warm, interesting and fun, all for the least possible outlay?

Some would say why bother since most accommodation of this sort is usually fairly short term. But it's vitally important for the morale to live in surroundings that are as pleasant as you can make them, and there are lots of ways of doing this that don't cost a fortune.

Inexpensive improvements
Here are twelve ways of improving temporary accommodation, without breaking the bank or leaving a present for the landlord. Impoverished property owners might also benefit from these ideas.

● If you are not allowed to leave nail marks on walls, hang pictures from the old-fashioned picture rail if there is one. If not, create your own rail with the kind of extendable, spring-loaded rod available from photographic stores. It should be slightly longer than the length of your wall. Hang all your art work from it with nylon wire or ribbon.

● You can change your wall colours at will by simply using the same extendable, spring-loaded rods mentioned above, and running them through a roll of seamless coloured paper—the kind normally used for photographic backdrops.

Cream prevails in this elegant but inexpensive room to the left. Cheesecloth draped over wooden poles forms the curtain while a deckchair provides seating. To the right, shabby chairs and table are made respectable with shawls.

You can then pull down a new wall colour at whim and the flick of a wrist. The rolls are available from good photographic equipment stores in a handsome palette of 30 or more colours in widths of either 2.75 m (9 ft) or 1.37 m (4½ ft), by 11 m (12 yd) long, and cost less than a roll of most wallpapers.

● Cheesecloth makes excellent temporary wallcovering to hide hideous paint colours or wallpaper, or just to freshen up dirty walls. Cut lengths to hang from ceiling to skirting or baseboards (or use traverse rods or extendable, spring-loaded rods which don't need fixing at all). Or you could just let the fabric hang loose. If you do this, loop the cheesecloth back over doors, windows and closets and fix them with thumb tacks if walls are reasonably soft—small picture hook nails if they are not. If you stretch it tight you will need to stop it either side of such openings or, for a neater finish, run cords or elastic or wire over the tops of doors and windows and suspend separate shorter lengths to hide the under surface.

● If you dislike the curtains but can't change them, just take them down and substitute hanging baskets of plants—or buy the cheapest possible bamboo blinds, which you can then take with you when you leave. They will almost certainly fit some window in any subsequent

place, and if they are too big, can be cut while flat with a pair of sharp scissors or a small saw.

● If the carpet is a horrible colour or very shabby, or both, buy whatever rugs you can afford (they are an investment and you will always be able to find room for them in another house or flat) and cover over the worst of the colour or the most worn bits. Rugs don't have to be expensive; you can make them yourself quite easily if you are nimble with your fingers.

● If lighting is the usual unsubtle centre fixture with the occasional lamp, don't worry. Invest in some uplights and stick them in corners, behind plants and pieces of furniture, or behind a sofa. Just use the centre light to see to put them on by and switch it off when it's not needed. The difference in light and shade and subtlety will be enormous. Invest too, in a small spot light to pinpoint anything interesting you have, even a plant. And if you really can't afford a spot, get one of those really cheap clip-on lamps from a hardware store and fix it so that it gives extra illumination to foliage or whatever.

● If you are allowed to paint but can't afford to buy much, try just painting the trims (base or skirting boards, door and window frames and any mouldings) with a contrast

Left: Screens, rugs, shawls, inexpensive, light cane furniture, plants and cushions or pillows are the absolute mainstay of the practised renter. Together with packing cases of books they can all be moved around easily to impart instant personality to dreary rooms.

Above: Good-looking coffee tables can be made out of almost any base and a sheet of plate glass. Here rounded terracotta planters make a handsome pair, but almost anything fairly heavy and solid would do.

Right: Photographic back drop paper comes in a rainbow of colours and can change the look of a wall – or make a divider – in a moment.

RENTED ROOMS AND BED-SITS

Right: Instant upholstery can be made by tucking fabric down the sides of and under the bottom of chairs as here. Fabric, of course, can then be taken away again if you move on.

Far right: Brighten a room by adding a fringe of fabric round the walls to make a cheerful frieze. Staple it or stick it with double-sided tape.

Below right: Cloths, shawls, sheets, quilts can all be thrown over tables for quick-change brighteners. Add more plants and the transformation is complete.

Below far right: Pieces of beautifully patterned fabric can make instant art. Stretch them on frames and hang them from picture hooks.

You can quickly give a room perspective and a sense of depth by adding a screen and placing some piece of furniture in front of it, as left. Here, a table, large plant, and a picture make an instantly distinguished corner which can be disbanded as speedily as it was set up. Cunningly placed lighting highlights the art and creates interesting dark shadows.

colour in semi-gloss. It will give an immediate lift to the room.

● If you are allowed to make minor decoration changes and the existing scheme is in good condition though dull, give it an instant cheap fillip with lengths of cheap braid or coloured tape. Any width from 2.5 cm (1 in) to 6.25 cm (2½ in) will do depending on the proportions of your room. Either run the braid or tape round the walls just below the ceiling and above the skirting boards, sticking it on, if it's not already adhesive, with appropriate glue. Or make the whole thing more elaborate by running it around doors and window frames as well, and down the corners too, if you think it looks good. It's quite easy to rip off before it has had a chance to dry, if you suddenly change your mind and think you've overdone it.

● An even more elaborate version of the same idea is to give instant glamour to a room by 'panelling' it with strips of picture framing. You can buy lengths of this in whatever style you like and can afford from most framers, and all you have to do is stick it to the wall (with an adhesive that works on wood and plaster) in squares or rectangles worked out in proportion to the room. Draw the elevation of the room to scale on graph paper first (see page 19 for instructions) and then work out the design. Or you can work it straight out on the walls with a long ruler, light pencil and an eraser (for mistakes).

● Do not underestimate the change plants can make to a room. Buy the fullest and best shapes you can afford and let them make a bold definite statement. Put them in corners, lit from behind with uplights or spots; mass them on windowsills, add them to arrangements of any kind of collection you may have. The fresh green of *well-kept* foliage will brighten the dullest of rental furnishings—and your spirits into the bargain.

● It sounds elementary to say add throw or scatter cushions wherever you can, but cushions in well-chosen colours and designs can add immediate zing, warmth and personality, injecting dashes of vitality where none existed before, as well as covering shabby and stained patches in upholstery.

It might seem odd to talk about entry halls as a postscript as it were but in practical terms most people put decorating their living rooms first. It is nevertheless the first part of your home that you and your visitors step into, and the last part that you leave. Obviously when you budget you have to allow the most money for the rooms you are actually going to live in, but once decided on this you must turn considerable thought and care – if not money – to making your hall as warm and welcoming and practical as you can. It might come last on your list of necessities, but there is no need for it to look the least.

Theoretically, halls should be easy to design, since there is generally little to purchase in the way of furniture and accessories unless you are blessed with the luxury of a wide, spacious and well-lit area. But whatever its size, you need to plan for convenience as well as impact, wear as well as warmth; a space that fits the feel of your home as well as it fits you.

The necessities

There should be at least one chair and a capacious table to take all the paraphernalia that inevitably col-lects in this clearing house for the home. If the hall is too narrow for this—and many entrance ways are barely more than a corridor, try to get in a long bench or a very narrow console, or at the very least a stool and a shelf.

If you have any built-in cup-boards or closets you are home and dry—literally—as far as storage is concerned; if you have not, and there really is no room at all for any sort of full-length closet, have a hat stand or, failing this, a row of hooks to take not only your own family's coats, but those of visitors.

Mirrors are unfail-ingly useful in halls so that you can check your own appearance going out while visitors can check theirs coming in. They are also useful for reflecting too small a space and exaggerating every last bit of light. The best place to site them is over the table, or shelf, or other handy surface.

Making an entrance—the unusually spacious lobby on the left has been used to advantage by the inclusion of a desk area complete with telephone in the small recess. In the much smaller hall to the right, bookshelves have been neatly fitted into the space under the stairs.

HALLS, STAIRS AND ENTRANCES

Suitability

What sort of furniture you have depends very much on the style of your home, your tastes and your pocket. Obviously if you have an essentially period home it is good to keep at least within the spirit of the place, although conversely, one old piece in a very modern hall can look stunning. Obviously too, if you have a country hall you will want to keep it as countryish and as relaxed as possible. Town halls should make an all out effort for interest and warmth to counteract the pervasive greyness outside. And houses by the sea should be well-prepared for sand and wet.

Durability

Any surface you choose should be as tough and durable as you can afford. People coming in from outside will bring in dirt and dust and damp as a matter of course so it's advisable to have both an outer and inner door mat. The most practical idea is to have a slight well let into the floor in front of the door and to fill it with coconut matting. This way, the mat will not shift, slip or kick-up, will not get frayed around the edges and cannot be by-passed.

The rest of the floor should be easily cleaned whatever material it is. Country halls look well in quarry tiles or French or Mexican tiles, flagstones, slate, brick or good old fashioned pavements. If you cannot

have any natural material for some reason, keep your bare boards, scraped, sanded and sealed, or painted if the boards are in bad condition or have vinyl or composition tiles. Carpet is acceptable in town houses or flats but it must be the best quality you can afford because hallways take a lot of through traffic. Add rugs to hard floors for softness and interest, but make sure they will not slip and cause accidents. Secure them to carpet with gripper tape or use the sticky weave that is sold especially to keep rugs in place. This is also good for rugs on wood or hard floors. Otherwise tack a rug down lightly. Hallways are at constant risk of getting scratched, marked or chipped, so wall finishes must be highly durable. Paint and wallpaper could be protected and hardened by a final coat of polyurethane. Vinyl wallcoverings are always practical in halls since they will withstand all sorts of rough treatment.

Decoration

Ideally, walls on halls, corridors and staircases (if any) should be decorated with the same colour or treatment unless they are in quite different parts of the home and cannot be seen, one from another. Whatever the colour chosen, make sure it leads naturally into the rooms leading off it. Warm-coloured walls like apricots, yellows, terracottas,

Above: A hall should be both welcoming and practical. This room achieves both objectives. Warmth is provided by a radiator, while pictures and fresh flowers give colour and character. The quarry-tiled floor is hard-wearing, easy to clean and echoes the country look of the white walls and natural timber. A row of hooks and a stand take your family's and any visitor's coats and umbrellas.

Right: This long corridor-like hall has become something like a mini-gallery. Floral wallpaper, table, chairs, plants, pictures and oriental rugs all add to the cheerful feeling it manages to impart.

deep roses, plums, reds, tawny browns and marmalades all look good in city homes with moderate climates and in country homes too, come to that, but hot climates benefit from the reverse treatment: whites, cool blues and greens, pale yellows and creams.

Quite apart from mirror, the hall, corridor, landing and staircase walls will take any number of pictures, and general memorabilia. If there is space, you can line walls with bookcases to enormous advantage, and use an alcove for a desk to make an extra-mural study. Odd corners, window sills, ledges and shelves might take plants, and if you have a wide enough hall, you might well be able to make the hall an extra, if not a permanent, dining place by adding a small table.

Playing with the walls

If you have partition walls and not much space or light you can try playing around with the walls a little. For example, in a narrow town or terrace house where the front door opens directly into a corridor-like space, you could either take the wall down altogether, or make an arch going into the living room, or take the wall down to seating level, literally making a seating ledge. This way you will get all the benefit of the extra light and space and still have the suggestion of a division.

Above: Diagonally-lined carpet repeats the strong angles of the staircase, and is echoed by the vertical lines and colours of the wool wallcovering which continues through to the living room beyond. It makes a strong impact for a small space.

Right: Here again, there is similar repetition of a theme: in this case the square balustrade repeats the square glass panels of the front door below but in larger scale.

Far right: A large healthy plant and a mirrored wall add interest and a sense of space to a cramped stairwell.

114

Another possibility, in say, a flat or an apartment where the living room door opens off the hall, is to cut two narrow floor-to-ceiling slits in the wall to give both extra light and interesting glimpses of the room ahead. Or you can cut out a large square or arched opening instead of a conventional door, and if the wall is big enough, a couple of openings or 'windows' either side—again to give different perspectives to the room ahead. Inset downlights into the top of the openings to light anything that you might care to place in these openings—a plant perhaps, flowers, an interesting object—and you will instantly dramatize the space.

Lighting

Lighting in halls, corridors and staircases should be clear and bright for reasons of safety as well as aesthetics. Downlights—recessed, semi-recessed, or ceiling-mounted—are good-looking and functional whatever the style of furnishings and collect fewer flies and less dirt than bowl-shaped or pendant fixtures. If you do not have many outlets, or cannot add extra lights, think of adding track-lighting to the ceiling since you can fix as many spots onto a track, trained to as many angles as you think it will take. If you have a lot of pictures on the walls this will light them beautifully as well as providing all the light you will need for comfort and safety. If your telephone is in the hall, a good light is essential for looking up numbers and writing down messages.

It might look particularly inviting to put a lamp on the table, chest or shelf and of course, if you have had room for a desk, it will certainly need a desk lamp. Very dark halls with little or no natural light will benefit from what the Americans call 'Plugmold'. This is a strip fixed with points on to which you can attach any number of bulbs that you like. The strip is placed behind a pelmet or soffit of some kind (a piece of wood or moulding running all round under the cornice, if there is one, or ceiling angle if there is not, and you then achieve the lighting expert's dream: light without a visible source.

Windows

Look carefully at any windows in hallways, corridors and on stairs to decide whether you should curtain them, blind them, shutter them or leave them alone. In general, unless you have very long and gracious windows, I think such windows look neater and let in more daylight if they are covered with blinds or shutters or even some sort of grill or trellis work. Very small windows are usually better just left, and given a plant, vase of flowers or object to cheer up the sill.

If kitchens are the most complicated rooms to plan they are also the most rewarding to get right, for we spend a large part of our lives by the stove and sink. The kitchen is above all a working room and although good looks are an integral part of its design, easy function should be the prime consideration. If it is a machine for cooking, as design writers are fond of saying, it must be a well oiled one.

A kitchen tends to fall into one of three categories depending on its physical limitations and your life pattern: it may be designed purely as a work room when all the other family activities go on in other rooms; or it may be a room where the work is done and some or all family meals are taken; or finally it may be the real centre of the house, where work is done, meals are taken and where the family congregates.

Over the decades since the First World War, with the introduction of new forms of energy, the development of labour saving devices and changes in food and menus, there have been radical changes in kitchen design. By the 1950s, designers had turned kitchens into streamlined boxes with aseptic, clinical, easily wipeable finishes. It looked as if all traces of the cluttered, lived-in, homey kitchen, the heart and hearth of the home, had gone for ever. The appliance manufacturers, the frozen food kings, the canners and food merchants exploited to the hilt the female desire to get out of the kitchen just as quickly as possible.

But that was before the great cooking revolution which has restored the kitchen as a family room, if not *the* family room: warm, friendly, relaxed and comfortable. Nevertheless, if it's going to work at all, a well planned kitchen has, first and foremost, to suit the cook.

Given all this, a book about kitchens and kitchen decoration would be illogical to say the least, if it failed to take into account the room or area where food is served, which should be as pleasant a place as possible. Not only is the one space the inevitable extension of the other, but as often as not these days, the kitchen and dining areas are in the same room anyway. Today's dining rooms are defined by *where* you eat, not by the furniture. How you arrange these cooking/eating functions in your home depends on your life style as well as the space and money available.

Unless you have ample funds to hand, it is of the utmost importance to think ahead when you are planning a kitchen. You might not be able to afford all the appliances you would like from the start, but if you think you will need them and will be able to afford them later you must leave the space and supply utilities for them. That is to say, if you want a dishwasher but know you won't be able to afford one for, say, three years, then make sure the plumbing is available and that there is a niche for a new fixture before you install your worktops and units.

If you are planning on a family and intending to stay in your present home, then allow for much more storage space than you need now. And whatever your current needs, try to get as much worktop or counter space as you possibly can. You always need far more dumping/preparation areas than you could ever imagine.

Finally, make sure that you have ample power points or outlets. They are much easier to fit earlier than later; wires can be more easily concealed and circuits worked out at the start of kitchen planning. Again, you will probably need more than you think at first reckoning. Start thinking along the right lines from the very beginning.

The main point of this book is to give ideas allied to practical information. But to get the most from ideas or information you will have to know how they can best be applied to your own particular situation and circumstances.

Compact, practical and stylish – this kitchen with dining area has all the ingredients which make it as attractive a place in which to eat as it is to prepare food.

If you are in the happy position of being able to plan your kitchen from scratch, rather than attempting to re-vamp existing layouts and equipment, it is worth giving the matter considerable thought.

It may even happen that you are able to choose *where* your kitchen will be, in which case bear in mind the following criteria. If your dining room is to be separate from your kitchen there should ideally be easy access from one room to the other. Long passages or stairs between the two make for difficulties in keeping food hot and clearing tables. Ease of access to the garden, especially if you grow your own herbs, vegetables and fruit, is also important, as is min-imising the time you spend answering the front and back doors. Good natural daylight and attractive views are less im-portant but should certainly be taken into consideration.

Once you have decided where you want your kitchen the next decision to make is what sort of kitchen you want. This will depend very much on what sort of cook you are. If you entertain a lot you may well prefer to have your kitchen separate from the dining area, unless you opt for a large and deliberately-

for-dining kitchen. A dedicated cook with a demanding job outside the home will probably need their kitchen to be that much more func-tional than someone with more leisure to shop – at least in the sense of providing good storage and extra-quick cooking facilities, such as a microwave oven and a freezer.

A single person, or a couple without children, extremely busy and not overly fond of cooking will almost certainly prefer a functional, working room that looks and is efficient.

If you really enjoy cooking you will pro-bably want to be able to take at least some meals in the kitchen and to have as much space as possible for herbs, spices, pots and pans, cook books and all the other impedimenta collected by the keen cook, quite apart from generous food storage and good kitchen aids.

If you cook constantly, have a

The sort of kitchen on the left would be ideal for some people with its generous work surfaces, storage and uncluttered feel. Others, especially dedicated cooks, might prefer the wood finishes and general organized chaos (right) of a room that is basically the same shape but arranged differently.

family and are forced to spend a lot of time in the kitchen, you will probably want to make it much more of a family room where people can sit around and talk, have a drink, do their homework, write notes, lists, letters, pay bills, and do a lot of eating.

Fit your space to your life style

If you are not quite sure of the sort of kitchen that will best suit you, ask yourself the following questions:

● Do you think your present situation will remain static or are you likely to have children and more children (their friends), guests and more guests to feed in the ensuing years?

● Do you know what kind of meals you are most likely to cook, for how many, and how often? (Remember that the *kind* of cooking you do is very much to the point, for if you only cook simple meals you will need far less preparation area than a more ambitious cook – though here again your aspirations may change with experience.)

● Do you work all day, and are you likely to go on doing so?

● Do you live far from a good shopping area so that you will need more than the average amount of food storage space and a large deep freeze?

● Even if you cannot afford them now, are you likely to acquire extra equipment in the future like a dishwasher, microwave oven, washing machine or freezer?

● Will there be more than one of you cooking or working in the kitchen at any one time? Kitchens that work really well for one, very seldom do for two (or more).

● Are you lucky enough to possess space for a utility or washing room? If so, you can hive off washing machine, dryers, ironing equipment and probably cleaning appliances and accessories, which is a great help when you are short of space.

● All these points should be thought about and considered in relation to the space you have to play with (a square room, rectangular room, cramped galley, and so on) as well as any existing appliances, and should certainly give you a clearer idea of the sort of room that will answer your needs.

What do you need? What can you afford?

Having decided that point, you should next make a list of the kitchen furniture and utensils that you would like, if not now, then later when you can better afford them so that you can plan your kitchen around specific objects.

Write down the items you need: basic essentials, then optional extras, then any luxuries. For the major items, make a note of the makes you would like, the price, and the dimensions, if relevant. Work out how much storage you will need for smaller pieces of equipment, serving equipment and foodstuffs: will one shelf in a cupboard be enough for tins, or do you need several? Can you hang saucepans on the wall near the cooker, or do you need cupboards or drawers for them? Will serving dishes, cutlery, table linen be kept in the kitchen or is there space for them near the dining table? Does cleaning and washing equipment have to live in the kitchen, or is there a utility room/cupboard under the stairs, or even a large bathroom where they can be stored?

Left: This purpose-built kitchen/dining/living room is unashamedly utilitarian, clean-cut and neat. It is also quite luxurious with its built-in tv and stereo units vying for place with rather more normal kitchen equipment.

Right: There is a totally different feel to this multi-purpose space viewed from the kitchen area. The kitchen equipment and utensils are used as homely decoration while a sofa and chairs provides comfortable seating in the living/dining area.

FIRST MAKE YOUR PLANS

Left: A satisfactory 'work-triangle' is formed by refrigerator, sink and stove in this awkwardly-shaped kitchen. Forethought and good planning has produced a room which is attractive to work in, well equipped, labour-saving and ergonomically sound.

Above: Neat and perfectly adequate cooking space for a couple has been squeezed into this compact and corridor-like area.

When you have completed your list, think about the basic services you will need: how many electrical appliances are on the list? Where will each one be plugged in? New tracking devices are coming on to the market to make this stage of planning easier, but most of us still have to plan where we want our socket outlets and lighting long before any kitchen equipment can be installed.

It might sound elementary, but it is only too easy to leave out quite obvious necessities in the trauma of getting everything done and easier still to discount the quite alarming final costs. This way, you can at least work out the essentials and plan from there.

How to plan your space
The chief rule for any successful kitchen plan is that it should always follow a work diagram based on the sequence of operations. Because food preparation generally involves a good deal of doubling back to and from the refrigerator, sink, stove and different work surfaces, the walking distance between all the main work areas should not be excessive. And each work area needs careful thought to ensure that all necessary equipment and ingredients are conveniently to hand.

The three principal work areas—preparation, cooking and washing-up—are centred on the fridge, the cooker and the sink. Professional kitchen planners use the term 'work triangle' to describe the imaginary lines linking the three areas. While you must allow enough space in each area to work efficiently, they must not be spaced too far apart, or you will be walking backwards and forwards much more than is necessary.

Consider the operation involved in cooking something as simple as frozen peas:

1 Take pan to sink and fill.
2 Take pan to cooker. Add salt. Bring to boil.
3 Remove peas from refrigerator. Open bag with scissors. Add to pan. Discard bag.
4 When cooked, take pan to sink. Use colander to strain.
5 Tip peas into serving dish.
6 Get butter from refrigerator. Use knife to add a knob of butter.
7 Return butter to fridge. Put dirty utensils in sink or dishwasher.
8 Take peas to table.

Even a task as simple as this involves two trips to the sink, three trips to the refrigerator, and two trips to the cooker (more if you warmed the serving dish first). You also need to visit the cupboards and drawers where the pan, salt, scissors, knife and colander are kept, and dispose of the bag in the rubbish bin.

So the distances between the work areas are crucial: each side of the work triangle should be between 1250 and 2150 mm (4–7 ft). If its perimeter is more than 6.6 m (22 ft) you will be walking around more than necessary. If it is less than 4 m (13 ft) you won't have enough room to be able to manoeuvre yourself comfortably.

You must organize your storage around the work areas according to what is needed: knives near the preparation area; spices between the preparation and cooking areas; wooden spoons near the cooker; coffee, tea and mugs near the kettle and so on. It may not be possible to get everything precisely where you want it, so think about the things you do most often (such as making a cup of tea, cooking a casserole) or in most of a hurry (preparing breakfast) and try to make the work flow for these tasks as simple and streamlined as possible.

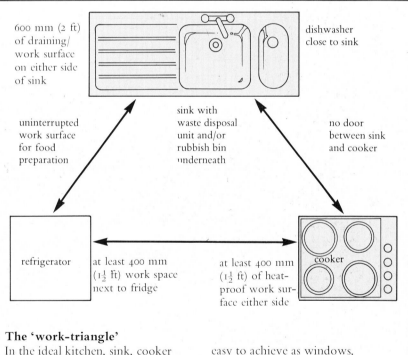

600 mm (2 ft) of draining/ work surface on either side of sink

dishwasher close to sink

uninterrupted work surface for food preparation

sink with waste disposal unit and/or rubbish bin underneath

no door between sink and cooker

refrigerator

at least 400 mm (1½ ft) work space next to fridge

cooker

at least 400 mm (1½ ft) of heat-proof work surface either side

The 'work-triangle'
In the ideal kitchen, sink, cooker and refrigerator are spaced evenly apart from one another to form a compact work triangle. Unfortunately this is not always easy to achieve as windows, irregular walls and limited space need to be taken into account. You will find some examples of typical solutions on page 146.

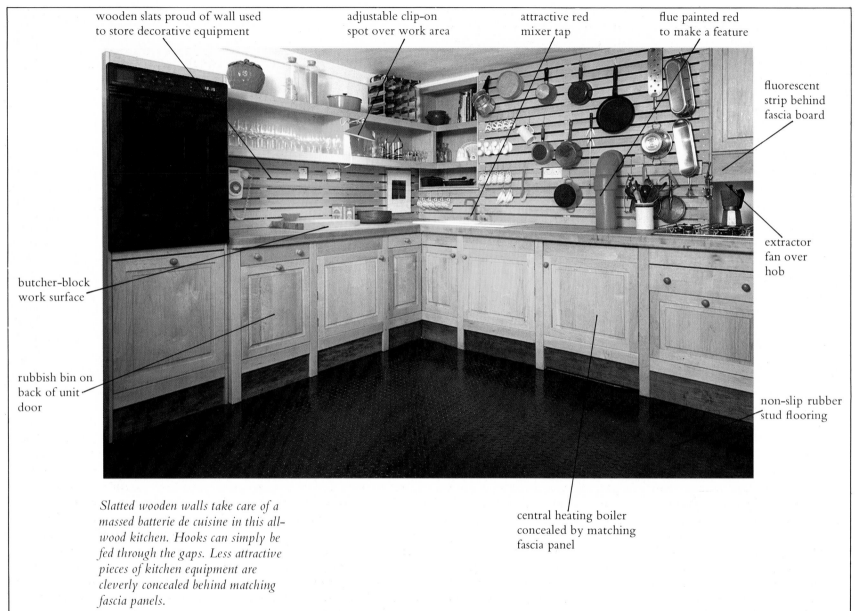

wooden slats proud of wall used to store decorative equipment

adjustable clip-on spot over work area

attractive red mixer tap

flue painted red to make a feature

fluorescent strip behind fascia board

extractor fan over hob

butcher-block work surface

rubbish bin on back of unit door

non-slip rubber stud flooring

Slatted wooden walls take care of a massed batterie de cuisine in this all-wood kitchen. Hooks can simply be fed through the gaps. Less attractive pieces of kitchen equipment are cleverly concealed behind matching fascia panels.

central heating boiler concealed by matching fascia panel

Put it on paper

Obviously, the actual dimensions of your particular work triangle are going to be determined by the basic floor plan of your kitchen. So you need to draw up a plan of what you've got already, then you can work out how best to improve it. This is the procedure to follow, whether you're planning a new kitchen entirely from scratch, or reorganizing an existing one.

You will need some graph paper, a tape measure, a sharp pencil, ruler and eraser. Measure the room's dimensions (length and width, allowing exactly the right space for doors, windows, breaks in walls, structural columns, radiators, fixtures and so on) and draw them out to scale making sure that they are absolutely exact. The slightest error can be disastrous when you have to fit in appliances and units. If you have awkward pipes, low windows, a hatch or power points already in position, mark them on the plan, and measure up and draw elevations of the walls as well.

Measure up any items which have to stay in the kitchen, and cut out shapes from graph paper to represent them. If they can't be moved (for example you may prefer not to call in a plumber to move the sink), stick them down. Try to be as flexible as possible: it may be well worth moving, say, the cooker as little as 1 metre (3 ft) from its existing position

in order to create a better work flow. Play around with the shapes and don't stick things down on your plan unless you are sure they can't be moved.

Work out the best way to organize your work triangle, then connect the points of the triangle. If the triangle does not seem as efficient as professional planners would like, see if you can move the appliances or work surfaces to give a better arrangement. For example, to increase working and manoeuvring space in an existing work triangle you could set up a second food preparation or cooking area with perhaps a microwave oven outside your main work area. To lessen the distance between, say, the refrigerator and the sink, you could add an island unit to the centre of the room, or a freestanding butcher-block work surface, or even a mobile work trolley.

Your particular triangle may well be unique, as it results from a combination of your particular space, and your particular needs. But there are some standard arrangements which may give you some helpful ideas. You can look at these in more detail on page 146.

Once you have traced out your basic floor plan and work triangle you can develop the rest of the kitchen to include more work space (like a pastry or baking preparation area), more storage, other appliances, an eating area (if there's

room), perhaps a desk area, and look into more technical details like electric outlets, and lighting. Finally, you will be able to add the finishing touches with decoration. If you cannot do everything at once, or want to start making staged improvements, either concentrate on your first priorities (leaving space for the next stages) or your worst problems—depending on whether you are planning a first-time kitchen or updating an existing one.

Corridor or galley kitchens are often particularly easy to work in – as long as there are not more than two people. This one is a model of its kind with clean lines, red and white scheme, wire grid hanging areas and careful use of every bit of space. Note the shelves across the window and over the door. Vivid red sinks, red and white checked vinyl flooring, red-topped stools, and fine red edging to the door frame to match the accessories, all contribute to the scheme.

Basic kitchen with big ideas

With a little ingenuity you can make a
perfectly adequate and cheerful
kitchen on the smallest of budgets in
the most awkward of spaces. This
room has a low and sloping ceiling
and very little natural light yet
manages to look airy, bright and well-
equipped even though the only
appliances are the most basic models
of sink, stove and fridge. There are no
units and very little equipment apart
from the versatile wok. With such a
low ceiling and lack of light the first
priority was lighting—achieved with
inset eyeball spots. There was no
money for tiles but walls and ceiling
were covered in a red and white check
paper given a toughening coat of clear
eggshell polyurethane. Appliances
were linked by a run of white
laminate work top which formed a
counter at one end. This serves as an
eating bar now but later can
accommodate a dishwasher. In the
absence of wall units storage is taken
care of by red plastic coated open
shelving, open shelving built into the
recess and cupboard with home-hung
louvre doors. The floor is covered
with red and white sheet vinyl in a
smaller square design. The detailing is
completed by the red taps, red handles
on the cupboard under the sink and
the pullout red vegetable baskets on
wheels.

FIRST MAKE YOUR PLANS

The importance of lighting

The same rules for planning light fittings apply in the kitchen as everywhere else in the home: general light to see by; work light to work by; an accent light to show off anything particularly worth looking at. The special rule of the kitchen is to make sure that there is light over every work surface so that you never work in your own shadow.

Insert general pendant lighting or inset downlights or wallwashers for the overall light; fix baffled light below cabinets to shine directly onto the worktop, and try to install special lights over stove and sink. If you are going to eat in the kitchen make sure overall lights are on a dimmer switch and that there is enough light over the table—use a rise-and-fall light fixture for example—which can, of course, be substituted for or combined with candlelight at night. Independent switches for each light will make it easier to create the appropriate atmosphere.

Fluorescent tubes are best for under cabinet/worktop lighting. They last much longer than incandescent tubes, offer more light per watt but need to be carefully chosen in the right colours for the most accurate presentation of food. That is to say, choose warm white de luxe (not just warm white) or cool white de luxe (not just cool white). There is no point in dimming fluorescent

Top left: Lighting, albeit slightly unconventional, is placed exactly where it matters in this kitchen; that is over the cook top and over the work surface, where spotlights are intertwined through a suspended wire grid.

Left: A square of centrally-placed tubular track has mobile spotlights trained on all the relevant parts of the kitchen as well as on the sink and grill area immediately underneath.

Above: In this deliberately old-fashioned and eclectic-style room with its prettily stencilled walls, a series of pendant lights is hung above the butcher block and dining table.

light; although it is possible, it is extremely costly and unnecessary. Mount tubes as close to the front of cabinets as possible and shield them with a baffle or small valance or cornice attached to the bottom of units. This will subdue any glare.

Sinks will need a minimum of two 100 watt incandescent bulbs or two 75 watt reflector floodlights which will focus light directly onto the bowls and draining boards.

If you have a hood over your hob or stove you should see that bulbs are enclosed to protect them from spattered grease and heat. Most manufacturers recommend a 60 watt maximum; or use fluorescent tubes.

Island work areas can be lit by general light, a rise-and-fall fixture or a fluorescent fixture containing at least two 30 or 40 watt tubes. Alternatively, try recessed or surface-mounted downlights using, say, 75 watt reflector floods. Good results for considerably less money can be achieved with clamp-on work lights.

Almost all light sources are concealed in the working area of this good-looking Hi-Tech kitchen. The exception—the long tubular green-cased fluorescent suspended from the ceiling—is as much sculptural decoration as lighting fixture. Note the large green-painted galvanized steel extractor fan over the cook top and supporting green columns.

If you find your kitchen hard to work in, tiring, cramped for space, uninspiring, or shabby, you can at least take comfort in the fact that you are not alone. The trouble is that the majority of kitchens in the majority of homes were designed years ago with appliances, storage cabinets, work surfaces and lighting that is now either inadequate or unsuitable. Alternatively it may be that your kitchen actually functions with great efficiency and is relatively modern but simply lacks character. Whatever the problem, there is always a solution, so long as you are prepared to use your ingenuity, be flexible and remember that rules were made to be broken—or at least bent a little.

Unfortunately some solutions rely on structural changes for effect, but these don't always have to involve vast expense. For example, if you are short of wall space and have a door off the kitchen leading to a room which can also be approached from another door, block off the kitchen door. This could either involve removing it altogether and blocking up the space with bricks and mortar, or simply locking it and putting furniture against it on both sides.

Similarly, if your problem is one of poor ventilation leading to a steamy or smoke-filled room in which it is difficult to see anything, the solution is obviously an air extractor. This could be let into the wall, which would mean taking up valuable wall space and also involving duct work. You could, however, if there is a window in the room, replace a pane of glass with one heavy enough to resist the weight and pressure of an air extractor. This will save on time, convenience and expense. If more drastic action is called for, some alternatives are outlined on page 145.

It may be that all that is required is a little lateral thinking. For example, if you are short of storage space, a perennial complaint, perhaps you should consider the ceiling. You would be amazed at what can be stored at this level. A high ceiling is, of course, a prerequisite if you wish to avoid constantly banging your head.

The charmingly rustic kitchen on the left could scarcely be called custom-built; but it does have good storage facilities and refreshing touches like the yellow window frames. Even more decorative treatment has been given to the all-wood kitchen on the right.

ROOM FOR IMPROVEMENT

Luckily, as most of us have neither the money nor the time to undertake major remodelling, it is quite possible to make significant changes without going to the bank for a loan or calling in a builder.

If you have not really thought how you could improve your space, or can't quite place what is wrong, ask yourself the following questions:

● Do you find you are walking around a lot, even to prepare the simplest of meals?

● Do you always seem to be shifting things along on your worktops in order to make room to prepare something?

● Do you have to keep looking for things? A particular knife perhaps, or some other essential-at-the-time utensil?

● Are you constantly having to move things around in your cabinet in order to find what you need?

● Are all your cupboards or closets crammed full?

● Can you see items on your shelves or in your cabinets which you have not used for at least a year?

● Has the size of your household changed since the last time you bought a kitchen appliance?

● Do people tend to stand around in your kitchen when they are eating a snack or drinking the odd cup of coffee because there is no place to sit?

● Is your kitchen the sort of place where family and friends congregate for chats as a matter of course. If not, would you like it to be?

● Would you like to change the whole look but don't think you have the money?

● Are you in rented property so feel you just have to put up with what you have?

If you have answered yes to at least three of these questions, some sort of change is certainly due, if not overdue. Here's how to achieve it.

The answer to the first problem is obviously to try to do something about your domestic traffic problems. If you do seem to be walking around a lot during meal preparations try to count the number of times you walk to various work areas and even the number of steps you take. You might well find that another work counter will help a good deal. If there is no room to add any extra counter space try importing a free-standing butcher-block worktop or a trolley or cart. Again, if you find you are always walking back and forth to a larder or pantry, or to shelves at the other end of the kitchen, a storage trolley or cart which you could wheel up when necessary should help.

Far left: A free-standing butcher-block worktop adds useful extra working space in just the right area. The walls, stripped down to the bare brick, could accept more shelves in the future. The use of light wood on all surfaces unifies the eclectic mixture.

Left: Extra pull-out worktops have been built in to this run of units. The deep pelmet adds interest.

Above: More storage and workspace, complete with integral steps, have been provided here by a kind of kitchen 'tower'. A further space-saving idea is the white-painted sliding door with its sculptural hanging chair.

133

Ringing the changes

However good-looking a room might seem there is nothing like day-to-day use to point up its shortcomings. The drawbacks of this dining-kitchen were soon realised to be lack of storage and worktop space and the hardness and noisiness of the otherwise splendid brick floor. The easiest solutions were to build storage around the large window and to cover the floor with coir matting—softer underfoot than bare brick but tough and hard-wearing. To keep the general character of the room a pine unit was built to the same size and style of the old dresser base which formed the original worktop and storage units. Its tiled top was replaced with solid butcher block and this was continued onto the new unit. A butcher-block trolley/cart added extra work space. The window shutters were removed and glass shelves and a rod were hung right across the panes to hold herbs, plants and pots, pans and implements. On one side of the window there was room for a capacious wooden cabinet, matched on the other side by a pine bookshelf unit about the same size. This takes all the cook books. The old beige cotton chair cushions were re-covered in a green Provençal print and teamed with a flower bordered tablecloth in another print. The result is a very pleasing kitchen which also works well.

Make good use of storage space. Top left: Industrial shelving and wire grid have been used to excellent effect in this Hi-Tech kitchen. Above: Almost every surface except the window has been utilised here for storage. Far left: This storage unit pulls out on wheels to reveal pots and pans. The painted outlines make quick replacement easy. Left: A plate drying rack and storage shelves suspended over the sink.

Sensible storage

Several more of the problems are clearly to do with your current storage or methods of storage. People are always complaining that they do not have enough work space/dumping space, but it may well be what they really need is better organized storage. Look at the work spaces at your disposal. Are you using them to their best advantage? Or are they so cluttered up that there isn't any real space to work on? If clutter is your only problem, be ruthless and get rid of anything hanging around that you have not used for the last six months, and put anything else away in a cupboard, cabinet or closet somewhere.

If there does not seem any room to get rid of storage jars, canisters, cook tools and so on, you might need to add more shelves and hooks. You can often use the space between the bottom of wall-hung cabinets and the counter top to put up small shelves which will take a variety of objects; this is often a good place to stand your collection of dried herbs in small pots or jars–it keeps them together, clearly visible and to hand. And if you add cup hooks to the edges you can hang things from them as well. Another useful extra storage space is behind cabinet doors where again you might fix narrow shelves or hooks. And don't overlook the exposed sides of end base or wall-hung cabinets.

fold-away
wall-mounted grill

spotlight on track
for effective lighting

jolly red accessories
tone with colour scheme

decorative dresser
provides extra storage

portable
countertop
oven takes
large turkey

work surface
made from
renovated
old timber

mobile
dual-function
worktop/sideboard

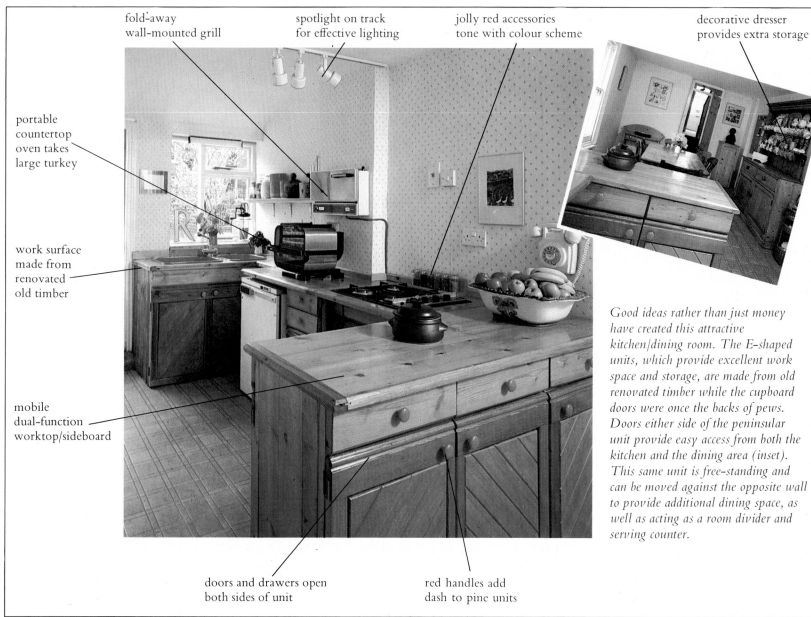

doors and drawers open
both sides of unit

red handles add
dash to pine units

*Good ideas rather than just money
have created this attractive
kitchen/dining room. The E-shaped
units, which provide excellent work
space and storage, are made from old
renovated timber while the cupboard
doors were once the backs of pews.
Doors either side of the peninsular
unit provide easy access from both the
kitchen and the dining area (inset).
This same unit is free-standing and
can be moved against the opposite wall
to provide additional dining space, as
well as acting as a room divider and
serving counter.*

Streamlined surfaces

A quick way to re-vamp a tired looking kitchen is to re-cover or replace the work surface.

Butcher-block, though expensive, will turn your food preparation area into one long chopping board. Oil it frequently, sand it occasionally and it will last for years. But avoid using it near the sink (where it might warp or the surface might rise) or close to the cooker (unless you have tiles and trivets for hot pans).

Tiles are a popular choice in country-style kitchens, but not to be recommended if you are heavy-handed with pots and pans. You can lay them on chipboard or plywood, or use them to cover your existing work surface. Rub down the surface with glasspaper, stick the tiles down with a suitable adhesive and grout in between them with a synthetic plastic bathroom or kitchen sealant (which won't pick up stains). Or use special coloured pigment (food colouring works too) to darken it. Edge the new surface with wooden beading, painted or varnished to suit the style of the kitchen.

If you have access to woodworking equipment or are employing a handyman, you can use planks of beech or hardwood, butted together and edged with rounded beading. Give the surface at least three coats of yacht varnish, rubbing down lightly with wire wool between coats.

Plastic laminate surfaces can be renewed: round-edged surfaces will have to be taken out and replaced. Square-edged surfaces can be re-covered with laminate, using edging strips of the same material, or lipping the edge with wooden beading.

If your kitchen is made up of separate units, each with its own worktop, you may be able to get a more streamlined look by installing a long run of worktop joining the separate units. If the units don't match the length of the wall, you can create a tray or vegetable storage area by leaving a space between units or continuing the worktop beyond the end of the unit, butting it up to the wall.

A cheerful but cheap way to renovate a worktop is to cover it with some sort of self-adhesive plastic. Smooth it tightly over the work surface, then give it a couple of coats of polyurethane for protection. It won't be as tough as plastic laminate, but it will be fairly hardwearing.

Many professional kitchens have stainless steel work surfaces, with wooden chopping blocks and marble sections (for pastry making) let into them. But stainless steel is expensive, and unless it is properly cushioned underneath it can be very noisy.

A complete work surface in marble would be impractical: cold, hard and expensive. But it might be worth topping one part of your work area (a single unit or a free-standing refrigerator) with marble for pastry making. But remember that it is easily stained by wine, acids and lemon juice.

Synthetic marble is an alternative: this new, durable material for work surfaces is proof against most stains, reasonably heat resistant, non-porous, and cuts like wood.

Sealed cork flooring tiles may also be used to re-cover a surface, but like butcher-block, they are not suitable for areas exposed to great heat or water.

Pale butcher-block makes a most elegant counter in this handsome room.

Slate is useful for pastry-making and also provides a decorative top.

This synthetic marble worktop comes complete with recessed sinks.

Extra work space

If you are satisfied that you have spirited away all possible clutter and still do not have adequate preparation space you could cover a sink with a portable chopping board, or turn a drawer into an extra work surface by fitting runners to a block of wood the same width as the drawer, so that it will glide in and out of the unit, resting on the top of the drawer when it is pulled out.

Cleaned up cupboards

If your cabinets seem to be constantly overcrowded, open up all the doors and look at the contents with a critical eye. If there are items around that you hardly ever use, remove them to more remote storage areas away from your work areas. Seldom used or once-a-year items like ham boiling pans, turkey roasting pans, fish kettles, picnic baskets etc, might well be parted from the day-to-day items. Or you can hang pot racks from the ceiling; and put up areas of peg boards to hang colanders, sieves, whisks, graters and so on.

If you have not bought any new appliances since you first moved into your home, or if your family has changed in numbers, you might well be due for some updated versions. The sort of choice available is explained on pages 157–165, but a new refrigerator or fridge-freezer, the addition of a microwave oven, or the purchase of a portable dishwasher if there is no room for a plumbed-in version, might make all the difference to your own work load.

Another salient question to ask yourself is: are you really using your space to its best advantage. I am not talking here about your work surfaces, or work triangles or the general space/work efficiency of your kitchen, but rather if you could use your kitchen as more of a family room—the sort of room which friends as well as family tend to migrate to at the first available opportunity. Obviously this is not relevant if you have a tiny galley kitchen, or a slit of corridor space, but if you can add a chair or two, or at least a couple of stools where there were none before; and some sort of bar, or at least an enlarged counter top if you can't fit in a decent table, then you are well on the way to making your kitchen a more welcoming place.

Another kitchen where every surface is made to work to maximum advantage. The counter top provides space for eating as well as cooking and preparation. Baskets, bowls and a fish kettle are hung on the stone wall. A suspended iron bar just under the ceiling holds a mass of decorative copper pans attached by butcher's hooks. Other walls have hooks for more equipment and still there is room for further expansion, if necessary, along the remaining walls.

ROOM FOR IMPROVEMENT

You might also think of adding a desk top somewhere: against a small wall; across a corner, as an extension of a worktop. A wooden counter with a couple of filing cabinets underneath, preferably on castors for easy manoeuvrability would be one excellent idea; or just a flip-down panel from a wall would be another. Try and have some shelves above for files and cook books, add a telephone, writing implements and note books, even a typewriter if you can, and you have a mini office to hand whenever you need it.

Finally, you should remember that it really is not necessary to totally re-vamp the kitchen or call in a decorator in order to give it a face lift. There are all sorts of comparatively small changes you can make which will transform your kitchen's looks out of all proportion to the time and expense.

Right: Painted blinds repeat the cherry pattern of the wallpaper and combine with the red accessories to set off the dominant pine.

Left: A compact galley kitchen with many of its original fittings has been given a totally fresh look by painting the units and appliances the background green of the bird-covered wallpaper. Plants enhance the bower image, while pieces of pretty china, paintings, prints and the birdcage inject further charm.

Changes for the better

● Cheer up dull-looking cabinets by painting them in a high gloss or eggshell finish. Or cut a stencil and re-spray the doors adding a simple motif – which can be repeated around the splashback, or around the top of a plain painted room.

● Take off cabinet doors: leave them off altogether for an open shelved look; replace them with new louvred or wooden doors with beading; replace them with glazed doors, or hang curtains in front of shelves instead (PVC fabric curtains won't pick up dirt so easily but cotton is cheaper and easier to wash).

● Re-tile the splashback between counter top and wall-hung cupboards. Plain white tiles are the cheapest: brighten them up with coloured grouting, or mix them with other plain tiles to build up an eye-catching pattern

● Paint everything white: walls, ceiling, units, and add new tiles as well. Even the floor can be painted (see below). The whole place will look amazingly different. Add colour and interest with brightly coloured or prettily patterned kitchen accessories–tea towels, canisters, cook books.

● Cover walls with a vinyl wallpaper (which can be wiped, or even scrubbed), in a pattern to suit your style–an all-over check or floral pattern for a soft, country look; splashy flowers in cheerful colours for a more lively country look; a sharp grid or smart stripe for a more clinical style. If you can't find the pattern you want in a vinyl, you can protect paper wallcoverings with a polyurethane varnish, but it may yellow the pattern slightly.

● Change your window treatment: café curtains instead of a tired roller blind; glass shelves stretched across the window to display bits of china and glass or a collection of old stone and glass bottles; or paint the wooden surround in a pretty colour to frame a crisp new roller blind.

● Either arrange trailing plants such as tradescantia and spider plants in hanging baskets slung from a brass or wooden pole fixed across the window, or intersperse them with herbs and African violets on glass shelves (see above). Some plants like kitchen windows, especially if they are over a steamy sink, but always check first. In a window which does not get much light, a single, showy Boston fern will make a focal point.

● Do the unexpected. 'White goods' (fridge, freezer, washing machine) needn't stay white: re-spray them (in a well-ventilated room) with cans of car paint – by using masking tape you can easily create simple but eye-catching patterns in bold stripes.

ROOM FOR IMPROVEMENT

● Change the walls. Make the room look warm and cheerful by panelling the walls: fix ordinary wooden lathes on the diagonal. Leave them natural or paint them to suit the rest of the decoration. Or cover the walls with tongue-and-groove panelling. Or do away with wallcovering altogether: strip away the plaster to expose the bare brick underneath. (This solution is only suitable for older properties—investigate the structure of the wall in an unobtrusive corner before setting to work.)

● Transform the floor: quarry tile it, or lay new ceramic tiles, Mexican tiles or bricks; put down a well-varnished wood block floor; or lay sheet vinyl, linoleum or vinyl tiles. Sealed cork tiles will create a warm atmosphere. Check the subfloor (is it solid concrete or suspended wood?) before you make your choice, as not all coverings are suitable for all subfloors.

Right: A radical transformation has been achieved in this room by stripping the walls to the brick beneath. The ceiling was tongue-and-grooved, the floor bricked and lights added in the right places.

Top right: Units here were wittily painted to match the upper walls.

Bottom right: Old dresser bases are used instead of modern units.

● For a really economical new floor, add a coat of paint. Lino paint is suitable for virtually any surface, and comes in a range of colours. Wood, cork and well-laid vinyl tiles can be painted with gloss paint and given extra protection with a few coats of polyurethane or yacht varnish.

● Add character and charisma: if the room is quite large but lacks personality, simply change some of the existing pieces of furniture: replace the table with an old pine one and add some old pine chairs (available in most junk shops); swap some units for a pine dresser; paint chairs cheerful colours; replace posters with a cork or fabric-covered noticeboard.

● Don't forget details: particularly in rented property, where you can't make substantial alterations, you can still make an enormous difference with carefully chosen accessories: sets of matching storage jars, wooden spice racks, kitchen roll holders, pretty tea towels, bunches of herbs, onions or dried flowers, interesting canisters—old or new; plants; posters; prints; and last, but by no means least, good-looking cookware.

I inherited one kitchen which had lemon yellow units with aluminium knobs, lemon yellow walls, a false flagstone vinyl floor and speckly plastic laminate worktops. I re-moved the units from one short wall, replaced them with a huge old pine dresser and painted all the walls, the ceiling and the rest of the units white. I changed the aluminium knobs for some more cheerful brass handles, covered the wall space between worktops and the bottom of cabinets with some blue and white Mexican tiles (which didn't cost the earth), re-topped the counters with butcher-block and changed the vinyl flagstones for quarry tiles. Result: a total change of character.

For other instant transformations you could jazz up an all-white kitchen say, by adding red and white tiles and red handles, or by just painting a stripe all along between drawers and cupboard doors. Another white kitchen could be given a totally different look by adding green plastic handles and importing masses of plants and some green painted bamboo blinds. Equally you could add wood counter tops to an otherwise all-laminate room, together with wooden slatted blinds, or the plain bamboo or matchstick variety, or some red and white or blue and white check gingham curtains or café curtains.

Once you really start to think of the components that can be changed in a room without too much ado you can come up with any number of ideas for a change of style, or more important, for adding style where none existed before.

143

When you come to re-vamp your kitchen on a more major scale, your choices are wider. You probably have a good idea of the atmosphere you want to create in your kitchen, and you will find some simplified pointers to style on the following pages. First, however, you have to look at how to make the best use of existing space.

Making sense of your space

The great advantage of starting from scratch in a kitchen is that you can, for very little extra cost, make major improvements by re-positioning services (gas, plumbing, electricity), doors, windows, even walls.

Since kitchens tend to be positioned at the back of the house, they are often in an ideal situation for extending into the back garden, or knocking through into a corridor or back room to create a more useful space. If you are planning major changes to your kitchen, it is worth finding out how neighbours with the same layout have solved the problem.

One of the first points to consider when reorganizing is the basic floor plan and convenient work triangle mentioned on page 123. There are several tried and tested arrange-ments of units and appliances which will give an idea of the use you can make of a given shape: The one-wall kitchen, the U-plan kitchen, the L-shaped kitchen and the galley kit-chen – for details see page 146. The shape of your room will probably dictate the arrangement.

When you get down to more detailed planning it is useful to know that in a standard European kitchen, base units are 600 mm (24 in) deep; wall units 300 mm (12 in) deep; most appliances are 600 mm (24 in) wide; units come in widths of 300, 500, 600, 1000 or 1200 mm (12, 20, 24, 39, or 48 in), counter tops are 900 mm (36 in) high, the bases of wall-hung cabinets 405 mm (16 in) above that. These dimensions have been tested ergonom-ically, and are designed to fit in with standard appliances, so they provide a useful guide if you are building your own units instead of buying ready-made.

The joy of starting afresh with a large budget shows on the left in marbled counter tops, built-in appliances, plenty of storage, elegant blinds and flooring, and a capacious skylight. Another high budget kitchen, right, with tiled floor, central cook top/eating counter, in clean red and white.

The U-shaped kitchen

This is usually considered the best shape for any kitchen: the triangle idea works well, everything should be within easy reach, and there should be plenty of counter/work space and plenty of storage. It does depend, however, on having a rectangular room.

Still, the U-plan has been proved efficient in both large and small rooms though it's as well to remember that a minimum of 1500 mm (5 ft) and a maximum of 3000 mm (10 ft) is necessary between base cabinets. If your room can take a U-shape and is reasonably large, one side of the U can form a natural dividing line between work and dining space, whether formal or informal. Raise and cantilever part of the counter top on this dividing line and it can act both as a breakfast counter by day, and a barrier against kitchen debris for diners by night.

The L-shaped kitchen

L-shaped kitchens make good dining areas because by locating appliances and cabinets on adjacent walls you create both a compact work space and still have room for a decent-sized dining table. Once again, this sort of arrangement works in a large or in a long narrow kitchen but can waste space in a smaller room where there isn't the same scope for counter and storage space as in a U-shaped plan.

The one-wall kitchen

This is a good idea in a small space, or in a family room or dining room kitchen where the emphasis is more on a general living room than a kitchen. The whole kitchen may be screened off with sliding or folding doors if necessary. Again, it can be useful for a kitchen area off a living room where work and leisure space are divided by a counter or island unit. Unless the wall is very long you do, of course, miss out on storage space unless that is taken care of in other areas.

The corridor or galley kitchen

As its name implies, this can be as neat and effective as a well-organized ship's kitchen—but can also be a disaster if the corridor or galley is open at both ends. When this plan works well it saves a great deal of wear and tear on the cook. However, it will not work for a family or dining/kitchen.

Since space will inevitably be very tight, planning should be as ingenious and imaginative as possible. Slide-out shelves, pull-out work surfaces and storage bins, revolving shelves, pot racks can all be brought into play for maximum effect. For manoeuvrability, there should be at least 1200 mm (4 ft) between the base units on either side. If space does not allow this it might be better to treat it as a one-wall or an L-shaped kitchen and build in narrow shelves down

the other long wall. You can even use 300 mm (1 ft) deep wall-hung units as base units, surfacing them with a narrow counter top, or you could combine a counter top and stools to make a breakfast bar, with storage space above.

The island kitchen

An island unit in a kitchen (if there is room for one) immediately adds extra work space, storage and interest. It is excellent in a large room which might otherwise lack focus and efficiency but it can also hinder the triangle work flow if the kitchen is not big enough to take it.

The usual function of an island unit is to hold a cook top (which can be self-venting or topped by an extractor hood), closet, shelf and extra work top space, but it can also incorporate an extra small fridge, an extra sink, dishwasher, wine storage, a bar, or an eating counter. If you do not have a cook top and extractor hood, the space above makes an ideal place for a pot or basket rack.

The peninsula kitchen

In a way, this is much the same as an island kitchen except the larger rectangular area is usually used to divide working kitchen space from a family or dining area. Again, you must have enough room for this arrangement but it is a neat way of getting extra storage, breakfast bar, work and buffet space.

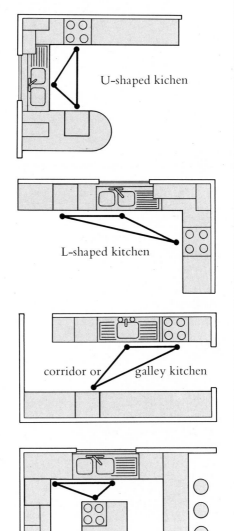

U-shaped kichen

L-shaped kitchen

corridor or galley kitchen

island kitchen

Left: This island unit in an immaculate kitchen-dining room holds dishwasher and sink side by side as well as providing a good counter top/serving space for the table. It also provides a useful focus for the large space. Note how the colours of plants, accessories and food come singing out against the all-white framework, including the stainless steel trim to the table and door.

Above: A one-wall kitchen with a difference—the addition of loud speakers nicely integrated with the back-splash between the units and the pop art displays of groceries. Not a cook's kitchen—more an efficient module for fast food service.

Creating a family room

If you are prepared to invest a lot of time and money in your new kitchen you might consider making a sort of kitchen/living or family room; a real 'heart of the home' area, more casual than a living room, more cosy than a working kitchen. If you would like to have this sort of feel but don't think your existing space is big enough, or light enough, or for one reason or another, does not seem to lend itself to such treatment, then consider the surrounding spaces.

What sort of room do you have next door? Is there a scullery for example? Or a lobby of some sort? A sun lounge, verandah or covered porch? A little used dining room or even a corridor or hall? If the walls separating the two are of the partition rather than supporting variety you could take them down and incorporate the space into one much larger room which will make more family sense.

Left and far left: Two different versions of corridor or galley kitchens. Both sides of the space are used for the homely kitchen (far left) which manages to incorporate a desk/eating counter as well as worktops and appliances. The narrower space (left) has made use of an L-shape to avoid too cluttered a look.

Right: An ideal kitchen/dining/living room for an active family.

The kitchen as family room

If a kitchen is big enough it's the obvious place for a general family room. It can do duty as a homework/play area, office and tv room as well as being used in the normal way for preparing, cooking and eating food. Here, a small, slightly awkward alcove to one side of the room has been turned into a useful home office with a typewriter and telephone, although the wall above, with its hanging grid panel for extra pans is still part of the kitchen storage. The large table is just as convenient for writing as for dining. The shelves stretched right across two windows and taking in the wall between make good use of the space to hold tv, cook books and lots of plants and herbs. Pale painted terracotta walls and ceiling are set off by a darker vinyl-tiled floor and plain white tiles above the counter tops are made to look more interesting by being laid on the diagonal. The green and white chair pads are tied on with toning ribbon and there are more green touches in the plants and the light shade. Other interesting features are the industrial serving cart, the spacious industrial shelving and the practical steel rod and hooks running the length of the counter top for utensils.

SPACE AND STYLE

Sometimes, too, it might make sense to turn most of a ground or basement floor into an open-plan kitchen/living/family room/study. As long as you consult the professionals, a surprising number of walls can be taken down with ease and the resulting increase in light and space is clearly amazing.

In a case like this, it might be best to keep most of the kitchen part of the room to one wall and hive it off from the rest of the area with a long island unit which could incorporate extra work and storage space and possibly a cook top, sink and refrigerator as well. A long dividing wall like this would make a good serving unit for every day and a splendid buffet area for a party.

Looking at style

Whatever the shape of your kitchen, it is worth giving some attention to the decoration and accessories to create a distinctive style. The choices are unlimited, but here are some of the characteristic elements which help to give a kitchen a particular atmosphere.

Mediterranean style would be designed to give a cool, smooth working atmosphere, with long slate or marble worktops, terracotta-style tiled floors, and large, walk-in cupboards with thick walls—lined with marble shelves for food storage or racks for pans and crockery.

Roughly plastered walls, shuttered windows and wall-mounted lighting typify this style, with open storage under the worktop and little wall-hung storage. Strings of garlic and bunches of herbs hang from the ceiling, and extra preparation space is provided by a solid table with upright, rush seated chairs around it.

Farmhouse style kitchens are typified by stripped pine, bare brick and perhaps a dresser. Many manufacturers produce pine or pine-effect units, but none will give the easy-on-the-eye, mellow effect that you can get from old pine. Worktops, where they exist, should be in natural materials—wood or tiles. But by using old pieces of furniture of odd shapes and sizes you may well sacrifice the conventional work surface to retain character. A pine or oak refectory table, forming an island unit in the middle of the room, would make up for this. Quarry tyles, brick paviour or wooden boards are typical choices for the floor. For real farmhouse style, you'll need a traditional range (or one of the newer versions). Back up the cooking facilities of the range with a modern oven, and you'll have all the character with the advantage of modern technology. Go for pretty floral fabrics, patchwork or fresh ginghams, and dot farmhouse chairs and rockers round the room to encourage visitors.

The fresh, country look has evolved over the last few years as people have begun to paint wooden units and replace solid doors with glazed doors to create a lighter atmosphere. Keep to pale colours, even for work surfaces, and choose pale, pretty floral patterns or plain cream for walls and accessories. Coloured tiles or sheet vinyl are ideal for country flooring, or a wooden floor looks equally at home. Use the glazed cupboards to display attractive china and to provide storage space for attractively packaged dry goods.

City slick style can add life to a dull urban kitchen. Go for strong colours and simple geometric patterns. All-white units are cheap, and can be brightened up with coloured tiles and accessories. Or be bold and use more dramatically coloured cupboards. Efficiency is essential in the fast food world of city life, so storage has to be well organized and cleverly designed to leave worktops clear and uncluttered.

Hi-tech is characterized by the use of functional glass and metal. In its extreme form, the domestic Hi-tech kitchen is indistinguishable from a professional kitchen in a good restaurant. Long runs of built-in stainless steel worktop, with hob, sink, chopping board and pastry board built in. Separate cooking areas for different types of food: a pastry chef's corner, a vegetable prepar-

Top right: This kitchen can only be described as not typical (but none the worse for that) with its long sweep of a table incorporating both gas and electric rings and a griddle, its amazing roll-top desk-cum-dresser with its pull-out shelves and enormous storage capacity; its old Raffles Hotel-style rattan long chair and its well stocked wooden shelves.

Bottom right: This is a deliberately Farmhouse-style kitchen. Note all the ingredients: the old pine dresser and well-used refectory table which can also do duty as a preparation area; the capacious old plate rack which holds so much more and drips so much better than a modern version; and the slightly haphazard but practical notion of curtaining the bottom part of the work top rather than filling it in with conventional units. Note too another decorative touch: the frieze of old produce advertisements.

Far right: A highly sophisticated corridor or galley kitchen with the useful addition of one mirrored wall with a small area of floor and wall-hung storage at the end. If these units had been extended all along the now mirrored wall there would hardly have been space to walk the length of the room in comfort. Note how the diagonally-tiled floor, creating an interesting chevron pattern by reflection, gives a further illusion of width and light.

ation area and so on. Cupboards are replaced by open steel shelves, lined with glass storage jars. Flooring is usually synthetic but essentially practical–stud rubber tiles for instance.

Of course, it is possible (even desirable) to draw the best elements of each of these distinctive styles together, to form a perfect, hybrid kitchen, adapted to your needs. They are not to be looked at in isolation and followed to the letter, but if you're not sure about style, they will give you some useful ideas.

These are only some ideas. Many more will be seen in the illustrations and prove that given the will and a bit of imagination you can inject style into almost any space you care to mention.

Left: A good description of this would be cheerful family kitchen designed with ultra-modern Hi-Tech efficiency. The details count: the bright yellow touches in floor border, lamp shade, sofa and accessories; the neat dark blue grid for easy wall attachments; the glass-fronted modular wall units dovetailing in so nicely with the units below and the blue tubular steel for chair frames and sofa legs. The general effect is clean, bright and smart.

Right: Hi-Tech par excellence . . . . with plants and flowers adding just the right sort of contrast.

Very few of us can afford all of the appliances we would like all at the same time. What we can do, however, is plan for them. Whether you are designing a kitchen from scratch or updating an old one you must think in terms of priorities, define your most pressing needs, and start from there. Do remember that, contrary to the cynics' view of built-in obsolescence, most major appliances—refrigerators, stoves, dishwashers and so on—are built to last for years, so, as far as possible, you should keep future changes of circumstances in mind as well as your present needs. If your household is likely to expand in any way it might be cheaper in the long run to buy a large model than the more modest affair you had thought of first.

In any case, it is perfectly possible to buy second-hand or re-conditioned models at a fraction of the price of new ones as long as you are prepared to accept the risk that they might eventually develop faults which could prove expensive. Still, they can make good stop-gaps till you can afford new models.

Obviously existing kitchens can be made more efficient with more up-to-date equipment – bigger freezer and/or fridge, a dishwasher, waste disposal unit and so on—but only if the appliances work hard for you, save time and labour and generally make your particular way of life easier and more enjoyable. A new cooker or whatever can be a tremendous boon and investment but before you go out and spend money ask yourself questions about the way you live: is the pace hectic or leisurely? how many and what sort of meals do you have to provide? are you far from a good supermarket or freezer centre? how much time do you have for shopping? are you out at work all day? do you grow your own vegetables? how often do you entertain? can you spend time on cooking and food preparation or is it always meals in a hurry? The answers will help you decide whether you need say, one vast freezer, or a large one in the garage and a small one in the kitchen, or a microwave plus freezer.

There is plenty of excellent equipment in the kitchen (left), and plenty of room for more to come (an extra fridge or small deep freeze cabinet could be tucked underneath the centre island unit for example). On the right, however, maximum effect is made with the very minimum.

CHOOSING EQUIPMENT

Gas or electricity?

This is really a matter of personal preference and the sort of facilities available in your building (or area – because, of course, nearby gas can be piped in at some cost, or use gas from cylinders if you really prefer gas). If you have the possibility of both services in a kitchen, you could opt for a gas cook top and an electric oven; or vice versa; or a mixture of both gas and electric plates to hedge bets should anything go wrong with one or other service, or to take advantage of both sorts of energy for different cooking needs (slow simmering; fast boiling etc.)

Stoves and Ovens

We've come a long way from the free-standing stove with four burners and an oven with maybe a separate grill or broiler. Now you can get models to suit every size, shape and style of kitchen from separate hobs and ovens, to catering-size free-standing models and makes that can be slid or dropped into your work run or counter top for maximum sleekness. Ceramic cook tops can give the semblance of an almost unbroken work surface, and so do the new magnetic induction units that look like tiles, but do not heat up because they use magnetic energy to cook food by energising molecules both in the food and the pan. Both types of cooker top are very smooth in appearance and easy to clean.

Some cook tops combine both gas and electric burners, others have interchangeable parts including a grill, a griddle and a rotisserie. Some tops have built-in deep fryers, and there are stoves with both a conventional and a microwave oven. Some British cooker tops still tend to be niggardly in size and don't make sufficient allowance for four large pans. Other countries seem to manage this better – British manufacturers please copy.

But there are plenty of other refinements to look for: self-cleaning ovens, automatic ignition gas ranges without pilot lights, automatic timers, automatic meat thermometers for perfect roasts, capacious drawer space underneath for plate warming and storing pots and pans, and tops with built-in grills and their own surface-venting systems.

Check the size Most free-standing cookers are 550–600 mm (22–24 ins) deep and extend slightly beyond most cabinets. Standard widths are 510–600 mm (20–24 ins). If you have the space and the cash, you will find that American and some continental cookers are much larger than this. You will be able to choose between a single or a double oven, with an eye-level grill or a grill at waist level, often set into a small top oven. New American models often feature a small, eye-level oven.

Built-in ovens may be designed to

Far left: This particular stove has been neatly dropped into a white wood-trimmed plastic laminate top and is flanked by a pair of pale oak cupboards for pots and pan storage. In fact the whole unit is happily fitted into the alcove left by an old solid fuel kitchen range.

Left: This handsome room with its white hexagonal tiles and interestingly white-stained wood units is extremely well off for cooking power with two full-size wall-mounted ovens and seven burners. With this number of working rings you would certainly need the enormous extractor hood and its inset powerful lighting. There is useful laminated counter space around the cook top and lots of extra cupboards built in underneath. In fact there is as enviable an amount of storage space as there are generous cooking facilities.

Hob design depends to a certain extent on the type of energy used. Top left: This wall-mounted oven and grill has been built into a substantial brick unit and is close to the stainless steel gas hob. Above: Deep set T-shaped shelves, painted a strong blue to contrast with white-tiled walls look bold and dramatic above the ceramic hob set into a butcher-block top. Far left: Gas rings are set into an elegantly green-rimmed top in a brilliantly designed green and white kitchen. The wine racks are stored behind the extractor fan. Left: The tray-like electric cook top here has been neatly fitted into a corner of a small kitchen.

go under the worktop (built-under), either beneath the hob or away from it, or they may fit into housing units so that the oven(s) are more accessible. Built-ins are usually just under 600 mm (24 in) wide, to fit neatly into standard units. Heights vary from about 500 mm (20 in) to 1000 mm (39 in). When you select a model, the literature which comes with it will tell you the exact size of opening and amount of ventilation space you need.

Compact hobs are about 550 × 450 mm (21 × 17 in) but if you have space, go for a large hob to take awkward-sized pans: you don't have to limit yourself to a simple, square configuration—there's no reason why you shouldn't have two or three small hobs in different places.

If you lead a hectically busy life, a microwave oven can be a real life –and time–saver, cooking food in a fraction of the time required by a normal oven. The snag has often been their lack of browning capacity—pale food doesn't look very appealing. But now there are special browning versions that take care of this. And the introduction of a turntable means that food is cooked evenly. Microwaves may be portable (but bulky) counter top models, wall-mounted, or built-in. Their measurements are less than those of standard ovens, although built-in models are the same width as built-in conventional ovens.

Above: Refrigerator and deep freeze are concealed behind wood fascia panels, which tone with the tongue-and-groove of the kitchen units, on either side of a wall-mounted oven in this spacious kitchen/dining room. A dark high level storage unit which matches the table is topped by rattan roller blinds to divide the workmanlike kitchen area from the more elegant dining space.

Left: Another housing unit, this time in white and blue, conceals a well-fitted fridge and freezer. Note how units have been cleverly fitted all around the small window.

Refrigerators and Freezers

The model of refrigerator and freezer you choose should depend on the size—or potential size—of your family and your work and cooking habits. Generally speaking, a 140 litre (5 cubic feet) refrigerator and 140–170 litres (5–6 cubic feet) of freezer space is ample for a couple and you should add another cubic foot per person in your household. If you can shop only once a week for example, you will need much more deep freeze space than if you can shop every day. If you cannot have a separate freezer you should look at a refrigerator with maximum freezer space and capacious food storage compartments. A good many of the latest models have sealed meat and vegetable drawers with adjustable temperature and humidity control to keep food fresher for longer.

Obviously frost-free models which mean you never have to defrost are as useful as self-cleaning ovens, and additional luxuries include iced water and crushed ice dispensers, automatic ice makers *and* the kind of American model with almost instant (that is to say about an hour) automatic ice cream and sorbet or sherbert-makers.

Separate deep freezers come in chest or upright models and are ideal for people with large gardens and plenty of produce to store and also for stashing away bulk buys and supermarket bargains.

Dishwashers

Really good dishwashers will clean everything from fine china and glass to encrusted saucepans and casseroles with settings that range from gentle wash to super scrub cycles. If you are a small family, look for models with the sort of controls that allow you rinse-and-hold cycles—a short cycle which rinses dishes for a short time to get rid of dried-on food and any smells so that they can then wait till you have a full load to put through. If you are a large family, or cook a lot, you should definitely look for a machine with a scrub cycle so you are not always hand-scouring pots and pans. Look too, for models with the sort of shelving that allows you to programme the machine to start work hours later and will make the operation a whole lot quieter, and the kinds that have soft food disposal units to prevent blocked drains.

If you do not have space for a build-in model beside or under the sink, there are portables available on wheels so that they can be rolled to the table for loading and back to the sink where they can be connected to the taps and drains for washing. Some have butcher-block tops so that they can double as extra work tops. If you move and have more space, many portables are convertible and can be built-in.

Most models are 60 cm (24 in) wide to fit in with average counter top measurements.

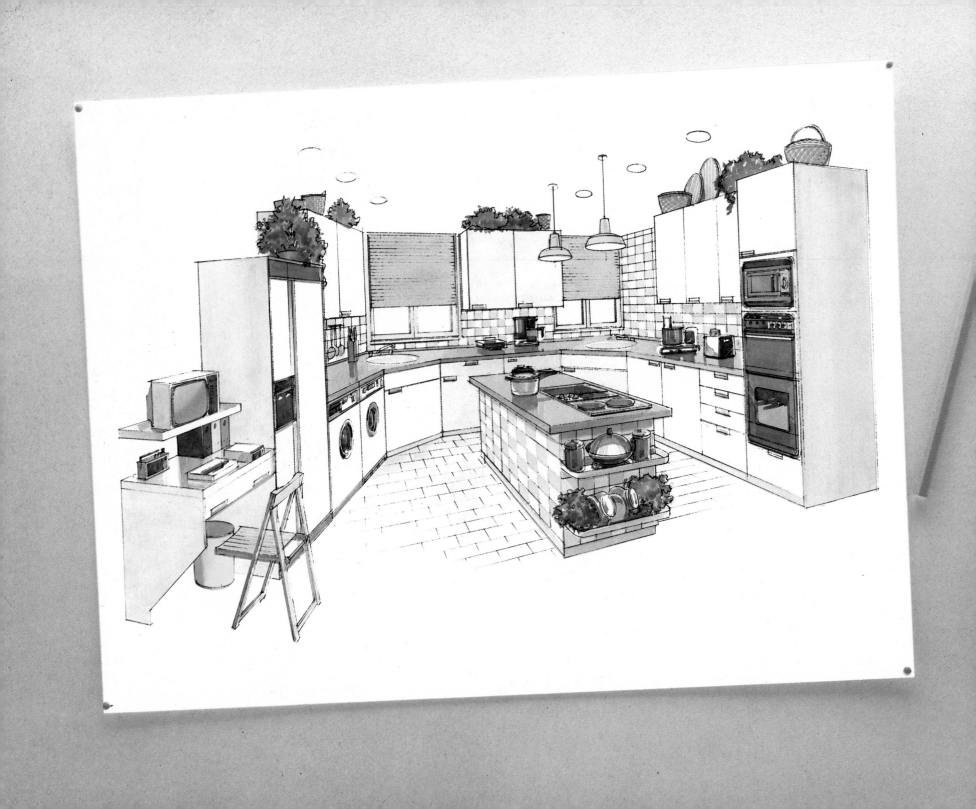

Fitting in the equipment

This is a good-sized working kitchen which has to accommodate a wealth of laundry as well as cooking equipment and make room for all the extra appliances essential to modern living. The most sensible way to arrange them all within the given space is to use the U-shaped layout, perfectly possible here because the room has the required width to make it work. One end of the room has windows at each corner and these make it easy to divide the space fairly naturally into two reasonably separate areas. Corner sinks make it possible to provide one area for clothes washing and another for dishes and vegetable preparation. The left-hand side of the kitchen takes the washing and drying machines, fridge, deep freeze and a desk unit with a shelf above it for a small home computer. This is used for keeping accounts, recipes and vital household information. The right-hand run includes dishwasher, drawer and cupboard storage and double oven and microwave. A centre island unit incorporates a cook top with both grill and electric hob and extra work surface. Wall units on both sides provide plenty of general storage. The whole room is given a fresh light look with yellow and white ceramic tiles, white lozenge-shaped floor tiles, white units and wooden Venetian blinds.

CHOOSING EQUIPMENT

Top: Washing machine and tumble dryer are set below oven and refrigerator and are flanked by a ceramic hob in this display of appliances.

Above, left and right: The same pair of sinks, set into a tiled worktop, has

been photographed twice to show its versatility. The rounded sink on the left is fitted with a drainer in one and with a wooden chopping block top, complete with cut-out for rinsing, in the other which has the effect of increasing the work space.

Sinks

If you have the space (and the money) it is useful to have two and even three sinks: one for soaking dishes, one for preparing vegetables and one smaller one for a waste or garbage disposer. A waste disposer can, of course, be fitted into a single main sink, but do make sure your building or house has the sort of drainage system that will not be fouled up by liquid refuse in bulk. Some sinks come complete with extra wood cutting board surface to fit across the top when necessary and so provide extra work space; others have small spray attachments at the side to aid cleaning. If you are short of space do not forget the inch-saving corner varieties.

The most common choice for taps is a single swing spout with either one or two handles. Materials are generally stainless steel, porcelain-covered cast iron, or the new plastic substance which looks like marble and makes a neat and effective all-in-one counter and sink.

Waste disposers and rubbish (trash) compactors

The newest waste disposers can handle up to 1 litre (2 pints) of waste food at a time very much more quickly than the old bone-chilling (and bone-crunching) models. Rubbish or trash compactors can squash up cardboard boxes, cartons, tins, cans and bottles to a quarter of

their original size. They may be worth considering if you live in a high-rise flat, or have infrequent refuse collection, but they do take up space. They can be located almost anywhere in the kitchen and attached to the same sort of outlet as an electric stove.

Cooker hoods

Although some stoves have built-in self-venting outlets, there is an enormous market for hoods of every description and style with built-in fans for ventilation and to remove cooking smells. Most units need to be on an outside wall or ducted to vent outdoors but others can be bought which are ventless, recirculating the air through activated charcoal filters which should be changed regularly.

All of them have incorporated light bulbs to give extra light over the work top.

Washing machines and dryers

If there is any possibility of placing washing machines and dryers away from the kitchen you should consider it. Detergents and dirty clothes don't mix very well with food preparation and in any case the most sensible place to position both appliances is somewhere near the bedroom/bath area. Standard machines measure 600 mm ($23\frac{5}{8}$ in) deep by 595 mm ($23\frac{3}{8}$ in) wide, to fit between units and can be stacked one above the other. But, unless you have a separate utility room, that does not leave much space nearby for storing laundry supplies and accessories or setting down the just-cleaned laundry. If there is room for a 1300 mm (5 ft) cupboard or closet just outside the kitchen, bedroom or bathroom, say in a corridor, or lobby, this would be a better solution. It would give room for a washer and dryer to stand side by side under a convenient counter top. Better still, if there is room, would be a 2500 mm (8 ft) wide louvre-fronted closet which would give you space for washing machine, dryer, clothes hamper and general purpose cabinet with a metre wide (3 ft) double door wall cabinet above and a clothes rod to hang out just dried permanent press clothing. The units could have a counter top and there would need to be efficient lighting.

If you really cannot find the space anywhere else in the home you will have to try to squeeze space in the kitchen (or go to a launderette). It would be best to install the appliances side by side in order to keep worktop continuity, and do not forget that most dryers need to be vented to an outside wall.

Appliances and units alike in this modern kitchen/dining room are all fronted by an interesting closed louvre finish which resembles an updated version of the old roll-topped desks.

CHOOSING EQUIPMENT

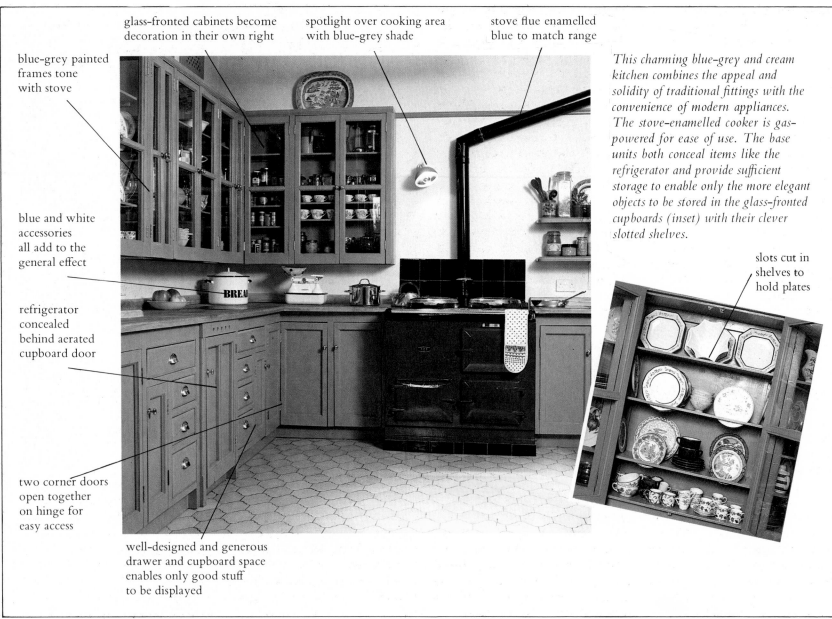

glass-fronted cabinets become decoration in their own right

spotlight over cooking area with blue-grey shade

stove flue enamelled blue to match range

blue-grey painted frames tone with stove

blue and white accessories all add to the general effect

refrigerator concealed behind aerated cupboard door

two corner doors open together on hinge for easy access

well-designed and generous drawer and cupboard space enables only good stuff to be displayed

This charming blue-grey and cream kitchen combines the appeal and solidity of traditional fittings with the convenience of modern appliances. The stove-enamelled cooker is gas-powered for ease of use. The base units both conceal items like the refrigerator and provide sufficient storage to enable only the more elegant objects to be stored in the glass-fronted cupboards (inset) with their clever slotted shelves.

slots cut in shelves to hold plates

Kitchen units and cabinets

If you are handy yourself, can employ a good carpenter, or go to a custom cabinet maker, you can make or obtain literally any size or type of unit to fit the most awkward spaces. Another ploy is to buy unfinished or whitewood cabinets and fit them into your space, finishing them off yourself with paint or stain.

If you are going for a fully fitted kitchen, you will find the units are made up of three elements: the carcass (basic cupboard and shelves), the doors and drawer fronts, and the work surface which runs along the top. Usually, all can be bought separately. In some ranges, you can buy decor panels to fit the front of specially designed built-in appliances, making them match the cupboards.

Ready made cabinets come in a huge choice of finishes, colours, and measurements. Heights for wall cabinets range from 300 mm (12 in) –good for the space over a refrigerator– to 1000 mm (39 in). The depth from wall to face is a standard 300 mm (12 in) and widths run from 230 mm (9 in) to 600 mm (24 in) for single door cabinets to 1000 mm (39 in) to 1200 mm (48 in) for double door models. Corner cabinets with a single door and either fixed or revolving shelves can be mounted diagonally across a corner to use every inch of available space.

Base units generally stand 900 mm (36 in) from the floor if you count the worktop as well and widths match the wall hung cabinets, though the depth is generally twice as much. You can buy them with doors, drawers, or both, and with different depths for different drawers. Again, there are many refinements to choose from: glide-out vegetable storage equipment, wine racks, slide-out chopping blocks, bottle drawers, silver storage drawers, pot lid holders, tray storage, sliding trays for linens and cutlery racks. Alternatively, you can buy standard but empty units and fill them with your own choice of such 'organizers' from other sources.

Pantry or food storage cabinets are specially made to accommodate cans and dry goods (breakfast cereals, jams, flour and other packaged goods). Often they are heavily hinged with one can deep shelving from top to bottom of the doors for maximum use of space. You can buy them in wall, floor or full length sizes.

Utility or broom cupboards are generally 300 mm (12 in) or 600 mm (24 in) deep, 1950 mm (7 ft) tall and from 500 mm (22 in) to 600 mm (24 in) wide. They consist of one tall space with an upper shelf for brooms, vacuum cleaners, mops and cleaning supplies. Similarly-shaped cabinets can be bought as housing units for particular models of wall oven and for refrigerators.

All these four pictures show the sort of variations and refinements that you can expect to find in the various ranges of units currently on the market. Top left: Swing out stove-enamelled (for easy cleaning) trays for corner units. Top right:

Open-shelved corner unit – ideal for better-looking possessions. Bottom left: Pull-out trash container drawer which neatly holds rubbish bin. Bottom right: Deep drawers have aerated wire racks for saucepans and their lids.

167

The central fact to acknowledge about any sort of storage is that there is rarely enough of it, and this is certainly true in the kitchen.

Be ruthless

The kitchen is the one room where you should literally use every inch, nook, cranny, piece of ceiling, window, door or side of cabinet; in fact the key to successful and efficient kitchen storage is to use every possible surface, and to assemble equipment and accessories by the places where they are the most needed. Start your kitchen reorganization with a drastic sort-out and throw-out. Don't weaken. If you do not use an object once a day, or at least once a week, it does not deserve prime storage space (that is within easy reach and somewhere between knee and eye level). Put it instead at the back of a base cabinet or high up on a wall cabinet, or in the space, if there is one, between wall cabinets and ceiling which you can always turn into a second tier of cabinets by adding fronts to match your other units. Things which are used once or twice a year—turkey roasting pans, huge party casseroles, picnic baskets, should be rigorously stashed right away, if possible out of the kitchen

altogether—under the stairs, in an attic, in the basement or garage in a house; in some more remote cupboard in a flat or apartment. And what about all those gadgets lying loose in drawers? Would they be tidier and more accessible hung on pegboards?

If you have not used something for literally years the chances are that it won't come in useful for a rainy day (the hoarder's excuse) and that you probably won't *ever* use it. So give it away, send it to a jumble sale, sell it if you can, or just throw it away. Whatever you do, be tough . . . Don't keep it. If you do, it will almost certainly be the beginning of the end and you will never get properly organized. Perhaps one should keep a picture of hideous confusion pinned to the kitchen door in the same way as slimmers keep a fat photo taped to the fridge as a deterrent to snacking.

Lovely storage for the tidy-minded (left), it could become a mess for anyone else. Still, the open shelves make life easy for the organized cook and the pull-out wire baskets are a good idea for fruit and vegetables. If you are not so tidy the kitchen on the right is a better bet.

ORGANIZED STORAGE

Far left: A clever pull-out unit the full height of the run of cabinets makes day-to-day necessities clearly visible and easily accessible.

Above: Two wood plate drainers flank the window here to provide excellent storage. A shelf across the window connects the racks and gives further storage space. A wooden rod suspended from the ceiling holds yet more equipment.

Left: Even the space between these handsome units has been used for storage.

Right: The staggered top cupboards of these good-looking units allow more wall space for hanging equipment that is decorative and functional.

Be logical

This simply means that instead of bending and scuffling around for saucepans stacked up in a dark base unit, try hanging them from hooks near the sink (where you are going to fill them with water) or near the stove. Keep herbs and spices on small racks just above or by the cook top. Store pulses, rice, pasta, sugar, flour and condiments by the worktop or preparation area. Stash old plastic or paper shopping bags near the rubbish or garbage bin and then you can re-cycle them as bin liners. Everyday plates can be stored upright in a wooden plate rack above the dishwasher or by the sink. This is much easier than keeping them in piles in a cupboard or closet. Similarly, mugs and cups used regularly can be kept on hooks near the stove top, and glasses can be kept in a cabinet near the washing machine. Store wooden spoons, whisks, colanders, sieves in containers or from hooks by the worktop or cooker top, wherever you need them most, and keep oil, vinegars, condiments, herbs and garlic near salad bowls.

Be ingenious

Once you have thoroughly reorganized your existing storage you can look around for new surfaces to conquer. Bunches of herbs and pot and saucepan racks can be hung from the ceiling. You can fix tiny narrow shelves or racks to the inside of cabinet doors; attach spice racks, hooks, more shelves (to take cook books?) to the sides of cabinets; add further shelves just above worktops on the splashback areas, and add shallow shelves 300–450 mm (12–18 in) above cook tops and sinks with hooks attached to the edges for various bits of equipment such as measuring jugs and ladles.

As usual in most rooms, corners are often a wasted area. You might be able to build a corner unit across the angle of two worktops for cook books, or more spices and condiments, with more storage space for jars on top. If there is not room for this you might utilize the space by making slots in the counter top to take your cooking knives, or you could suspend them from a magnetic bar just above out of reach of children. Think too, about using the underside of your cabinets for kitchen paper holders, more suspended spice racks, or for hooks to hang just about anything.

Spare bits of wall which are too small for conventional cabinets can be used for mounting peg boards for small implements and utensils; or pin-board for recipes, bills, receipts, reminders to the family and to yourself. Make better use of your base cabinets by fixing slide-out towel racks to the doors, and by installing swivel storage shelves to do away with all that groping around for things at the back. Shallow alcoves can be used for yet more narrow shelves just the depth of one can or bottle or for mounting a magnetic knife-rack; awkward spaces, say between stove and storage cabinets, can be used for trays.

171

Eating in the kitchen

This kitchen-dining room is first and foremost a good working kitchen which happens to have space to fit in table and chairs. Neatly checked and sprigged wallpaper is teamed with cream tiles which have thin blue grouting between them. This has the effect of giving continuity of colour and pattern to the background. The cream paintwork and cream Holland roller blinds at the window keep to the theme. The floor is deeper and warmer with ochre bricks. The wood-framed kitchen units have dark blue laminate panels and the same blue is repeated in accessories like the kettle. The cooker top set in the island unit, which makes a useful serving area for the dining table, is surrounded with more cream tiles and the blue and cream scheme is carried right through to the hanging light over the dining table. Track lighting in the centre of the ceiling provides good overall illumination and strip lights are recessed under the top units by the window. For all its neat simplicity it's a cheerful kitchen. The rounded curves of the wood table and chairs add a homely relaxed note to all the clean straight lines of the room.

ORGANIZED STORAGE

Right: The pull-out work table in the middle of this cheerful kitchen divides cooking and workroom space as well as providing an excellent sewing/writing surface with telephone conveniently to hand. Such bonus workspace means that one can take advantage of lulls in the middle of cooking and preparation to get on with other jobs—or catch up with bills, lists and letters and still keep an eye on the meal. After all, the table could just as well hold a typewriter, or drawing materials or any other working equipment.

Far right: A counter top has been extended here to take a typewriter, filing tray and a good worklight with again a telephone at arm's length. Of course, the same space can equally well be used as a serving area for the table.

A place for paperwork

It is useful to have some sort of desk where you can write lists, pay bills, file receipts, copy recipes, and take messages. Again there might be some odd space between units that you could span to make a desk top, or you might add a swing-up flap at the end of a worktop which can be raised and lowered as required. Another alternative is to widen or deepen a counter top so that you can sit at it with a stool; or you can convert a drawer to a small work counter/worktop/cutting board by fitting a block of wood on top which you can draw out and sit at..

Think about the benefits of a kitchen telephone installed on or near the improvised desk top within, if possible, easy reach of the stove. It is infuriating to have to run and answer the telephone in the middle of some intricate sauce or dish. To have a phone within arm's length of the cook top makes a world of difference to your general convenience so see that any phone has a long extension cord.

Such comparatively slight and inexpensive changes can make an enormous improvement to the way your kitchen works, by reducing the amount of to-ing and fro-ing and getting rid of many possible sources of irritation, inconvenience and interruption. After all, the less hassle enjoy being the more you'll there.

Making a pin-board

One of the simplest ways to make a pin-board is to buy a cork bath mat and mount it on the wall. For a more substantial board, fix unsealed cork tiles to the wall, and surround them with beading or picture framing (architraving to

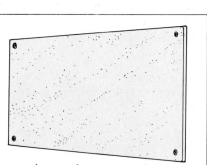

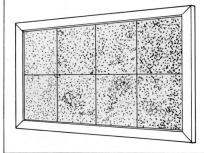

match your door surrounds is a neat solution), mitring the corners for a neat finish.

For a fabric-covered board, use coloured felt to cover a piece of softboard, wrapping excess fabric over the edges and glueing it to the back. Mount the board on the wall, using round-headed screws.

Only when you have made your plans, decided on your work sequence, bought your appliances and thought about the style of room you would like to create, can you focus on the treatment of the rest: the framework of walls, floor, window and ceiling as well as the sort of tiles, splashback and worktop you would like. This, of course, is the actual decoration of the room, the process which comes first in most areas, but certainly last in the kitchen planning sequence. Last, but *never* least: colours, surfaces and embellishments have their own particular and important role to play in kitchen comfort.

Walls

By the time you have put up an appropriate amount of cabinets and storage there is not usually much wall left to cover. It is often possible to tile a large proportion of the wall for guaranteed ease of maintenance. Paint, however, should always be washable – do not use emulsion because you will not be able to wash grease and smoke off easily, but rather use gloss or eggshell finishes.

White or earth colours – tobaccos, umbers, sand, sludgy green, pine green – are particularly appropriate with food, while blue and white, green and white, red or pink and white and a sunny chrome yellow, always look good and fresh. Try painting walls white and colouring woodwork, or vice versa. It depends very much on the units you choose. Obviously, if they are a colour as opposed to white or wood, you should choose a background that blends with them.

If you decide on a wallpaper, try to use a paper-backed vinyl, a vinyl impregnated fabric paper, or a PVC wallcovering. Or else paint the surface of ordinary paper with a coat or two of eggshell or gloss polyurethane for a practical protective finish.

Stripped or new brick makes a good kitchen background, so does tongue-and-groove wood panelling or panelling of wide wooden planks. Bricks should be sealed with a masonry stabiliser, while wood should be waxed, varnished or painted.

The units are in place, the floor is stripped, sanded and polished and there is still plenty of scope and general living space to play with in this large loft, left. Very positive decorating decisions in this kitchen, right; co-ordinating red and white fabric and paper everywhere.

SUITABLE SURFACES

shelf unit suspended
from ceiling provides
additional storage

glossy red diagonal
tongue-and-groove
boarding adds space

charcoal-filter
extractor hood

light
positioned
over work
area

double sink
unit with
drainer rack
fitting

*The warm and cheerful
look of this small kitchen
has been achieved with a
fairly low outlay.
Tongue-and-groove
boarding set on the
diagonal has been given a
coating of brilliant red
paint. The suspended shelf
over the worktop holds
plants and spices and also
supports a charcoal
extractor hood.*

mosaic-
tiled work
surface

curtains conceal
food and utensils

If you have a kitchen/dining room and want to make it look particularly warm and comfortable you could make a visual division between working and eating areas by stapling the dining walls with a cheap cotton treated with a protective spray. Or you could give your room an interesting old country look by adding a 'wainscot' of boarding to a free wall, or at least some moulding at dado level.

Ceilings

Unless you have a particular pretty beamed or coved ceiling it is often a good idea to lower the ceiling area in a kitchen. This enables you to put in recessed lighting, or to add an acoustic or tongue-and-groove wood finish. Acoustic tiles are used for ceilings rather than walls and are made to absorb sound. They have to be suspended from battens and are most often made from pre-finished, slotted insulation board, polystyrene or fibreglass. Tongue-and-groove pine boarding looks good; it should be sealed with polyurethane to protect the wood and needs hardly any maintenance—just wiping over occasionally. In America, the virtues of the old pressed metal ceilings have been rediscovered and redeployed. But if you do not want to add a ceiling covering, simply paint the surface with white, or very pale emulsion to reflect as much light as possible.

Left: The glass roof to the ceiling of this kitchen lets light flood in but keeps heat out. It has been fitted with a stretched, diagonally-striped green and white roller blind which gives good protection and also looks cool and decorative. The all-cream units and walls blend with the tiled floor and provide an excellent background colour for the intense green of the plants which underline the greenhouse feel, as do the vertical louvered blinds.

Above: Mini-print hexagonal tiles and floor tiles that match in shape if not colour, are nicely offset by the strawberry print curtains in this wood-trimmed, friendly little kitchen.

SUITABLE SURFACES

Floors

Kitchen floors need to be tough enough to withstand all sorts of spills, grease and damp, comfortable enough to stand on for long periods, and handsome to look at. The choice of covering in fact, very much depends on the sort of style you have set yourself. If you want a rustic kitchen, then quarry, brick or Mexican or French terracotta tiles look very splendid. Slate is marvellous to look at but at a marvellous price, and there is an enormous choice in ceramic tiles which can be mixed in among the terracottas for an ethnic Mexican or Provencale, Italian, Spanish or Portuguese look. Terracotta tiles, brick, flagstone, slate, terrazzo and non-slip ceramic are all durable, impressive, good to look at and easy to clean. They generally come in a range of beautiful colours and pleasing shapes. Most are heavy and therefore only suitable for laying at ground-floor level or where floors are exceptionally strong. All

Left: A bright cheerful kitchen where vivid colours are carefully balanced. Red/white/yellow checked vinyl flooring co-ordinates the red and white checked tiles and red stripes with the yellow in the accessories.

Right: Brick-shaped terracotta tiles have a country look to them and nicely bridge the gap between rusticity and modernity in this pleasant kitchen.

Sensible surfaces

Kitchen, floor, walls, counter tops, table, units and windows all need covering in as practical and harmonious a way as possible. Choosing the appropriate materials for all these various surfaces requires careful budgeting as well as serious thought since they have to look good, wear well and be just right for their particular purpose. In this predominantly blue and white room the major investment was in the synthetic marble counter top and sink. French blue and white ceramic tiles look fresh and pretty and their cost is reasonable considering how durable and maintenance free they are. The blue and white floor tiles are vinyl—easy on the feet and easy to keep clean. Here they have been cut into interesting patterns. The blue and white theme is taken up again at the window where the cotton blinds are white with a vertical blue stripe and their pelmets are dark blue with horizontal white stripe, all given protective treatment. The same dark blue fabric is used for the seat cushions, tied with blue tape. Table, chairs and louvre door units are all in the same handsome mellow pine.

SUITABLE SURFACES

of these treatments are as hard on the feet as they are easy on the eye – but sometimes, as I have said, good appearances win over practical considerations. If both price and hardness bother you, there are acceptable alternatives in vinyl, and cork coated with vinyl which can look very good too. Both vinyl – in sheet or tile form – and vinyl-coated cork are easy to maintain.

Hi-Tech and more sleekly designed kitchens look good with white tiled floors whether ceramic

or vinyl, but again you could use cork and vinyl, or composition tiles or even linoleum which has taken on a new lease of life now that people have realised how well it can look inserted with other colours.

Wood treated with polyurethane to withstand spills and grease can look very handsome, especially in a dining kitchen, and old floors can be spruced up with paint, various painted finishes and stencilling, protected with extra coats of varnish.

When choosing flooring for a

kitchen/diner, make sure the surface is suitable for both functions, or delineate one area from another by using different types of flooring. For example, if you have quarry tiles in the kitchen, they may be rather cold on the feet for dinner guests lingering over coffee, as well as being noisy when chairs scrape across them. You may find that people are encouraged to use the room as more of a gathering place if the floor of the dining area is covered with colourful rugs, and even with vinyl flooring

Above left: Polyurethaned wood boards are a handsome contrast to this mainly white kitchen with its distinctive blue and white tiled border. Note the repetition of the boarding on the ceiling – here painted white – and the linear effect of the blinds.

Above right: Graduated hexagonal tiles look quietly handsome against white units and butcher-block tops. For the accident prone, vinyl tiles simulated to look like earthenware tiles might be better.

Emphatic flooring. Top left:
Brilliant blocks of primary colours
set into black make imaginative use
of composition tiles. The bold
colours are picked up again in the
flowers and also repeated in the
accessories. Above: Gleaming
ceramic tiles cover floor, counter
tops and walls in a kitchen
planned to last. Far left: Neat
herringbone parquet makes a
warm-looking expanse in an
otherwise fairly austere kitchen.
Left: Both ceiling and floor
have been painted a stunning
red in this compact kitchen.

SUITABLE SURFACES

you can create a change of atmosphere around the table by changing the colour of the floor or simply by adding a rug.

Windows

There is no point at all in elaborate window coverings in the kitchen. They only get dirty, greasy and in the way. It is far better to use café curtains, short, tied-back curtains, or blinds. Fabric should be easily washed or cleaned cotton, or vinylised cotton (for roller blinds). Otherwise use Venetian blinds in plastic or wood which can be easily wiped, or wooden shutters, or no covering at all. Shelves look good and are practical across a window and can be made of glass, or wood, or metal grid for a Hi-Tech look. Alternatively, just hang plants from hooks above the window, or stand small pots of plants along the windowsill, making sure that the ones you select are going to be happy with the kind of light, temperature and humidity you are providing. Used this way, with massed greenery, or collections of glass on glass shelves, the kitchen window becomes a strong focal point.

If your kitchen has a whole wall of window, this needn't be a problem. Either treat it as a feature in its own right, with a striking blind or shutters; give it as much impact as possible and let the view and the light pour in. Or, if you think it steals

too much potential storage space you could consider sacrificing some of it. If you're desparate for storage space it's often possible to build units right around a window so that the window acquires a recessed effect and becomes an essential part of the arrangement. In this case, the simpler the window treatment the better; plain blinds, café curtains or just left bare.

Worktops

Worktops have to be as durable as floors, able to withstand chopping, hot utensils and spills, and still be good to look at. The plastic laminated top is very popular but you must be careful not to chop directly on to it (use a chopping board) or to put down hot pots and saucepans. Once ruined it is extremely difficult to put right.

Ceramic tiles—which can be continued up the space between counter top and unit to make a handsome splashback—come in a huge range of colours and designs and can look spectacular, gentle or fresh depending on the effect you want. However, the grouting can easily get discoloured and dirty-looking, so it might be better to start off with a dark grouting from the beginning. Also, you should be wary of putting down pots and pans straight from the stove; this might cause the ceramic to crack.

Butcher-block and wood counter

186

Left: This terracotta-tile effect vinyl floor is almost indistinguishable from the real thing and makes a smart contrast to the white tiled units and brilliant yellows and greens of the rest of the kitchen/dining room.

Above: The red sink fits neatly into the white-tiled counter top and blends with the dotted wallpaper.

Right: This continuous work surface with its moulded integral sinks and generous depth, not only looks good with its marble appearance but could hardly be more practical. It is hardwearing and relatively stain-resistant. Damage, like scratches, can be removed with reasonable ease.

SUITABLE SURFACES

tops are sturdy and look good but they are not very practical near the sink surrounds or anywhere where there is water because they can warp and the grain can rise up. If you are using wood as a continuous work surface, introduce some variety; let in a square of marble or ceramic tile for making pastry; surround your sink with stainless steel, tile or plastic laminate rather than wood, which tends to lift up and warp.

There is a new plastic substance that feels like marble but is immensely more practical. This material is ideal for countertops and pastry surfaces since it is very durable, resistant to most stains, and does not burn or warp. It comes in white, cream and a slightly veined beige. It may be cut and glued to give a virtually seamless surface.

For more ideas on renewing or replacing worktops, see page 138.

Splashbacks
These can be made of plastic laminate, synthetic marble or, the most popular, ceramic tile. They can be plain, patterned or flowered, bevelled, or a mixture. Tiles can be laid on the diagonal or in a basket weave design to produce handsome effects.

A calm, pretty pink and white kitchen. The laminate top to match the units beneath, contrasts happily with the pink tiles, painted ceiling and ceiling-mounted spots.

Safety rules

Statistics reveal the horrifying truth that there are more accidents in the home than on the road and that most of these take place in the kitchen and to children. So safety should be a priority, whether starting from scratch, or just re-vamping.

To avoid all possible causes of accidents take the following precautions:

Always unplug small appliances when they are not in use, and don't let appliance cords dangle over the edge of counters where they can be reached by children. Keep flexes as short as is convenient to avoid a spaghetti of cables.

Choose non-slip flooring and always mop up spills immediately.

Treat food processor blades with the greatest respect. Handle them gingerly; wash them carefully; don't ever leave them soaking, submerged in water in case someone else unsuspectingly puts their hand in. They can be lethal. Equally, if they are in the dishwasher, pick them out very carefully.

Whenever possible, cook on the back burners of cook tops or stoves, especially when children are around. Make sure pot handles are turned towards the back of the stove and that the oven door is firmly closed.

If you have small children around cover electric outlets with safety caps or tape.

Never pull any appliance—kettle, mixer—out of its socket without switching off first.

Never add dishwasher detergent (which is toxic) until the last moment, then close door immediately. Make sure that dishwasher doors are always latched tight. Left down they are a temptation to children who might climb onto them and tip the whole appliance.

Place all poisonous, potentially poisonous and toxic household cleaners, detergents and scourers on the highest possible shelf. Never keep any of these in innocent looking old lemonade bottles particularly if the original labels are still on.

Keep all trash and garbage out of children's reach and place any old container which held a toxic substance into the outside dustbin or garbage can as soon as it is finished.

Don't ever leave your children alone in the kitchen; they have even been known to get trapped inside fridges and freezers.

Never leave an iron on if you leave the room, and never let young children near an ironing board while you are ironing.

When you are serving up hot dishes make sure that toddlers and young children are well out of the way.

Keep sharp knives well out of the reach of children—either on a magnetic panel set back and above the worktop; in slots made at the back of the worktop, or in a knife block set well back too.

Try not to use long tablecloths, or at least tablecloths within the reach of a yank from small hands.

If you have high shelves keep a proper, solid stepladder within easy reach and do not climb on chairs or worktops.

Always keep a first aid and burn treatment kit in the kitchen, near the stove, ready for emergencies.

If you possibly can, keep a small fire extinguisher to hand near the stove and make sure that everyone knows how to use it. It's too late to absorb the instructions when the kitchen is in flames. Ensure it is suitable for fat fires and electric fires. A fire blanket, hung to one side of the cooker, may also be useful, as long as you understand how to use it.

Do not keep any fabrics near the stove or cook top: if the window is near the stove top do not use curtains. Nor should you keep drying up cloths or oven gloves in the sort of position where they could drop or drag on a burner.

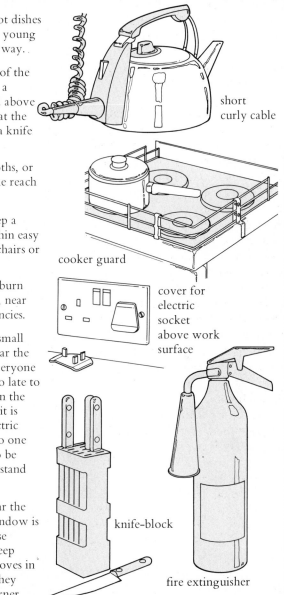

short curly cable

cooker guard

cover for electric socket above work surface

knife-block

fire extinguisher

Cooking and eating go together, so naturally the next step is to decide where and in what sort of style you are going to serve and eat meals. It really hardly matters if this happens in a room of its own, in the kitchen, the living room, or even the hall. Dining rooms today, are wherever the food is served.

If you do have a separate dining room, you're lucky. It need contain no more than a sideboard, table and chairs and can be decorated in its own individual way. If you do a great deal of formal or business entertaining then this sort of dining room is essential. But these days, with space at a premium, a room kept solely for dining is rare; the chances are that it has to double as a work room, say for hobbies like model making, or as a quiet place where the family can get on with homework, studying or other paperwork. And far more likely is the dining room which is no more than a corner of another room. This, of course, makes it simple to furnish; all you really need are a table and chairs which fit in well with the rest of the room. A kitchen-dining room is ideal for a family; its cosy, convenient and economical since it saves heating another room. In tiny flats and bed-sitters it's more often the living room that has to make space for dining, in which case it's a good idea to separate the two functions with either a physical division–like an arch, trellis or shelving–or with visual treatment like different lighting or flooring, or perhaps a change of colour or mood.

But whatever your dining area consists of, organizing it, giving it character and interest can be challenging and stimulating. In fact, the dining room should be a particularly interesting room to decorate, because, like the bathroom, it is generally used for comparatively short periods at a time, and then mostly at night. As long as its main purpose is borne in mind–that of providing a relaxed, comfortable and enjoyable area for eating which is also a good background for the food that is served–it can,

The clean-lined dining area in this white-tiled kitchen left, is neatly separated from the work part by handsome structural columns. The clever updated chandelier effect is achieved by hooking up five green and white lights to one outlet. The summery dining area, right, is divided from the work area by kitchen units.

191

theoretically, be as inventive, curious, and as experimental as you like.

Before you embark on the decoration, however, you need to have the practical considerations firmly in mind. Decide exactly what functions the room has to fulfil. Ask yourself these questions:

● How many people will eat in the dining room regularly?

● What is the maximum number of diners which will have to be accommodated at a sit-down meal?

● How much storage space is necessary for china and cutlery; for dining accessories; for other items not related to eating – books, papers, sewing equipment and so on?

● Is the room the only dining space or are family meals usually taken elsewhere?

● Will it be used mainly at night, or does it need to look fresh for breakfast, serviceable for lunch and intimate for dinner parties?

● Are your needs likely to change over the next few years – will you have children to cope with; are you likely to entertain more often than you do at present?

Would a very bold, outrageous, or dramatic look be too overwhelming in a dining room which all the family are going to want to use at different times? I remember an all-black room I saw years ago which has always stuck in my mind: black velvet walls, black carpet, ebony table and chairs, black lacquer side table. The only relief was in the tablecloth, napkins, china and flowers which varied from spanking white, to black and white, to brilliant yellow or green. The lighting was subtle: concealed behind pelmets, inset into the ceiling, bounced up from uplights on the floor, flickering from candles. And the room always looked beautiful, except on a gloomy winter's day, when it was frightful. Such rooms are definitely not for breakfast.

Another room I remember for its verve was all shiny dark green lacquered walls, gilded carpet and *trompe l'oeil* painted walls which looked like real draperies: a theatrical, stunning experience. But the fact that so few rooms stand out in my memory is not so surprising. On the whole, dining rooms fall into pretty familiar categories, furnished with pretty familiar types of furniture, colours and accessories, And perhaps that is as it should be. The serious diner likes to feel comfortable, at ease, to have a sense of well-being, but does not want his attention to be distracted.

Having worked out how your room will be used, you should consider what sort of finishes are going to be suitable. With food

Left: Built–in bench seating round a corner–placed table provides a lot of seating in small space. The continuation of the white and blue colour scheme also ensures that the dining area is in tune with the kitchen.

Above: This dining room is fitted into a convenient alcove and delineated by the red light, chairs and checked table-cloth as well as by its island of matting.

Right: The kitchen area is one convenient step down from the dining room with its nice use of pine, well-stocked bookshelves and gleaming wood floor. The kitchen area is tiled to continue the rustic effect.

WHERE TO EAT

Getting seated

Dining tables come in a vast range of shapes and sizes—square, round, rectangular or oval: but there are some basic rules to follow when it comes to choosing a table for a room of a particular size.

Each place setting (with an armless chair) takes about 66 cm (2 ft 3 in) with 5 cm (2 in) added to the width for chairs with arms. A long table should be at least 75 cm (2 ft 6 in) wide if both sides are to be used. Each person will need at least 75 cm (2 ft 6 in) to give space for getting in and out. And, of course, there must be an ample passageway around the table: 100 cm from table to wall is really the minimum allowance.

When buying a table and chairs, if possible spend some time sitting in the chairs *at* the table. Make sure they are a good height for the table, that any chairs with arms will fit under the table, and that seats stay supportive through long sitting sessions. If cushions are used on chairs, remember this may change their height. Further equivalents of the measurements given opposite are:
25 cm (10 in); 32 cm (13 in)
35 cm (14 in); 50 cm (20 in)
73 cm (29 in); 90 cm (35 in)
100 cm (39 in); 110 cm (43 in)
115 cm (45 in); 130 cm (51 in)
150 cm (59 in); 175 cm (69 in)
210 cm (83 in); 250 cm (98 in)

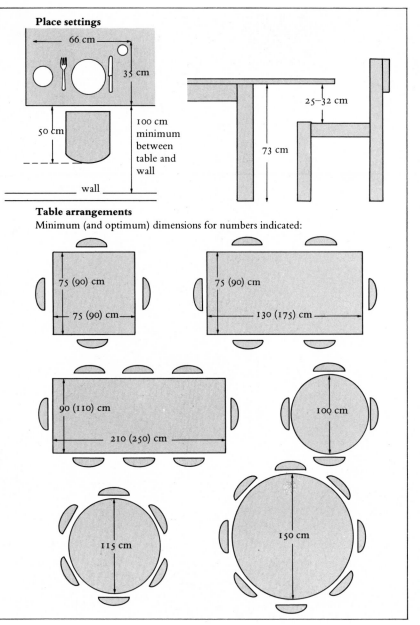

Place settings

66 cm · 35 cm · 50 cm · 100 cm minimum between table and wall · wall · 25–32 cm · 73 cm

Table arrangements

Minimum (and optimum) dimensions for numbers indicated:

75 (90) cm · 75 (90) cm · 75 (90) cm · 130 (175) cm · 90 (110) cm · 210 (250) cm · 100 cm · 115 cm · 150 cm

around, surfaces should be as practical as possible: choose flooring which will not show crumbs and can be mopped up easily; sideboards should be provided with protective covers if they are not heatproof; traditional polished tables might look good, but with children around, you may be better off going for a heatproof, scrubbable surface which can be wiped over quickly; upholstery should be washable; wallpaper need not be as tough as the vinyl-coated varieties.

In short what you should aim to create in a dining room is a special atmosphere within a very practical framework, so when you've provided for the basics you can add to the mood with window treatments, interesting lighting and decorative tricks to make the room as comfortable, as functional and as good looking as you can.

Eating in the dining end of this extremely pretty dining-kitchen is like eating in a conservatory. Floor to ceiling glass doors and window open directly onto an equally charming paved garden. It all looks beautifully casual until you notice the careful transition from dining area tiles to garden paving with the fresh grey and white blinds as a demarcation point. Wine racks are tucked neatly and accessibly under the marble serving top with its vaguely rural wood supports.

When you know where your dining area is going to be and what size table and chairs will fit best into the space, you can start thinking about how you plan to treat the other important elements in the room—the walls, floor and windows.

Walls, floors and windows

There are any number of suitable treatments for walls in a dining room: there is not going to be much wear and tear, and no need for waterproof surfaces, as in kitchens or bathrooms so you can afford to have some fun. Paint them deep matt, eggshell or shiny gloss and hang them with pictures or a collection of some sort. Use one of the attractive paint techniques which are re-gaining popularity: spongeing, rag rolling or dragging. Stencil a border round the ceiling, around the door and windows, and above the skirting boards. Wallpaper them or cover them with fabric: felt, hessian, sacking, lining fabric or printed cotton. Panel them with wood, line them with cork, strip the plaster back to the brick; the choice is endless. Tongue-and-groove panelling will make a complete transformation: stain it, varnish it or paint it. Or finish with one of the *trompe*

l'oeil paint techniques like murals or marbling. If you do a lot of entertaining and want it to look spectacular at night then mirror tiles will gleam and sparkle and reflect candlelight beautifully.

If floorboards are in reasonable condition, they could be stripped, sanded and polished. Or they could be painted, or stencilled or both. I, personally, do not think it a very good idea to have carpet in the dining room where it only picks up smells and gets dirtier more quickly than in most places, since people do, without fail, drop things. But there is nothing against rugs of any description. Bricks, old tiles, new tiles, quarry tiles, Mexican, French or Spanish tiles, ceramic tiles, slate and even marble facing all look spectacular if you are prepared to put up with the clattering noise from chairs pulled up to the table and pushed back again. Vinyl is

A clever feature of this living/dining/guest room, left, is that half the table top can be removed and pushed against a wall when not in use. In another kitchen-diner, right, old linoleum has been painted a milky cream to go with walls, ceiling and units.

Above: Cork tiles are given a smart black border to echo the lines of the octagonal table as well as the colour of the marble counter top. The arched windows are too pretty to be covered.

Top right: Bleached boards are in keeping with the various shades of pine in a spacious country room.

Right: Grey lattice paper, silver grey paint and lavish baskets of orchids, set against botanical drawings, make this room look especially cool, airy and expensive. And with the sort of view shown here, curtains or blinds would be quite unnecessary.

practical, so is vinyl-coated cork, and lineoleum, which now comes in all colours and can be inlaid or arranged in a pattern in various shades with quite spectacular results. Black and white vinyl tiles can look particularly effective, and hardboard or chipboard, painted or varnished, make cheap cover-ups. I was always immensely impressed with the vinyl flooring we had in the dining room when my children were small. It seemed to withstand the onslaught of bicycles, tricycles and roller skates with scarcely a scratch to show.

Windows give you a chance to go to town. The obvious window treatments in traditional dining rooms are curtains on rods, or under pelmets, or hung from various headings, tied back at the sides, and used with roller, Roman or festoon blinds if you wanted to cut a particular dash. Blinds on their own can fit any atmosphere, particularly if windows are awkward, small or you did not want to lose too much light. Vertical or louvred blinds, pinoleum or matchstick blinds or Venetian blinds are more appropriate in modern settings. Add colour with roller blinds, atmosphere with Austrian blinds, or create an entirely different mood with cottagey patterned curtains. Match them with other patterns in the room.

Then there are shutters in natural or white-painted wood: if you have

Victorian shutters, strip them, and hang a pretty lace panel at the window. Close the shutters over it at night. Or have no window treatment at all except glass shelves full of plants, or plants hanging from the ceiling or from poles slung across the window. There are enormous numbers of possibilities when you get over the thought that you must have some sort of fabric at the windows.

Seeing to eat

Whatever the style of your dining room, traditional, modern or something in between, the same broad principles of lighting apply. People need to see what they're eating but the light must never be so bright that it kills any atmosphere you're trying to achieve. Although the fittings can be totally different according to the room itself, the effect should be the same: subtle lighting, capable of creating different moods but in plentiful supply over those places that need it.

Obviously the table and sideboard or carving table need to be well lit, but whether you use a light right over the table, a chandelier, candelabra or side lights, they really should be used in conjunction with a dimmer switch. If you do have a hanging light over the table it should not hang more than 85 cm to 90 cm (34 in to 36 in) from the table top. A rise-and-fall fitting ensures it will be right. This could be discreetly boost-

Window treatments for dining rooms. Top left: Grey walls, Roman blinds and a grey-covered table tucked into a panelled bay window make a pretty dining oasis. Top right: Dinner for two among a symphony of nutmeg shades in this mellow dining hall with its romantic curtains. Right: Sheer lace curtains share the same flowing fern design as the wallpaper. The bare pine table set right by the window is a cheerful breakfast or lunch place. Far right: The window treatment here reinforces the clean lines of this uncluttered dining area. The table accessories have been chosen to reflect the same colours.

ed by concealed uplights in corners, or by strip lights running round the room just below the ceiling and concealed by a pelmet or valance.

There are, of course, all sorts of chandeliers available for traditional rooms in brass, iron, wood, wrought iron and crystal, but again the effect can be discreetly boosted by recessed downlights set in the ceiling to light up the chandelier itself. This is especially effective with crystal.

To add special accent, use spots round the room to highlight pictures or fireplace, and take any collections you may have into consideration when you are planning lighting: a lit display is always very dramatic. Wallwashers, downlights or up-lighters can be used to highlight areas of the room, or sculptural halogen floor lamps with dimmers can be ready to flood a room with sunshine-like light, or give a warm and cosy glow.

Setting the table

The table setting—china, glass, cut-lery, linen—is as much a part of dining room decoration as the furni-ture and framework. There's no point in getting all the other decorat-ive details perfect if your plates and knives and forks are all wrong. It doesn't matter whether they are family heirlooms or bargains from the market stall; if they're right for the setting, that's all that counts.

China, cutlery and glass all need to

Far left: A wide-brimmed pendant light adds sparkle as well as light to the transparent table setting of glass and clear plastic beneath. Flowers stand out with clarity against the see-through surfaces and floor. Note the upright radiator in the recess.

Left: The downlight shining through the lavish indoor tree gives dramatic but subtle light to this good-looking room. Large Mexican terracotta tiles make a mellow base for the russets of the chairs and table. Note the table centre of pots of mustard and cress.

Above: Clever neon lighting above this table means that the whole feel —and colour—of the room can be changed at a touch of a switch.

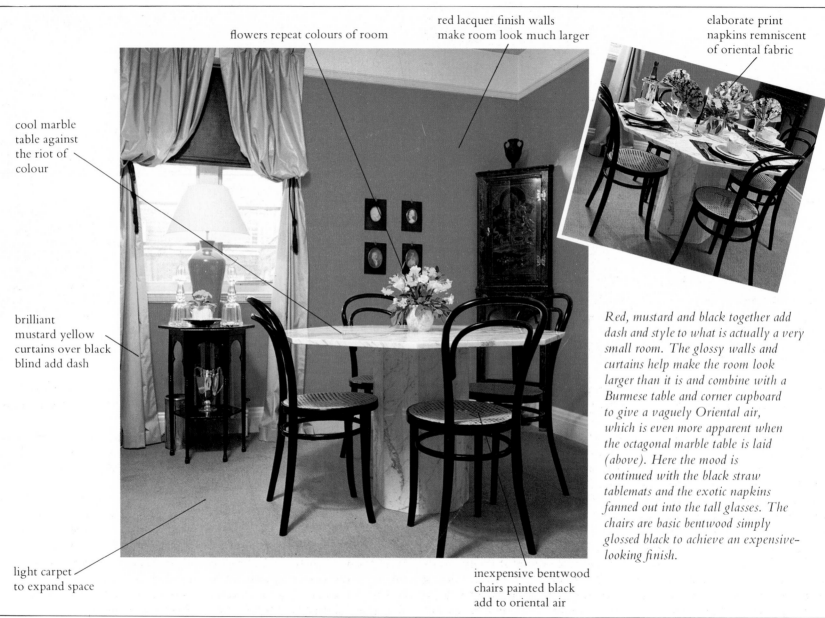

flowers repeat colours of room

red lacquer finish walls
make room look much larger

elaborate print
napkins remniscent
of oriental fabric

cool marble
table against
the riot of
colour

brilliant
mustard yellow
curtains over black
blind add dash

light carpet
to expand space

inexpensive bentwood
chairs painted black
add to oriental air

Red, mustard and black together add dash and style to what is actually a very small room. The glossy walls and curtains help make the room look larger than it is and combine with a Burmese table and corner cupboard to give a vaguely Oriental air, which is even more apparent when the octagonal marble table is laid (above). Here the mood is continued with the black straw tablemats and the exotic napkins fanned out into the tall glasses. The chairs are basic bentwood simply glossed black to achieve an expensive-looking finish.

be useful as well as decorative. When you're choosing them think as much about shapes and sizes as about colour and pattern. Do they come in a wide range to suit all your needs? Are they going to be your serviceable everyday sets or only used on special occasions? Will they stand up to family wear and tear or look too sturdy for dinner parties? Are they all dishwasher/oven/freezer proof? Do they need to look equally at home in kitchen, dining room or living room? Do you want to be able to add to them over the years or is the manufacturer likely to discontinue that particular pattern? Good table linen is also essential – to show off the food and add to the atmosphere. By changing cloths and napkins you can alter the feeling and style of the room quite spectacularly without going to a lot of expense – bright paper tablewear for children's parties, sophisticated damask or fine linen for a formal dinner party or cheerful gingham for casual or family meals.

One of my most favourite dining rooms was in an old country farmhouse with brick floors, uneven nutmeg brown walls and a huge fireplace where there was almost always a fire. There was a long elm table, an old chestnut French provincial armoire, a rather well-worn 17th century velvet-covered Spanish chest and thick white cotton Roman blinds, edged with a brown and apricot cotton to match the tablecloth.

The matching or contrasting of tablecloths, napkins and window fabrics is always a pretty thing to do and by changing them you change the mood effectively at little cost.

Left: Silky festoon blinds make a sumptuous backdrop for a nicely faded wood table full of sparkle and gleaming silver. Lace mats and velvet seated Regency chairs complete the traditional dining room elegance.

Right: Breakfast by the sea, and what could be more appropriate than the blue and white china on a blue and white tablecloth under a full vase of roses. The striped rug fits quite happily into the unashamedly romantic setting which even has a flower-filled fireplace.

203

Once you have decided which facts you have to face, and whittled down the possibilities according to space, family and pocket, you can decide much more easily on the feeling you would like to introduce. Clearly, in a family dining room with several small children to cater for you are not likely to plump for any sort of exotica, or even the favourite splendours of velvet and mahogany. You are much more likely to go for old pine, or oak, tough lacquer or vinyl—at least for several years, but there is no reason why these cannot work just as well and create a feeling of their own.

Even if you don't have children, there may be other limitations that turn out to be more inhibiting than inspiring. Here's where it pays to borrow a little inspiration. Think which public places, which restaurants, in particular, have made you feel comfortable and at ease. Do you go for the opulent feel of linen, sparkle of cut glass and rich warm colouring, or do you prefer the more casual look of bare wood and brick? Do you like a clean-lined, pale wood, Scandinavian feel? The lightness of glass and wicker and white-painted plaster or brick? Or the softness of long sweeping print tablecloths and fabric-covered walls?

These days you do not have to go for matching suites of furniture in the dining room, any more than you have to go for three piece suites in the living room. No one will look askance if you have a makeshift wooden table disguised by a floor length tablecloth (with interchangeable overcloths), painted or lacquered ex-kitchen chairs, and an old dresser for a sideboard, or an old Victorian or Edwardian wardrobe for glass and china storage. Why should they? What you are achieving with such a happy mix is very much more personal and, therefore, interesting than the blandness of the careful match.

Set the mood

Colour is a useful tool to achieving a particular atmosphere: dark colours—rust, deep green, earth colours, dark woods—create a warm, inviting atmosphere

Unit furniture, spreading plants and an even more spreading Arco light, left, divide dining from living area in a long, clean-lined room. A different effect, right; a happy mix of pretty pine dresser and table, white-painted directors' chairs, old stove and cane side tables is still homogeneous.

and show off food well. Bright, primary colours make for a cheerful, family room. Fashionable pastels are fresh and clean for daytime eating and cool and subtle for evening atmosphere. Whatever the colour scheme, there are certain characteristic styles.

Traditional with polished wood furniture and fine accessories to create a feeling of opulence. Walls in dark, warm colours, with rich fitted carpets or traditional rugs make for a quietly splendid effect. Panelled walls enhance the atmosphere.

Farmhouse follows the style of the farmhouse kitchen, and has a pine dresser or armoire as its focal point. Traditionally, flooring is of flagstones or quarry tiles, softened by rugs or matting. Old fashioned pine tables are expensive, but you could cover a modern one with a PVC cloth in a rustic pattern for everyday use and a more prettily patterned cotton cloth for special occasions. Window treatments should be fairly simple: floral or gingham curtains with tie-backs are ideal.

Scandinavian freshness is characterised by modern pine or beech and clean lines. Colour and design are all important; plants, clear colours (but not strong primary ones) and lots of white (paint, walls, floor or accessories) help to achieve this healthy non-fussy look.

Top left: Grapefruit yellow walls, an abundance of marguerites, a spanking white floor and pale wood furniture for a Scandinavian look.

Above: Chunky furniture, black-painted bentwood chairs, matting and a cheerful garden view for a nice no-nonsense dining-living room.

Left: Up-dated traditional with slightly oriental overtones in the Chinese chairs, art, blossom trees and rattan blinds. Co-ordinated cloths, napkins and curtains owe rather more to the West.

Right: Farmhouse style furniture assisted by the charming rustic nature of the room itself.

DINING IN STYLE

Above: This is a fair approximation of French café style, with its bentwood chairs, marble-topped table and turn-of-the-century tiled floor.

Right: Not so much Hi-Tech as high ingenuity, because this dining room is actually a corridor with a mirrored wall just by the front door. Note the interesting idea of suspended spots operated by a dimmer switch.

Top, far right: Here is a touch of Eastern fantasy with the tented ceiling, kimono-style print, which is also used on the cushions, cane furniture and basketware.

Bottom, far right: Weird, wonderful and slightly film-set-ish.

Eastern fantasy runs riot with fabric decorations in either plain or delicately patterned style. Tented ceilings, fabric-covered walls, floor-length cloths and extravagant combinations of curtains and blinds at the window give a luxurious exotic feeling. Use lining fabrics for economy, trimmed with pattern border or edged with braid. If you are at home with colour and pattern, you could go for a Persian look, with patterned Indian cotton bedspreads draped round windows and tented over the table.

Thirties style cries out for a dining suite. Although this is generally considered a thing of the past, there has been a revival in the popularity of the solidly built, veneered Thirties suite with its square lines. You need panache to carry it off, with carefully selected ornaments and crockery from the period–fortunately, there's still quite a lot of it around; geometric patterned wallpaper or plain walls with a border pattern in peaches and rusts.

French café is reminiscent of the local bistro. The French are masters of restaurant cooking and atmosphere, so why not take a leaf from their book? Bentwood chairs, small circular tables and wall-mounted globe café lights are the key. Walls need to be mellow: dark creams, possibly sponged or rag rolled to give a textured effect. A dado rail, fixed round the room at the level of chair backs, with painted panelling below it will add more character.

Hi-tech says modern finishes and colours which give a bright, space-age feel. Go for angular-shaped chairs, softening them with cushions in bright, geometric prints. Trestle tables of either laminate or glass suit the wood. Flooring should be non-committal: plain, functional cord fitted carpet, or rubber stud flooring. Simple window treatments, such as vertical louvres or slick Venetian blinds are the most appropriate.

But don't be tied by necessity or convention to furnish all in one style. It is quite acceptable to mix, say, the feeling of the 17th century with the very modern; country pieces with glass and chrome; modern bentwood with early Victorian; a nice Regency side table with a scrubbed pine table. If you can't afford, or can't find, a good antique table to suit your style, get a second-hand, junk table, cover it with cloths, and invest as much as you can in comfortable chairs. Then again, you can still get a traditional feeling without having to spend money on a set of antique chairs. Old deal or pine kitchen chairs can be picked up reasonably in junk shops and painted or stained; not particularly nice reproduction chairs can be lacquered in unexpected colours. And so on.

Stylish transformations

As well as these pointers to distinctive style, there are many finishing touches which will add personality to a dining room, whether it is newly decorated, or a dining room you can't afford to re-vamp (or don't want to re-decorate, because it is in a rented home).

Put in a dado rail round the room, level with the backs of the chairs: it will protect the wallcovering, and change the proportions of the room. Polish it, or paint it to match the woodwork.

Fireplaces with real fires can be awkward in a very small dining room. Go for background heat, which is more controllable, and put an arrangement of dried flowers in the redundant grate.

Cover the walls with large panels of fabric—wall hangings, rugs or (appropriately) tablecloths. Staple them in place or stretch them on battens.

Add light to a room, and increase its apparent size by putting up mirror tiles (or fixing panels of mirror) in alcoves.

Make the room an extension of the garden by keeping potted plants by the window. Patio plants can be moved to 'winter over' in the dining room. Windowsills serve as greenhouse staging.

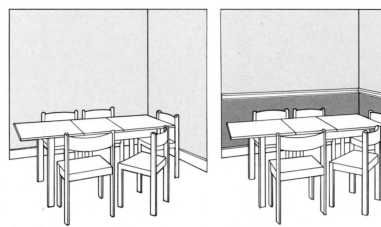

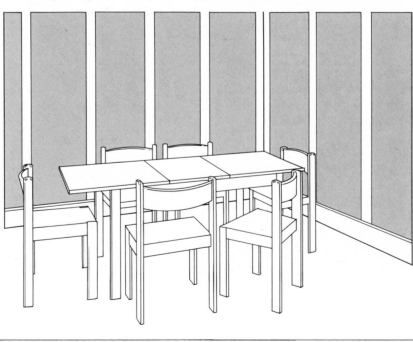

a plain dining room (above left) given character by adding a dado rail (above right) or covering the walls with panels of fabric (below).

The collector's room

Because of the nature of the furnishings in a dining room (a large, flat surface, empty walls) and because it is needed to serve its purpose only at regular, specified times during the day (meal times), it is an ideal room to serve as a collector's library. Collections can be displayed and made into a decorative asset, and if you are a serious collector you can use the room as a quiet retreat to pursue your hobby, cleaning or mending plates, checking hallmarks on silver, valuing new purchases from relevant text books, cataloguing details—whatever might be involved in your particular field.

● Use wire plate hangers to hang a collection of plates on the walls, grouped according to colour, size or origin.

● Line the walls with shelves to house a library of books or magazines.

● Build storage cabinets and shelves to hold a collection of records.

● Display a collection of models—houses, soldiers, toys, cars—on shelves, carefully lit by strip lights behind baffles.

● Frame a collection of samplers—or something more unusual like lace collars or handkerchieves (or table napkins), and hang them in groups on the wall.

real candles in
candelabra and sconces

Regency column
and bust

wood glued
to produce
'gothic' shape

pediment is
actually hardboard

inexpensive
muslin curtain
with quality trim

dado panelling,
door and cabinet
(inset) painted
for 'oak graining'
effect

Regency
fire-screen

'lace' is
cut out
paper

genuine Regency
table and chairs

*A graceful Regency dining room in
which period features, such as the
dado, with its 'faux bois' oak-grained
treatment, have been restored for effect.
The candle-lit candelabra and chairs
are genuine but the curtains and
skirting board heating are welcome
modern introductions. The equally
modern cabinet (inset) is ingeniously
aged with paper 'lace' and a hardboard
pediment.*

Dining room proper

The style of this dining room is a very successful mix: the furniture is modern and so is the sculptural halogen floor lamp but the general effect and feel is formal and traditional, even rather Victorian. The walls set the tone and the theme. They have been lacquered an Indian red and panelled over with lengths of an Indian red and cream paper. A matching fabric is used for the overcloth on the table. The same colours are followed through at the window with its Indian red curtains edged with cream and its cream blind. This time the undercloth of the table matches the curtains. Chairs, sideboard and halogen lamp are all a glossy black. And just as the lamp adds height to one corner of the room, so the pedestal, urn and oversize fern balance the effect and do the same in the opposite corner. Lighting is all important here. A subdued background light comes from strip light running all the way round the room just under the ceiling but concealed by a pelmet papered in the wall design. The halogen lamp with its own dimmer gives whatever extra light is required. An uplight behind the pedestal shines through the leaves of the plant to create quite a different effect of gently diffused light.

Above: Terracotta-coloured painted boards in this dining room make a spectacular background for part of a collection of blue and white china. There is more of it on the table which is given additional emphasis by the blue and white chair covers. Note too, the interesting barley-sugar twist candlesticks and the old chest. The russet colour is the perfect complement to the blue/white scheme.

Right: The vivid painting clearly dominates everything else in a small red lacquered room and not only dictates the other colours, for example in the flowers and rug, but also the slightly tropical feel of the table, napkins and chairs.

● Collect old kitchen equipment—bread boards, wicker carpet beaters, jelly moulds—and hang them on the walls.

● Put up a pin board and start a collection of cards from restaurants. Each time you visit a new eating place, pick up a card, write your verdict on the back, and pin it on the board for future reference.

● Display your children's art lesson masterpieces round the room—it will encourage and gratify them and will certainly provide talking points.

● Certain collections—Mickey Mouse ephemera or period memorabilia need a range of different treatments to display them to their best advantage: dot pictures and plaques round the wall, arrange toys and crockery on shelves, lay rugs on the floor. Even the table setting can be part of the collection.

● Collect something that you can actually use: a collection of cruets is both amusing and practical; give each guest a different set to use.

Whatever your collection, display it thoughtfully. Try to give pride of place to one prized item: maybe the most valuable, or the most spectacular, perhaps the very *first* of your collection, or the one that was a special gift or heirloom.

Position it in the centre of the mantelpiece, stand it on a shelf on its own, shine a spotlight on to it, or hang it on an empty wall where it will attract attention.

Clever lighting can make all the difference to the look of a collection, drawing attention to it and showing it off to its best advantage at the same time. The kind of fixtures that are best for this sort of accent lighting are the various types of spotlights, wallwashers, pinhole or framing projectors, as well as uplights and candles. If you are lighting a single object, aim to place your fixture so that there is no distracting reflection. You need to experiment, lighting from above, or below or straight on, to see which gives the best effect. Glass shelves are often particularly effective, especially when set in a mirrored alcove, and lit from above or below, or both.

Above: Almost everything else is subjugated to the neatly arranged collection of art in this dining room where both decor and furniture are firmly restrained. The long glass table is dramatic but not distracting and the only other colours are in the plant life and the mahogany-finish arched door frame. Note too, how everything in the room—table, chairs, all the pictures—is framed in steel.

I like to think that one can make provision to eat almost anywhere in the home, just as one should be able to move small tables about to different parts of the garden. It is obviously nice to be able to eat in the kitchen or in the living room. But why not the hall for a change? The bedroom for a breakfast *à deux* or cosy supper? Even in the bathroom –if you happen to have sufficient space, and money, for a luxurious bathroom/exercise room, bathroom/study, bathroom/ sitting room, bathroom/ bedroom–you could fit in a small health bar with fruit and vitamin drinks.

All you need is a table and chairs that do not look out of place in whatever room they are put– though, of course, folding varieties of both can be brought out for the occasion.

In any case, in any home where space is at a premium, you have to learn to use that space for all it's worth. If you do not have the luxury of a dining room used just for dining–and most of us do not, the trick is to make your dining table look as if it is not a dining table most of the time. And that means that you do not have a table surrounded by chairs–except, of course, when you are actually going to use it for eating.

Dining/work room

If you use what was the dining room for a work room/study as well, you should either have a round table which can be piled with books when necessary, a table set off-centre, or a drop-leaf table that can be pulled out and set up in the centre of the room as required. All of them can then double as a desk, homework table, sewing or drawing table. If you occasionally have quite big parties it would be worth buying a table with extra leaves (store them under a bed, or behind a door). Bookshelves can have cupboards underneath to take china, glass, cutlery and table linen as well as files, stationery and normal work room apparatus. It is just a question of organization. Keep the breakfront surface (the top of the cupboard part) about twice as deep as the shelves above, and you will have a ready-made serving area for meals as well as an effective room divider.

This small study/dining room, left, is thoroughly light-hearted with its floor like an abstract painting and its delicious stripy fabric. White dining table and chairs blend happily into this chunky white living room, right, with its dividing chimney breast.

DUAL-PURPOSE DINING AREAS

Another great aid to any part-time dining area is the trolley or serving cart which makes the valuable link between kitchen and eating area, and is useful for transportation of food and dishes, and in addition provides storage and an extra serving surface.

The problem of where to put all those extra chairs is not really so very difficult. There are several solutions. For example in a flat or apartment, you could buy chairs that would act as occasional chairs; have them covered in the sort of colour that will go in every room and they can then be distributed throughout bedrooms, living rooms, hall if it is big enough, and brought together as and when needed.

Alternatively, you could buy folding chairs that could either be put away in, say, a hall cupboard and taken out when needed, or hung on a wall. The clear perspex or plexiglass variety will take very little visual space since you can look right through them and the brightly coloured wooden varieties are a decoration in themselves, looking rather like modern sculptures against the wall's surface.

This kitchen/dining room, with its useful draughtsman-like table and mobile chairs, works equally efficiently as an office. Altogether a practical, useful room.

magistretti chair

plia chair

modern movement
tubular steel chair

medici chair

wheelback chair

director's chair

bauhaus chair

wicker chair

bentwood chair

DUAL-PURPOSE DINING AREAS

Dining/guest rooms

Much the same suggestions can apply to a room that also acts as part-time guest room. Here, of course, you will also need to make provision for a bed and clothes storage. The bed could either be a sofa bed or a studio couch with, perhaps, extra drawers underneath, or, in a smaller room, an armchair that transforms itself into a bed. The bed/storage area could be neatly screened off with matchstick blinds.

If at all possible, you should provide a wardrobe either by having a wall of storage with shelves, drawers and cupboards to take both dining accessories and clothes, or by having a separate armoire or old wardrobe (which can also take silver, china, glass etc.). And there is almost no limit to the ways you can reorganize the space in some of those old Victorian and Edwardian wardrobes that can still be found. Even with dire shortage of cash and space, hooks fixed on the back of the door will take an overnight clothes hanger or two.

If you wanted to make the room seem more like a bedroom/sitting room than a study/library/dining room that will also accommodate a guest, you could make much more of the sofa bed and have a rectangular or drop-leaf table like a sofa table behind it. This can then be pulled out and opened out as the occasion demands.

Living/dining rooms

This is a pretty usual arrangement nowadays, and again the trick is to disguise the dining table when not in use for dining. Round tables and drop-leafs can be bought to act as library tables and sofa tables as described above, or there are large adjustable coffee and cocktail tables which can be raised to dining or lowered to coffee table height as desired.

Table tops can also be concealed within a storage wall in much the same way as fold-up beds, so that the leaf can be pulled down when wanted and shut up later to look like a piece of smooth wall. Or, more ingeniously, the underside can be mirrored so that when it is flipped up it will look for all the world like a large looking glass.

Obviously, tables can be a visible part of a storage wall, acting as either a desk or for dining, and some of them have an extendable top so that they can be pulled right out when you have company.

If you have a dining alcove in your living room you could make the division more complete by building a low storage wall of shelves or cupboards with plenty of room inside for all your dining equipment and serving space on top. Or you could line the walls with bookshelves with cupboards underneath to provide storage and serving space, as in the dining/workroom.

Alcoves like this can also be treated like separate small rooms and lined with mirror or mirror tiles; or with the curtain or shade fabric; or painted or papered in a colour out of the room which is at the same time different from the main walls. Any cloths used on the table could be made from the same fabric as the main room curtains or upholstery.

Above: In this living room the round table under the large pine mirror is perfect for dining and looks just as good when it is not laid for a meal. The handsome 19th century chairs can be used as occasional seating in other parts of the room.

Right: A kitchen/dining room with a distinctly conservatory feel.

DUAL-PURPOSE DINING AREAS

If the alcove is very narrow, use an upholstered bench with suspended cushions for back rests on one side of the table and chairs on the other.

If the style of the main room will take it, a dining alcove can sometimes be semi-curtained off as in a box at the theatre or in one of those titillating little areas off famous turn-of-the-century Paris restaurants used for discreet entertaining.

When there is no separate alcove or eating area allowed for, a distinct dining place can be made by raising a table on a plywood platform at whatever height is preferred. Again, it can be separated a little from the mainstream area with a low wall of cupboards and shelves, or, providing the main area is big enough, a high wall of shelves.

If, of course, the room is quite big, all sorts of divider devices can be used to partition off a dining area, from screens of one sort or another to large indoor plants or trees.

Another good solution for dining if the room will take it, is a long old refectory table which, like the library table idea, can be used for piling books and magazines on, for displaying flowers and objects and to provide both work and eating surfaces.

Dining halls

A nice wide hall is a natural for dining, and again, the table should be an object in its own right, in use for

Left: The dark gate-legged table at the dining end of this all-white living room looks just as charming devoid of chairs, which can be easily folded away when not in use.

Top right: Although long and narrow, the space in this open-plan kitchen-dining-living area has been cleverly planned and furnished. The kitchen area towards the garden crams in most necessities including adequate storage, and the round table can act as a desk as well as dining table. Note the metal chairs stacked neatly by the garden door.

Bottom right: Landings, if they're a reasonable size and shape, can make good dining areas too. This space, somewhat exotically divided from the living area by what looks like a christening font, makes a very pleasant place for eating, for sitting chatting or even for playing cards.

Far right: Sometimes, squeezing in dining space is more a matter of courage than anything else. One could hardly imagine a table for six in this tiny bedsitting room (the bed is up the other end), but it works. And pushed against the wall when not in use for dining, the table makes an excellent desk/work surface as well.

display and general dumping space when not in use for eating. If you are lucky enough to have full length cupboards in the hallway, they can easily be reorganized to take china, cutlery, glass and linen and maybe even a trolley or serving cart.

Small tables for two can make very good use of the wasted space at the end of a corridor. Good lighting, a picture or two or a rug fixed to the end wall will give a whole new lease of life to what could have been a boring dead end.

Dining/kitchens

There is no doubt that eating in the kitchen has an attraction all its own. It is more informal, warmer somehow (both in fact as well as in atmosphere), and, naturally, there is no feeling of separation from the action or the cook, for whom, of course, it is also more practical. Many more dishes can be made that go direct from stove to table than could ever be produced for a separate dining room or area.

It's important to have enough space and a well-thought out arrangement that allows both eating and cooking to take place without the one interfering with the other. The cook needs room to get at the cooker, sink and cupboards without hindrance and to move around the kitchen comfortably. Lots of worktops and dumping space is essential. It's more pleasant for the diners too

if the cooking paraphernalia–dirty pans and plates–can be kept out of sight

So if the kitchen is large enough to take any sort of eating surface–even if it is only an extension of a counter top to make a breakfast and supper bar, this is obviously a bonus. If

breakfast is a cut-and-run meal then a bar counter is a good idea and a nice compromise between setting a proper table and snatching a cup of coffee on the wing. And children enjoy perching on stools. But you still have to decide whether you want to make a kitchen you can eat

There is a very clever use of space in this kitchen-dining-family room. The central green tiled island unit, here laid for supper, acts as dining table and is also the main work surface. Every surface is used for cupboard space including the area over the island unit as well as beneath it.

The right setting for the right room. A round skirted table makes a pleasant place for breakfast (and supper too) by the window seat in a country bedroom, top, far left. Two trestle tables, placed end to end, provide generous dining or work space in this celadon green living room, bottom, far left. Hallways can be dramatic places to eat in, especially a soaring space like this one, top left, where the hexagonal marbled table is echoed in the dinner service. Once candles are lit the table becomes an oasis, as here in the room shown bottom left. Wherever there is space for a table and chairs, there is space for a dining area. This landing, below, by French doors makes a pretty indoor/outdoor dining space.

Left: The dining corner of this basement living room comes straight up against the kitchen alcove and uses the half partition wall for a wrap-around seating support. Shutters on the bay window are painted in an abstract design to match other colours in the room.

Above: The dining area counter top of this apricot and white room acts as a kind of visual partition.

Right: The eating area is divided off from the working part of this kitchen by an island of matting and a nicely detailed window treatment with green edged scalloped pelmet and green checked shade to match the chair seats and napkins.

in, or an eating place which is also the kitchen. There is quite a difference.

Either way, you will probably want to put more emphasis on decoration than you would do normally. You could, for example, divide the table area off from the working area with a storage/serving wall or the sort of peninsular unit described on pages 137 and 146. Or install some sort of screen, dividing panel, a blind that lets down from the ceiling, and even a stack of wine racks which would make a substantial and permanent wall in themselves. You could too, choose rather different wall treatments for the dining part: flame-proofed fabric; wallpaper, a warm, dark paint, and add pictures, prints, objects, favourite collections, bookshelves, anything that emphasises that the space is as much for living as for working in.

Use pretty table cloths and napkins. Go for well-designed china that delights the eye and sets off the food. Pay attention to plants and flowers and make sure that you have your lighting on dimmer switches so that you can dim it right down for dining as well as drawing a veil over any kitchen clutter.

In fact, if you always bear in mind that once a table is set for dining, lights lowered, candles lit, that table becomes an oasis, complete in itself, you can make a dining room wherever the table is.

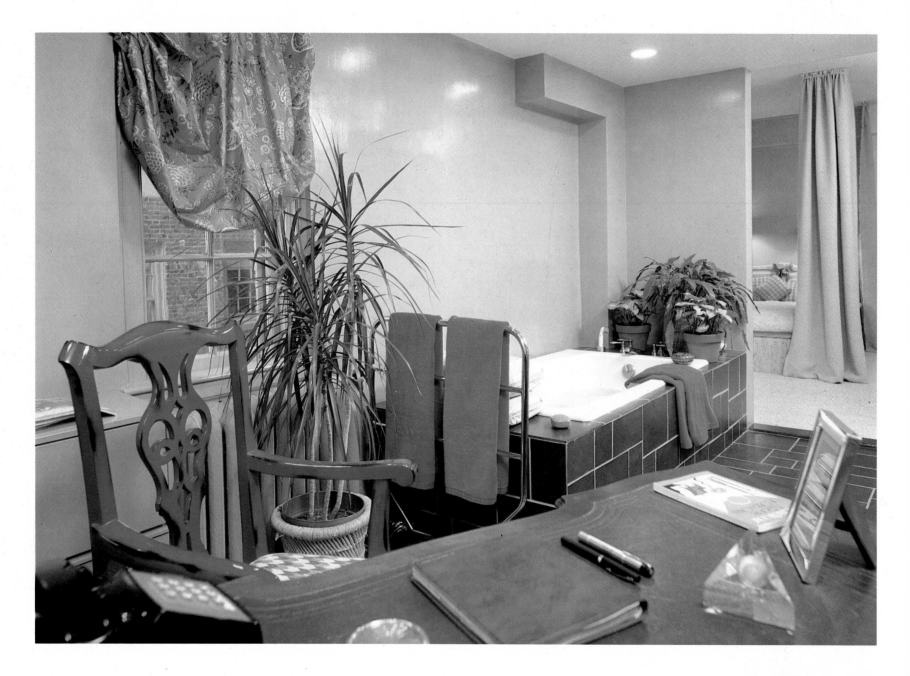

Bedrooms and bathrooms are the rooms in which we are supposed to relax our bodies, restore our energies, and take comfort. In short, they need not be just for sleeping, for storing clothes, dressing, bathing, washing and shaving.

So there is no reason – especially given the general shortage of space – why bedrooms should not be on 24-hour duty, used for working in as well as sleeping – and for watching television, listening to music, and even for eating; a small table for leisurely breakfasts and comfortable little suppers could be a great luxury.

Bathrooms too – given the square footage – can be multi-functional. Some people deliberately turn a large bedroom into a comfortable bathroom/study/dressing/exercise room, keeping a smaller room for actual sleeping. But even a very small room could probably be made considerably more luxurious and comforting than it is at present.

The first priority in any bedroom or bathroom, whatever its use, should be comfort. In the case of bedrooms this is not just a comfortable bed and bedclothes, although they are essential since we spend one-third of our lives in bed – but also really good lighting. And that means good to make-up by, good to read in bed and work by, good for general dressing and easy on the eye. You will want comfort underfoot too. If ever there was a place for carpet, or at least generous rugs, the bedroom is that place. Heating too, should be well regulated so that the temperature can be as good for sitting in as it is for sleeping. Quiet is an essential. If you live in a busy area or over a much-used street, you will certainly need to consider fabric-covered walls as well as carpet and multi-layered window treatments, if not double glazing, all of which will help to deaden outdoor sounds.

Bathrooms too, need good lighting and heating and warm, non-slip floors. Some kind of ventilation, e.g. an extractor fan, may be necessary to combat condensation. Handgrips on baths might seem a small detail but it is an important one if you have children, elderly people or invalids to consider.

Whether you do it all at once or aim for a series of staged improvements will depend on your budget and your circumstances.

If you are planning bedrooms and bathrooms from scratch you are lucky, because with a very limited budget you can decide your priorities and plan sensibly to achieve them as and when you have the cash. If you are hoping to improve existing rooms but cannot do it all at once you will find that even the slightest change can uplift the spirits . . . cushions on a bed, a new bedcover, tie-backs on curtains, pictures, new towels, an added plant.

The aim of this book is to define the functions of both rooms and show you how to make the best use of your available space, how to achieve an appropriate style, how to plan children's rooms so that you do not have to keep on spending as the child grows up, how to plan storage, lighting and heating, and how to choose the best furniture and equipment or improve what you've got.

Most importantly, it aims to show you how to fit your rooms to the way you live; how to make them really work for you. After all, bedrooms and bathrooms are, or should be, the foundations of your personal comfort. They deserve to be well-planned.

This splendid bathroom-cum-study, en suite to the bedroom glimpsed beyond, shows how the original function of such rooms can be extended. The mahogany colour of the desk and blind is cleverly repeated in the lining to the fabric at the four corners of the bed.

Most people would like, and indeed need, to think of their bedrooms as more than just a place for sleep, storing clothes, dressing and making up. In today's world the bedroom often has to be office, study and second living room as well. The ideal would be to have a desk as well as a bed, an armchair or two and a couch, generous bedside tables and storage, bookshelves, television, stereo, space to stash away a sewing machine and an exercise machine so that they do not spoil the elegant harmony of the whole. There should also be space for storing impedimenta like files, records, tapes and sewing stuff. Space in fact, to ensure that the bedroom really is a room for quiet and rest, a room away from the family for pursuing your own interests and work, and above all a room for comfort.

Alas, the reality is that most bedrooms are far too small for most people's ideals and need to be meticulously planned if they are to hold more than the minimum of a bed, a couple of bedside tables, clothes storage and a chair. Almost everywhere, except in roomy country or suburban houses and old-fashioned mansion flats or apartments, bedrooms are sacrificed for the greater good of the general living space. Cottage bedrooms, small flat bedrooms, new house bedrooms, conversions and bedsitting rooms all suffer from lack of the square footage that is desperately needed for real comfort. And if so-called master bedrooms are small, rooms meant for children are often no more than cells fit for a couple of bunk beds.

Luckily, a number of furniture designers are now producing modular furniture that can be shaped and re-shaped to suit awkward spaces and differing needs. If you can afford it, fine; if not, you can still do a great deal with decoration and ingenuity.

Space, one cannot stress too often, is as much a matter of *feeling* spacious as of actual room measurement. If you can foster the illusion by clever and imaginative use of mirror, lighting, pattern and multi-purpose furniture (beds that have storage underneath, chests of drawers that are also

Limited colours, the wall design repeated on bed quilting, and the bed placed cornerwise, all help the feeling of space in the bedroom on the left, while the small room on the right gets its fresh look from the blue and white scheme, deep window and plants.

Three very different small bedrooms that benefit from clever use of mirror. Light colours and a wall of mirror effectively double the size of the tailored guest room, top left. Mirror tiles set on the diagonal completely cover the end wall and cupboard doors, with their clever glass handles, on the small room above. The trellis structure makes an original bedhead and gives the illusion of an airy room divider halving a much longer space. In the tiny bedroom, left, large mirrors at right angles, framed to match the handsome chest, matching fabrics and wallpaper and pale beige carpeting all produce a tranquil effect.

work surfaces; cupboards and closets that hold files and equipment as well as clothes) you are well on the way to manipulating every inch to its best advantage—and every inch well used in a bedroom really does make an enormous difference.

Adapting to partners

Adapting bachelor accommodation – whether male or female – to take a partner can be very testing. I am not talking here about the merits or de-merits of feminine or masculine decoration, but rather of making room for one more person's effects. It can come as a great shock, once the all-embracing, all-forgiving 'honeymoon' period is over, to wake up to somebody else's clothes and clutter. So every possible inch of storage has to be utilized to cope with the changed circumstances and, if possible, to disguise the overflow of possessions. And all in such a way as to give each a fair share of the space, leaving no room for complaint or irritation.

Doors, and this includes wardrobe or closet doors, are often an under-used ingredient of the room ripe for conversion. Racks, hooks, the sort of spring clips used for holding brooms and cleaning apparatus can all be used to provide extra storage. Is there room for a window seat? If there is, make it one with a lift-up lid so that belongings can be stored inside.

The old-fashioned ottoman or a similar sort of chest is another good solution. Either can be put at the foot of a bed, in a corner, or under a window to provide extra seating as well as storage. If there is a dressing table think too about a hollow upholstered stool with a lift-up lid. Make as many things as possible do two jobs rather than one.

If there isn't room to add a dressing table and/or desk, think of buying three or four whitewood chests of drawers, or chests plus a cupboard and arranging them against a wall so that there is some knee hole space. Cover the lot with a long counter top, perhaps covered in plastic laminate, paint the chests in with the room and you have a desk, dressing table, work surface and clothes storage all in one.

Right: A large drop-leafed table set behind this bed acts as bedhead as well as drawing/work surface. Floor-to-ceiling open bookshelves effectively divide off sleeping from sitting/breakfast/casual eating area. The rose and cream colour scheme freshened by touches of white in light shades and chair cushions makes this multi-functional space seem light and welcoming. Long swing-armed work lamps provide powerful light when needed but can easily be pushed up and away; so can the rise-and-fall fixture over the pedestal table in the seating area of the room.

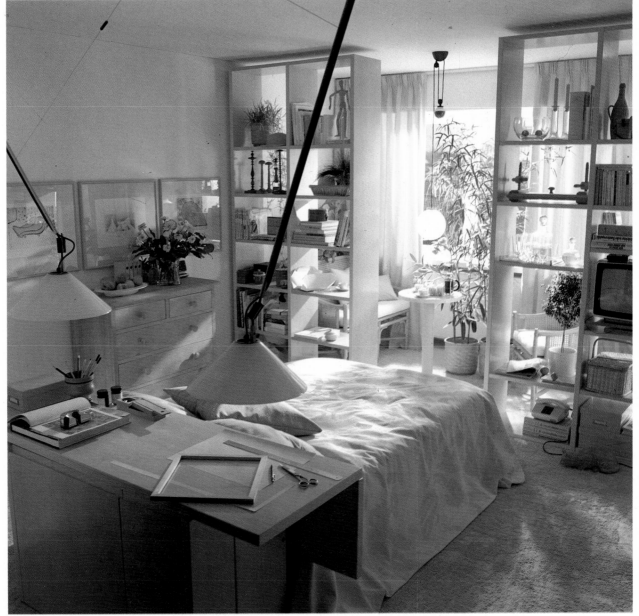

Use the window as a bedhead

At first glance there would seem to be
no hope at all of squeezing a double
bed into a room of this size—at least
with any semblance of elegance. But
by using the window as a headboard
and by covering the bed to blend in
with the walls the room looks fresh,
pretty and comparatively spacious; an
illusion helped by mirroring the door
between the wardrobes which gives
depth and extra light to the room, and
by painting the wooden floor a glossy
white. The green and white of the
wallpaper which covers cupboard
doors as well as walls, thus
minimizing their apparent size, is not
only repeated in the matching
bedcover and bolster, but echoed in
the neat white Roman blinds edged
with green and the updated rag rug
from Portugal. A nice touch is the
white edging on the bedcover which
reverses the green edging on the
blinds. Other good details to note are
the green ribbons used to hang the
miniatures either side of the bed
which repeats the colour of the velvet
chair upholstery—a nice contrast to the
crispness of the cotton; the differing
textures on the plain green cushions;
and the way the deep window sill and
reveals are used as bedside table and as
a convenient base for mounting the
pair of adjustable brass reading
lights. The chest at the end of the bed
holds spare linen and blankets or
duvets as well as making a useful extra
seat/bookshelf. There is even room for
a dressing/writing table.

Above: Bookshelves tucked under a window sill and permanently drawn-back curtains make a handsome bedhead as well as solving an awkward space problem in this small room. Adjustable wall lights provide the answer to where to put lamps when there is no room for bedside tables. A blind ensures privacy.

Left: Two built-in closets act as supports for bookshelves as well as providing guest bed/sofa space in this nicely book-lined work room, which also includes a desk and more shelves along the opposite wall.

Making room for guests

Today's tight spaces rarely allow for a spare room and rooms used exclusively for guests are practically non-existent in most current homes. More often than not the guest room is where the sofa bed or convertible happens to be, and it could be anywhere – in the living room, study, den, dining room or a convenient alcove in the hall. Happily, good hospitality is more a matter of *how* you accommodate your guests than *where*.

However, with a little careful planning and foresight you can make space for a guest almost anywhere in the home. If, for example, you have a sofa bed in the living room you could arrange to have a cupboard or closet in the hall which can be cleared enough to take visitor's clothes. If you can make a bed in the hall the same storage would naturally apply. If there is a sofa bed in a study, den or dining room you could try to fit a built-in closet in that room which would in any case be useful for other storage.

Most living rooms will already have a floor or table lamp and a small table which can be moved close to the sofa bed. All you need do is add books, a carafe of water or bottle of mineral water, a glass, generous towels and clean, tidy bathroom space and you are well on the way to making a guest feel just as much at home as in a self-contained bedroom.

Tricks for stretching space

When you are planning – or re-planning – a room remember the following well-tried space stretchers and see if you can apply any of them to your own particular situation and needs:

Mirror used at right angles to a window and, if possible, all along one wall, will make a room look twice as big and twice as light. A huge old mirror used as a bedhead will appear to double the space, particularly if the mirror reflects a window.

Flooring with a diagonal design will make the space seem larger, so will most geometric designs.

Using the same print on everything – walls, windows, bedspread, upholstery – will deceive the eye about the real size of the room and, by making you forget about limits, edges and boundaries of walls, seem to enlarge the space.

Disappearing wardrobes will appear to increase the wall space. Make them vanish by decorating them the same as the walls so that they don't stand out. Better still if you can merge the wardrobe frame with the walls *and* cover the front with mirror.

Screens can hide a multitude of unsightly but necessary equipment (like filing cabinets, if you use the room for working in) and at the same time give the illusion of space because of their angles.

Light colours make surfaces retreat. Use them on ceiling and floor and choose light backgrounds to fabric designs.

A platform will virtually give you two rooms for the price of one, so if you are able to plan a room from scratch and need to expand a comparatively small area, it's useful to know that you can do this.

The use of mirror always increases the feeling of space and light. It is particularly effective used at right-angles to a window to give the maximum reflection of light.

Shelving at the top and bottom of the bed can make an enormous difference. A low shelf at the foot can hold tv, stereo, books, magazines and could provide extra seating as well. High shelving at the top can act as bedhead as well as being used for books and general display purposes. If you build out such a storage and display wall a short distance from the wall proper, you could use the space behind as a study/work area.

Putting the bed in a corner or even in the middle of the room rather than against a wall, often makes the whole space more generous.

Uplights set in one or two corners of the room will make the space seem much bigger at night because it will bounce light up and soften the hard edges.

Small chests of drawers either side of the bed instead of bedside tables will make better use of the space.

A highish bed will free the space underneath for storage.

Cupboards and closets that go right to ceiling height will press into service all that otherwise wasted space, and cope with things that aren't used a lot and need to be out of sight most of the time.

The window used as sort of bedhead and curtains combined will save space in a very small room. Or if you have two windows, use the space in between for the bed.

An unused or unusable fireplace can provide extra storage: fit some shelves across the space and, if possible, a door in front.

Storage built around the bed will free the rest of the room and make it look much more open.

Use mirror panels at right-angles to a window to create an illusion of increased space and light

Build cupboards that go right up to the ceiling to make walls look longer and provide more storage

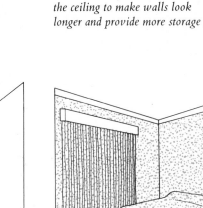

Position the bed at an angle to the corner of a room rather than flat against a wall

Use the same small print on a light background for walls, curtains and bedspread

dark blue velvet ribbon gives distinction

panels and bed head edged with blue

border gives definition to unruly angles

transparent perspex table and glass lamp take up no visual space

pale matting adds textural interest

skirted table gives softness and width to space

Attention is drawn away from the awkward angles of the room to the left by the pretty cornflower and white colouring, against which the pale furniture and matting, soft festoon blind and skirted, lace-covered table all take the eye. While above, another blue-white room is given definition by plain blue edging on door panels, the cushioned bedhead slotted onto a blue-painted pole and the blue china jardinière.

Of course, you are not limited to sofa beds. You might include a fold-up bed as part of a storage wall in the living room or study. (When shut up it is an innocent-looking cabinet – when down a bed pulls out.) Or there are deep armchairs that become single or double beds, stacking pillows or cushions or covered blocks of foam that pull together for night duty, as well as folding beds that can be hidden behind a screen or stored in a cupboard.

If you do have the luxury of a spare or guest room try to make it the sort of bedroom you yourself would enjoy staying in. Make sure it is pretty, cheerful and clean, with comfortable beds, good lighting, plenty of dressing table space, and if at all possible, a desk or writing table of some sort together with a comfortable chair. If there is a fireplace you could hardly do better than light it for guests; or have a gas flame fire.

Most important of all, try out a guest room from time to time yourself to make sure everything works and is in good order.

Right: A sleeping alcove lined and curtained with washable cheesecloth, and a matching archway, make brilliant use of space in the hallway to accommodate guests. The rather austere grey of the carpet and bed base is softened by the pastel patchwork quilt and heaped cushions.

PUTTING STYLE INTO THE BEDROOM

BEDROOMS

Bedrooms are obviously very personal. They are not on show to outsiders like the living room and can, therefore, be as idiosyncratic, or as fanciful as you like providing that they are quiet to be in and, I repeat, comfortable. If you have a good mattress, a window and some space to play with there is practically no limit to the way you can decorate a bedroom.

Most people, once grown up, have some sort of idea of how they would like their ideal bedroom. If you had a room all to yourself through childhood, or at least from adolescence on, it was the place where you spent hours reading, did your homework, thought great thoughts, made plans, practised an instrument, played music, experimented with make-up, hair and clothes styles, entertained your friends and was, in general, a real refuge. You may have been lucky enough to have had a free hand with its decoration, or you may have had to put up with the same old wallpaper and hand-me-down furnishings, but either way you would have evolved a deep gut feeling for the sort of room you would like to have, given an absolutely free rein.

When it comes to the crunch, of course, and you do have your own place, the bedroom is often the last place to be decorated, or at least decorated in the way you had imagined. But this is almost invariably from lack of funds rather than lack of ideas. People might be short on plans for living rooms but everyone can give a ready opinion on a bedroom.

What's your style?

There are clearly both very feminine and very masculine bedrooms at either end of the scale with compromises for couples made in between. But there are no rules and, interestingly, you often find in the most otherwise modern of households that the main bedroom has been decorated in a traditional way. Old brass, painted iron and pine bedsteads have made a tremendous comeback over the last decade or so. Now too, the

Red and white with strawberries on quilt and pillows, flowers on sheets and walls, add up to a clean, cheerful country bedroom, left, in contrast to the red on red print used for tented ceiling, walls and bedspread in the fantasy-style sleeping alcove of the converted barn, right, which is deliberately sophisticated.

241

PUTTING STYLE INTO THE BEDROOM

four-poster bed has become popular again, whether it is the real thing, a modern version of the same, or an approximation devised with fabric. Half-testers – beds with a canopy which only overshadows the pillow area; filmy drapes attached to a corona; back hangings – all these are currently much in vogue.

All the same, there are certain general styles which are firm favourites and can form a framework, if you like, within which you can incorporate your own personal touches and ideas.

Cottage-in-the-country style rooms with brass or pine beds or pretty fabric bedheads, pine chests and wash-stands; lace or broderie Anglaise or both combined with fresh mini-prints, co-ordinating plains; and stripped floors either covered with rugs or stencilled.

Prosperous Victorian style bedrooms with mahogany or brass beds or fabric four-posters with either a couch or chest at their feet; ruched or Austrian blinds, pelmeted and tied-back curtains; handsome carpets and equally handsome furniture.

Edwardian style bedrooms with brass or fabric-covered beds, possibly with muslin or lace hangings or drapes, dressing tables with muslin skirts and a wealth, as they say, of silver or ivory-backed brushes, combs, mirrors and boxes; probably

prettily flower-printed walls, and again, filmy pull-up curtains or festoon or Austrian or just white holland blinds; a period fireplace and an overmantel.

Real English style would be a mixture of both the above with flowery glazed chintz, probably with leaves and roses, or leaves and birds, deep carpet, deep, maybe well-worn arm chairs, nice mahogany or painted furniture, an imposing bed, lots of cushions, books, prints, pictures and memorabilia. There would be a desk complete with writing paper at the ready and, of course, pretty little posies of sweet-smelling garden flowers everywhere.

Thirties style with perhaps a limed-oak bed or polished mahogany, or a sumptuous Hollywood-style upholstered bedframe; perhaps Jazz Moderne rugs on a carpet, a whole bedroom suite to match the bed and all kinds of 30s details – lamps, cushions, vases, bedspreads – probably collectors items.

French country style might be small flowered patterns: flowered on walls and ceilings, matching fabric on bed, windows and chair covers. This can look splendid in a tiny room with pine, cane or painted furniture, and fruit or flower prints framed in bird's-eye walnut or fruitwood.

Fantasy style could be done entirely in fabric with a fabric tented ceiling,

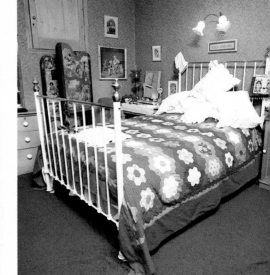

Top left: English eclectic style where practically anything goes as long as it's comfortable, pretty and well-flowered. The modern pine bedside table is quite different from the delicate 19th century bamboo and lacquer dressing chest, but the effect is still charming.

Bottom left: True Edwardiana with drooping lace, lots of wicker and elaborate silver frames.

Bottom near left: A late Victorian bedroom with William Morris-like walls, brass bed, early pine furniture, memorabilia and charming 19th century scrap screen. Only the bedspread is modern though it has the proper old-fashioned air and look to it.

Right: Difficult to define in style, this bedroom could be called prosperous but updated Victorian, or just prettified Mid-Atlantic. The half-tester with its mellow lining matching the eiderdown has two different scales of pattern in the same subtle colouring. The shawl on the upholstered stool blends gently with the cool greys of the dhurrie rug, and the frilly, lacy cushions are matched by the beautiful lace tablecloths. All nicely set off by the soft wicker chair and squashy basket.

243

Left: American Country, and how, with its display of rosettes strung along the mantelpiece, primitive paintings and its Colonial post bed complete with obligatory quilt. The window is always given interesting treatment, here elaborately pelmeted curtains. Upholstered chairs complete this mellow roomful of comfort.

Above: Tailored style with a hint of Japanese, visible in the screen above the bed and the collection of porcelain on the shelves. Colours are muted and disciplined. Furniture lines verge on the severe.

or a fabric four-poster with elaborately shirred top, padded fabric walls, padded bedhead, generously gathered flounce or bedskirt and masses of pretty, feminine cushions, frilled or trimmed with lace, round tables with luxurious skirts and over clothes; or all in Indian mirrored-fabric or lace, with bamboo or mirrored furniture.

American Country style could have a nice Colonial post bed with an old quilt – perhaps in one of the traditional American patchwork designs – polished floors with rag rugs, filmy lace curtains and interesting window treatments, comfortable chairs, good reading lights, naive portraits and masses of cushions. Or it might have a fabric four-poster lined with, perhaps, a check cotton with matching curtains and blinds, ribbon rugs on stripped floors.

Tailored style would be quite the antithesis of all these. Walls might be covered in suede wallcovering or felt or just dark paint or hessian, perhaps given a neat border of brass or contrast fabric of some sort. If there is wallpaper instead it might be dark and geometric. The bed would be neatly tucked with a tailored piped bolster. The window might have Roman blinds; furniture and possibly doors would be mahogany, wardrobe doors would be very well-appointed with interior lighting and mahogany linings.

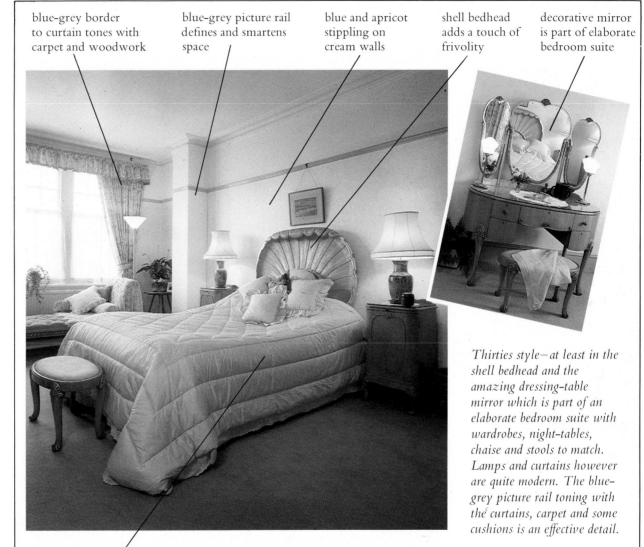

blue-grey border to curtain tones with carpet and woodwork

blue-grey picture rail defines and smartens space

blue and apricot stippling on cream walls

shell bedhead adds a touch of frivolity

decorative mirror is part of elaborate bedroom suite

luxurious bed cover completes opulent 30s feel

Thirties style – at least in the shell bedhead and the amazing dressing-table mirror which is part of an elaborate bedroom suite with wardrobes, night-tables, chaise and stools to match. Lamps and curtains however are quite modern. The blue-grey picture rail toning with the curtains, carpet and some cushions is an effective detail.

Adapting to partners

How to make an essentially feminine room look a little bit more masculine, or at least more asexual, without changing all the furnishings is a problem that faces a great number of couples. And of course the same problem can occur the other way round. In this particular case some clever juggling with colour plus a little sleight of hand resulted in an entirely different look. The only costs involved were for the new soft furnishings and the re-vamped junk couch at the end of the bed. To achieve this turn-around in looks, the ceiling was painted a pale, pale apple green and walls were covered in green felt superimposed with strips of red painted beading to give the illusion of panelling. The white carpet on the floor was exchanged for a green one, old quilt tablecloths were swapped for deep green velvet, and the lace-edged bedlinen was replaced by green, red and white checked sheets with a tartan throw-over and a red corduroy valance. The pink-lined white curtains were ousted by green felt Roman blinds with hardboard pelmets covered in tartan, and the same tartan was used for cushions on the white painted wicker sofa at the end of the bed. Final touches were green-painted woodwork to match blinds and walls and the white mantelpiece 'marbled' with paint to give the room a slightly more study-ish air. Most accessories, paintings and plants were left in exactly the same positions but the room is hardly recognizable.

Bed treatments

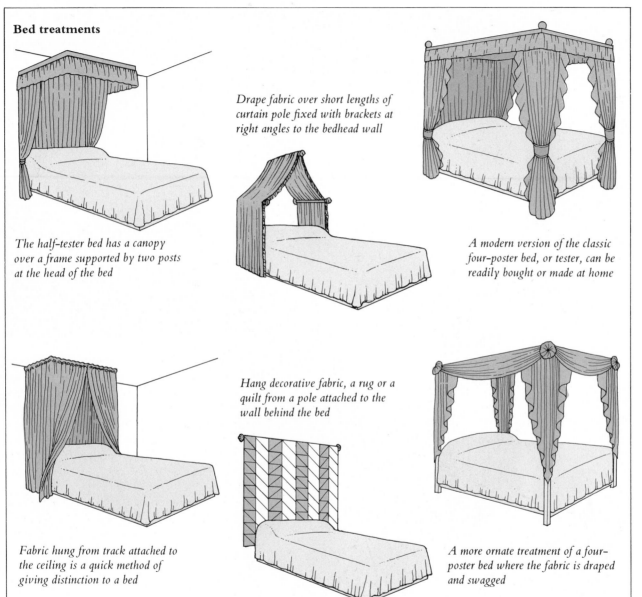

The half-tester bed has a canopy over a frame supported by two posts at the head of the bed

Drape fabric over short lengths of curtain pole fixed with brackets at right angles to the bedhead wall

A modern version of the classic four-poster bed, or tester, can be readily bought or made at home

Fabric hung from track attached to the ceiling is a quick method of giving distinction to a bed

Hang decorative fabric, a rug or a quilt from a pole attached to the wall behind the bed

A more ornate treatment of a four-poster bed where the fabric is draped and swagged

Bedroom-workrooms should manage to integrate a good working (as opposed to writing) desk and all the necessary files and clutter into a peaceful, relaxing bedroom. On the whole, the room would be rather tailored with carpeted floors, perhaps fabric walls, a neat bed which could easily look like, or even be, a sofa bed. Storage would cunningly have extra space for filing cabinets, bookshelves would be extra capacious to take reference works, there would be comfortable chairs and reading lights and perhaps a couch for restful contemplation.

Putting style into the basic bedroom

All the above vignettes are the ideals of course. Unless you are particularly fortunate, you are far more likely to have to try and inject some sort of style into an otherwise fairly basic room. Given that you have just about afforded to paint or paper the room, buy a good bed and carpet or rugs for the floor, what can you do to give it a quick shot of personality?

It is quite easy to make a significant difference with very few and often fairly inexpensive importations. You can add a heap of cushions on a bed, or cover pillows with pillow shams and leave them propped on top of a matching or coordinating bedspread. You might find a pretty chair in a junk shop which you could paint or re-cover the seat; or you could find an old shawl to drape across the foot of a bed or a chair. If there is room, you could get a round wooden table made up and cover it with a fabric skirt and an overskirt in a co-ordinating material. Add a lamp, some odds and ends, a framed photograph or two, a small plant perhaps, and the room will immediately look more inviting.

Then too, you could add a tall plant in a big cane basket, a whole lot of prints, a screen which you could either find and re-cover, or one that you've made yourself. Given the basic screen frame you could stain it mahogany and fill it in with voile or muslin shirred onto stretch wire like the Edwardians used to do. Or make your own version of a Victorian scrap screen either with traditional scrap pictures, which you can still buy, or with your own cut-outs.

Cane or bamboo chairs are cheap, light and attractive, and there will almost always be room, even in the smallest bedroom, for something of this sort. Add a pretty cushion and again you will make a difference. Attractive old bedside lights; a new mirror; an upholstered stool; tie-backs or a contrast border added to curtains, or a blind underneath; a paper border stuck all round the walls; such comfortable touches, and they are really no more than these, can make an amazing change to an undistinguished bedroom.

Left: The bedroom area of this Hi-Tech studio/loft has been divided, at least visually, from the living area by the blue-painted steel scaffolding-like structure slung just below the ceiling. The same sort of girders are criss-crossed across the window and covered by Venetian blinds.

Above: A vividly covered bed does not look out of place in this basically pine bed/workroom. In fact, it's just what the room needs.

249

PUTTING STYLE INTO THE BEDROOM

Designing from scratch

If you do have the chance to design a bedroom from scratch you are really very lucky, although couples might not think so after they have spent hours quarrelling about who should give in to whom about ideas! A sybarite might never have realized that he or she had linked up with a Spartan until the subject of decoration came up. The important thing, of course, is to learn how to compromise in a way that is comfortable and agreeable to both partners.

Discuss the subject thoroughly, pool your ideas, look around, see what you can afford and what you must discard and don't be afraid to take your time. If the bedroom is to be the restorative room it should be, then it is worth spending a long while to get it right. If you need to buy a bed, buy a good one, and a rug, and hang your clothes from hooks until you have worked out the best furnishings and methods of storage to suit you both.

If you do not have to consider a partner you are in luck again, and if you do not have to worry too much about a budget you are luckier still, although it actually helps to have the supporting framework of a limited budget. It immediately cuts down on the available choice and actually encourages you to compromise, to be ingenious, to think up new solutions which make for a much more

personal room in the end.

If you have no very set ideas on what you like, then the best thing to do, as always, is to buy what books and magazines you can, and go conscientiously through the pages marking the rooms that appeal. Or it may be that you like one idea here, another there. Note them all, see what you can afford, and go from there. There really has never been such a choice in co-ordinated wall-coverings and fabrics, bedheads, lamps, carpets, blinds, china, rugs and bedlinen. And don't forget that sheets can make splendid curtains, bedhangings and table-cloths.

Style with comfort

As I have said before, comfort should be the overriding theme of any bedroom. Of course, standards of comfort vary. What is comfortable for one, is suffocating for another. Some people are only comfortable with soft opulence; others thrive on simplicity and firm lines. The important thing to remember is that whatever style of room you choose, make sure that everything in it functions in the best possible way. Mattresses should be the best you can afford; storage should be really functional; lights should be the correct height and intensity for reading, bed linen should be comforting and beds should be easy to make.

Real comfort and style depend as much as anything else on the small

touches. The little details that count are things like inconspicuous but capacious waste paper baskets; containers of tissues and cotton wool always to hand; carafes and glasses for water, or bottles of mineral water; nicely lined drawers and cupboards complete with sweet-smelling sachets; curtains and blinds that pull easily and fit well. Some people like to wake up with a chink of light, others most decidedly do not, so try to determine this in the beginning. If you are having curtains

specially made for you, ask for them to be made light-proof, and be sure to stipulate this right at the beginning. If you possess curtains that are not sufficiently light-proof, consider putting up black-out blinds behind them, or ordinary roller blinds lined with black-out fabric. People often forget in the first rush of enthusiasm for romantic, filmy curtains, that the same fabric is not nearly so romantic during a cold night in winter, or first thing in the morning after a particularly late night.

Left: Mirrored alcoves and an all white room look luxurious, though the treatment is simple and fairly inexpensive.

Above: A skirted table to match the curtains, blue and white china and a blue painted wicker chair make this room instantly more romantic.

Right: A neutral scheme is given immediate impact by converting the standard double divan into a handsome draped four-poster.

Starting over again

If you are sick and tired of your old bedroom but cannot afford to start over again, don't despair. Go into action with one or two or more of the instant improvement suggestions mentioned earlier. A new wallpaper alone might do wonders. If that's too expensive, add one of the new borders around the room, or superimpose a fabric border, stuck with an appropriate adhesive.

A crisp, pretty new bedspread or valance wouldn't break the bank and there has never been a wider or more exciting choice around than there is now. If you hate throwing things away that still have life in them you could always cut up your old spread to make cushion covers or move it to another room.

A stunning and dramatic way to change the look of the whole room is simply to give the bed an entirely different treatment by making a fabric four-poster or half-tester or interesting back hangings.

Even changing your old bedside tables for two skirted round tables introduces a softer, more romantic look. If you have not got a tv in the room try bringing one in for your own private viewing away from the family; or add some bookshelves and more pictures, or a comfortable chair, stool or desk if you can afford it and have the space. The bedroom really is the easiest room to alter with the minimum of effort and expense.

BEDROOMS

Any problem is easier to solve if you can break it down into various components. It is the same with the decoration of a room. If you think – in the case of a bedroom – of walls, floor, ceiling, windows, bed, furniture, fabrics, and – last but not least – lighting, and then take each of them in turn, deciding what you can and cannot do, the whole exercise becomes very much more simple. It helps too, to commit it all to paper in the form of a check list which you can refer to and revise as you go.

Although most people would obviously think of the bed as the most important ingredient of a bedroom, it is still necessary, as in any room, to get the actual framework (walls, ceiling, floor and windows) planned out in detail even if it can't be done all at once. If you cannot afford to complete the whole room right away, at least knowing what you hope to do will help you avoid the sort of mistakes and compromises which could spoil the final look.

Walls and ceilings

Bedroom walls can either be painted, papered, or covered with fabric (or wood, or carpet, or some other covering if you are daring). Three things will guide and affect your choice: the position, condition, proportion and shape of the room, your existing furnishings and your budget. Although ceilings are very often neglected, the same applies to them, and they can make an enormous difference to the look of a room.

Paint

Paint is generally the cheapest way to cover a wall as long as the wall is in good condition to start with. If it is not, you should make it good and at the same time find out the cause of any stains on walls or ceiling and have them dealt with. If walls are merely uneven and the house is old and in the country, you might actually like to keep a slightly bumpy look. Or you might prefer to disguise the defects with an alternative wallcovering such as paper or fabric, which will cover a multitude of sins.

The fern theme gives unity to the bedroom on the left. They are printed on the creamy wallcovering, repeated in the cotton blinds, window seat and valance and woven into the lace tablecloths and bedspread. A nice bare room, right, where wood predominates and blue paint provides impact.

253

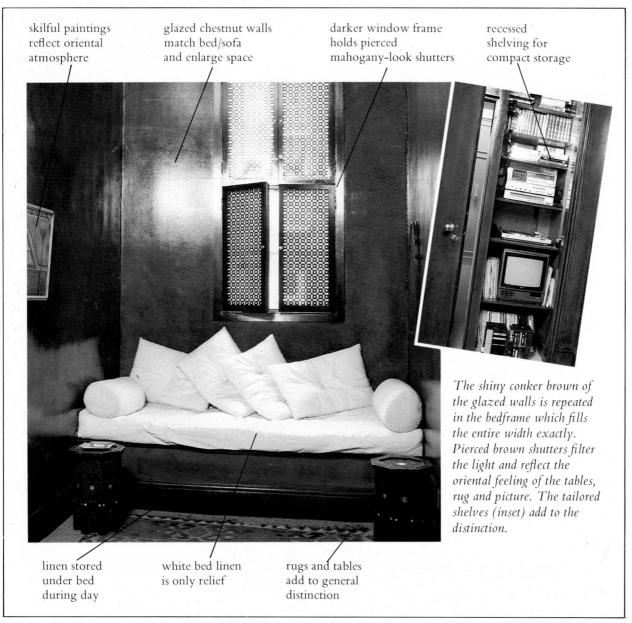

skilful paintings reflect oriental atmosphere

glazed chestnut walls match bed/sofa and enlarge space

darker window frame holds pierced mahogany-look shutters

recessed shelving for compact storage

The shiny conker brown of the glazed walls is repeated in the bedframe which fills the entire width exactly. Pierced brown shutters filter the light and reflect the oriental feeling of the tables, rug and picture. The tailored shelves (inset) add to the distinction.

linen stored under bed during day

white bed linen is only relief

rugs and tables add to general distinction

Colour counts If you do decide to paint, the next thing to consider is colour. If you want to put the focus on the furnishings and have a laid-back, relaxed scheme, choose neutral tones: soft white, soft cream; pearl grey, sand, camel or blush pink. Woodwork and ceiling could be white, or you could paint them the same shade as the walls if you want the space to seem as large as possible.

If the room receives little or no light, choose a warm colour, unless you are prepared to keep white walls very white all the time which means frequent re-painting. Make sure there is plenty of clear colour in the room as well: pinks, greens, apricots or yellows, with a lot of mirror and sparkle. One of the most spectacular bedrooms I have seen was mostly white, but the white curtains were lined with rose, there were white and rose cushions on the bed, great pots of marguerites in baskets, and above all the flicker of flames from a gas flame fire – the fireplace, of course, being a splendid extra bonus. All white-on-white rooms, pristine and beautiful as they can be, are really only good in a hot and sunny climate or in a well-staffed household. Dark walls can be restful in a bedroom. I once had a dark room with an off-white carpet, ceiling and wood-work, and the room always seemed to trap the light within itself in some mysterious way, mostly because the brown was sandwiched between very light colours. Darkish tones can also make a room seem much better funished than it is: dark green, dark rose, chestnut, dark blue, are all sophisticated and will give incidental colours used with them much more of a glow in contrast.

Finishing touches Painted walls can be pepped up in a variety of ways. You could add one of the many new paper borders just under the cornice or cove if there is one, or just under the ceiling if there is not. Or you could run a contrast fabric or webbing border (to match curtains say, or carpet) under the ceilings, around doors and windows and over the top of skirtings or base boards.

You could make your own panelled effect with lengths of beading or picture framing stuck on the walls in rectangles or squares or both. Framers will often sell it by the foot if you ask, and it comes in natural wood (paint it to suit your scheme), gilt and silver. If you can first work out the panels to scale on a plan of the room, so much the better. If not, at least draw it out on the walls carefully with a long ruler, chalk or pencil, and use a level. When this has been completed the 'panels' can be painted in a contrast of a darker or lighter tone to the main body of the wall.

Another idea is to make a dado, again with picture framing or

Top left: This heavily beamed and joisted room at the top of an old warehouse building was made light and charming with a simple coat of all-white paint.

Bottom left: An abstract pattern of yellow and blue allied to Indian cotton bedspread and cushions and an Indian carving makes the most of what could have been an unprepossessing space.

Top right: The walls were panelled out with carefully painted lines to make this room look larger and more distinguished.

GETTING THE FRAMEWORK RIGHT

moulding or even something like a double border of grosgrain ribbon. All you have to do is to run whatever frame you have chosen around the room at dado height about 90 cm (3 ft) and fill the space below with contrast paint, or paper.

Alternatively, you can try out one of the many decorative finishes like rag-rolling, stippling, dragging, colour washing, shading, glazing or lacquering which have now become fashionable again. Clear instructions for all these techniques can be found in specialist books on decorative paintwork. There is a variety of excellent manuals to choose from, full of ideas to spark you off.

Wallpaper

Quite apart from softening the look of a room wallpaper is also an excellent disguiser of awkward angles, architectural imperfections and wardrobes or closets which might otherwise break up the harmony of a space. It is also, of course, a splendid unifier for rooms that seem all doors and windows since the paper design will link the unbroken areas together, especially if woodwork is painted in one of the colours of the paper.

There is such an enormous choice of wallpapers now in every sort of scale, colour, design and price, many of them with their own co-ordinated borders, 'partner' papers (for alcoves, behind bookcases etc.)

Painted tendrils of flowers wind their way round walls, window frame and cotton blind in an otherwise all-white room, top left. Paint is used decoratively again, top right, in this yellow-ceilinged and carpeted room where painted graphics add further interest to an already colourful scheme. Swags of painted stencilled flowers on doors, bed curtains and border, bottom left, are echoed by stencilled garlands on walls and bed linen. A painted green landscape brings an element of surprise to a formerly rather dull room, bottom right.

Left: Green and white mini-print wallpaper and a matching border make the most of a tiny space which is dominated by a decorated pine bed and knitted patch quilt. The useful storage hampers under the bed are repeated in larger scale by the wicker laundry basket. Notice the build-up of colour in rug, towels, plants and cushions.

Top right: Wallpaper and paint have been cunningly used in this bedroom. The ceiling looks twice as high and twice as interesting with its two-tone, two-scale wallpaper and paper border separated by white painted mouldings. Walls are in a paler version of the same paper with mouldings on wardrobe doors picked out in white.

257

Finishing touches

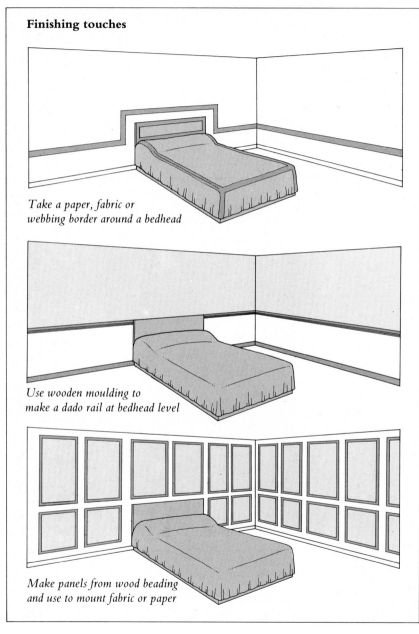

Take a paper, fabric or webbing border around a bedhead

Use wooden moulding to make a dado rail at bedhead level

Make panels from wood beading and use to mount fabric or paper

and fabrics for an effortlessly unified look, that the problem is rather eliminating the unsuitables than finding the right ones.

Small rooms can be made very much more interesting by using co-ordinated or matching wallpapers and fabrics for walls, ceilings, windows, soft furnishings and the bed. The repetition of a single pattern, the use of the positive and negative of a design, or different scales of the same pattern, will add immediate distinction to a space and an all-over flower design for example, will add instant summery freshness to an otherwise dingy area.

How to cheat with wallpaper
What happens if the particular paper you've set your heart on is hopelessly expensive? Don't abandon the idea. The answer is to cheat a little. You could have it, or at least the effect of it, by painting your walls the background colour of the paper with matt paint, and then using the paper itself in panels. By doing this you can get away with the minimum number of rolls – maybe only one if your room is not very big. Or you could use a small amount of paper up to dado height in much the same way as I suggested with paint earlier on.

At the other end of the scale, cheaper wallpaper can be made to look much better and will last much longer if it is given a coat or two of matt or eggshell polyurethane –

allowing the first coat to dry thoroughly before adding a second. The polyurethane will yellow the paper a little, but this often has the happy effect of making it look more mellow, and certainly more practical since it can then be wiped clean with a sponge or damp cloth.

Preparing the walls If there was a previous wallcovering it may need to be stripped off before you start with the new. Old wallpaper can only be left if it was well put up in the first place, that is to say butt-edged with no lumps, bumps or wrinkles. If you are putting up a vinyl covering, any old paper will have to come off first. Likewise any old vinyl wallcovering must always be removed before putting up new paper. Any previously painted walls must be free from grease and dirt otherwise the adhesive will not work. So wash the walls down with water mixed with detergent or household ammonia, and for a really professional job, line walls with good quality lining paper before applying your wallpaper.

Fabric wallcoverings
Fabric walls are particularly appropriate in the bedroom for their look of softness and luxury and for their sound and heat insulating properties. There are a good many specially treated fabrics, some of them paper-backed and flame-

proofed, sold especially for the purpose, the most common being felt, hessian or burlap, suede fabric, wool, silk, moiré, grasscloth, linen, cotton and denim, all of which should be spot cleanable.

But it is quite possible to put up just about any fabric, fixing it in position by one of the following methods:

Sticking Firmly woven fabric, which will deter any adhesive from seeping through the weave, may be stuck to the wall like wallpaper. The adhesive must be applied to the wall, not the fabric.

Stapling Use a proper electric staple-gun and choose materials with the sort of design which will help to conceal seams. If you can line the walls with a layer of padding so much the better: the effect will be very like the soft, upholstered look of battening but achieved with far less trouble. Seam the fabric first before you start applying it. Any frayed edges can be covered with a matching, contrasting or co-ordinated braid, or lengths of picture

Cool greeny-grey cotton is here gathered on rods fixed just below the cornice and just above the skirting. The top of the lace-edged Austrian blind is gathered to match, and the general softness is repeated in the generous fall of the flowered cloth.

259

Fabric techniques

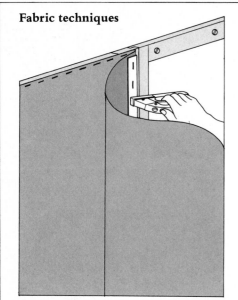

Fabric stapled over battens

Fabric may be staple-gunned either directly to the wall or stretched over wood battens which have been previously screwed into the wall

A wall-track system is an almost foolproof way of fixing fabric to walls and requires neither glue, nor battens nor staples.

Fabric hung loosely from poles provides instant drama and is easy to put up and take down

Gathered fabric stretched between curtain tracks, fixed immediately below the ceiling and above the skirting board, looks luxurious

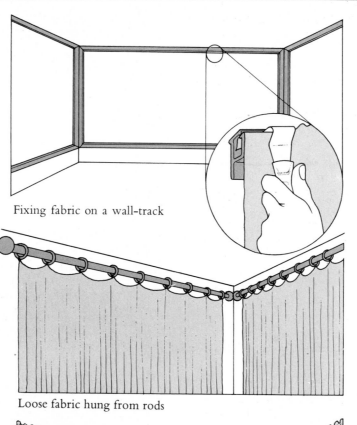

Fixing fabric on a wall-track

Loose fabric hung from rods

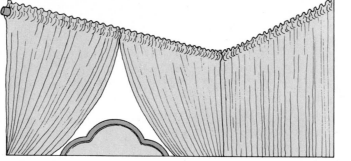

Gathered fabric on tracks

framing, or strips of brass, chrome or wood beading, depending on your taste and pocket.

The wall-track system This consists of lengths of track which you can fix all round the wall just below the ceiling and above the skirting or base boards. The seamed fabric is clipped into the track at the top and stretched down to be clipped into the bottom track. It is practical because fabric can be taken down for cleaning, moving or just changing.

Walling or battening Upholstering a wall, or 'walling' or 'battening' as it is called in the trade, means stretching pre-seamed fabric over strips of thin wood or battens which have been lined with strips of synthetic fibre padding. It is quite complicated, but well justified by the final result. It looks professional and luxurious and, in addition, its double layer helps to muffle sound and preserve heat.

Probably the best way to do it is to staple the battens horizontally, just below the ceiling or mouldings and just above the skirting. Take vertical strips of wood cut to the size required (i.e. the height from skirting board to ceiling) and fix them at metre (three foot) intervals all round the walls. If you plan to have paintings or prints on the wall, work out where their positions are likely to be and fix your battens in these places. Remember to make provision for wall-fixed lighting, sockets, and switches at the same time. When the fabric is up the battens can easily be felt through it and hooks or nails hammered through in seconds.

Thumb tack lengths of padding between the strips, then stretch the fabric and tack it to the battens. Cover the tack marks with lengths of braid which should also be used round the top and bottom of the fabric and around doors and windows to hide frayed edges.

Hanging Hung fabric looks especially soft and appealing when draped on the walls like curtains and is a useful method when money or time – or both – is short. It's good for temporary accommodation since the fabric can be taken down and moved. It can also be cleaned very easily since it can be removed from its fixings and put in the washing machine or sent to the cleaners.

There are several ways of hanging it. Very light (and inexpensive) fabrics like cheesecloth, muslin, or cotton can be shirred onto stretch wire or long thin poles attached just below the ceiling and just above the skirtings or baseboards in much the same way as fabric is fixed onto those nice old-fashioned fabric screens. Heavier fabrics can be suspended from more substantial poles, either shirred, or from rings, and left hanging loose and just touching the floor. Catch fabric back over win-

dows (use blinds underneath) and doors, fireplaces and wardrobes or closets and either cover any bits of wall thus exposed with matching wallpaper if it exists, or have extra short bits of fabric in those areas.

Be different, be daring
Although paint, wallpaper and fabric are the most popular wall-coverings for bedrooms there is nothing to stop you using unusual alternatives. Quilts or bedspreads for instance, can look very exotic – Indian cotton bedspreads make marvellously inexpensive wall-coverings if you can get matching, or nearly matching ones – or what about rolls of bamboo or oriental matchstick like the kind used for blinds – or even a series of blinds themselves let loose and hung side by side if the ceiling is fairly low and the blinds are long, or if you have a picture rail.

One of the simplest ideas is to use double sheets which are in any case the cheapest way of buying a lot of seamless fabric. Or you can buy sheeting by the metre (yard) in a wide range of beautiful colours and patterns. Even carpet, or fake fur if your tastes run to it. I once saw a bedroom entirely lined with sheepskin on ceiling, floor and walls and the effect was like a woolly igloo. All these alternatives can be coverings stapled or stuck according to the weight of the material.

Plain and patterned Indian cottons have been used to line this sleeping alcove, along with bordered Indian bedspreads. Ceiling and wall fabric have been stapled onto battens and stretched. Bedspreads used as curtains are pulled across a bamboo pole for privacy at night. By day the alcove becomes transformed into a comfortable, stylish sitting area.

GETTING THE FRAMEWORK RIGHT

Floors

On the whole, I think, bedroom floors should be soft, or at least have rugs by the bed, as much for comfort and warmth underfoot as for reducing noise.

If your choice is carpet, be sure to choose the right grade, usually described as bedroom grade; it does not need to be of the same hard-wearing quality, and therefore high price, as carpet for the living room, hall and staircase. In a guest room, you can get away with an even less hard-wearing carpet unless you have a perpetual stream of guests. If you feel you cannot afford carpet for the moment you can always compromise temporarily with extra thick felt topped with rugs to distribute the wear and tear. Or it might be worth while considering carpet tiles which are comparatively inexpensive, and can be taken up if you move.

If you have a wood floor in good condition, it can be stripped, sanded and polished, or bleached to a much paler colour and then adorned with rugs. Wood in not particularly good condition could be painted or painted and stencilled and again given rugs where necessary. Pick up a colour in the curtains or walls, or paint the floor a neutral colour, like white or cream or bluey grey or – very popular in America – Indian red or terracotta.

As long as you coat the paint with a couple of coats of eggshell polyurethane (left to dry a good twelve hours in between each coat) you do not need to use expensive gloss or enamels. Give the boards a couple of layers of undercoat tinted with the final colour and you can get away with just one coat of flat or eggshell oil or alkyd (oil-based) paint. Alternatively you could use yacht or deck paint for a denser effect.

If you feel like stencilling painted floors it should be done before the final coats of polyurethane. Stencil kits, complete with a charming choice of designs and detailed instructions, are sold in specialist stationers and art and craft shops. You could also cover old boards with vinyl tiles or sheeting or linoleum, especially if you livened it up with inset borders or a patterned inset of your own design.

Top right: Vividly-painted floor boards, tone with equally vivid bedspreads, and rugs echo the paintings in a painter's colourful room.

Bottom right: Large striped cotton rugs tone well with the quilts on wall and bed and the decorative cushions.

Far right: White carpet and matching white wool wall covering make a luxurious background for the tailored black and white bedspread, curtains and right-angled unit furniture.

GETTING THE FRAMEWORK RIGHT

Windows

Few of us have beautiful, elegant bedroom windows; sometimes they are downright ordinary but quite often they are just unusual enough to present problems when it comes to decorating. Whether you have bows, bays, casements, dormers, skylights, sloping or otherwise oddly shaped or proportioned windows, explore all the possibilities of curtains, sheers, blinds and shutters before deciding on the treatment. There are all sorts of decorative tricks you can resort to to overcome awkward or ugly windows and which will actually transform a negative feature into a very positive asset.

Windows worth looking at

Bedroom windows can be treated to look as romantic, as spare or as chaste as your taste, circumstances and the actual shape of the window – and its view – dictate. If a window is unusually beautiful or just plain unusual, it might be better to show it off rather than hide it with curtains. But you will almost certainly want some sort of covering for it in a bedroom, for even if you are not overlooked you might well want to block out the light occasionally. In this case it would be better to have a blind or café curtain which would still show off the frame and shape by day. Alternatively, translucent (but

not see-through) screening could be used if you only want occasional privacy.

Blinds and shades

Blinds might be the plain roller variety, or the more tailored Roman blinds which fold up on each other in flat horizontal pleats, or the softer festoon, or Austrian blinds or pull-up curtains or balloon blinds. All

these last five categories have vertical tapes through which pull cords are drawn to raise and lower the blind or shade. Or again, there are Venetian, bamboo, matchstick, pinoleum or vertical louvred varieties. In fact, whatever your style or requirements, there's a blind to match them. If there is nothing particularly extraordinary about the window or windows, and, let's face it, there very

Top left: Elegantly ruched Austrian blinds with gathered headings soften the rather harsh modern windows in an otherwise tailored room.

Top right: Shiny olive green painted shutters add just the right subtlety of colour in this Mediterranean-style room. Note the nice change of textures introduced by the creamy crocheted cushions and plant.

often is not, but you have a radiator under the sill which you do not want to cover, or a piece of furniture there like a desk or dressing table or even the bed itself, you could still use a blind rather than short curtains. Or if you want to be really lavish and like the look of it you can use blinds with dress curtains, or curtains proper which can be elegantly arranged and tied back either side. This sort of treatment will make any window look soft and graceful and will help to cut out any unwelcome morning light which could otherwise intrude around the edges of the blind.

Incidentally, if morning light is a problem, or if you work at night and have to sleep during the day make sure that the fabric of your blinds is backed with a black-out material or thermal lining. And if somebody else is making the blinds for you, inform them right at the start that you want black-out backings. It is pretty well impossible to laminate black-out material onto already-made roller blinds and cumbersome to do it on all other finished varieties. In any event, festoon or Austrian or pull-up curtains only really look good in light filmy fabrics, so if you want that effect have them in conjunction with properly lined and interlined curtains that can be drawn across on top of them. Or have them with concealed black-out-backed roller blinds that can be pulled down underneath beforehand.

Blind identikit
Blinds are a useful adjunct to window decoration, whether used on their own or in conjunction with curtains. They come in all kinds of textures, sizes and prices ranging from the relatively inexpensive pinoleum or matchstick and bamboo, through Venetian and vertical louvres to the more expensive custom-made fabric varieties.

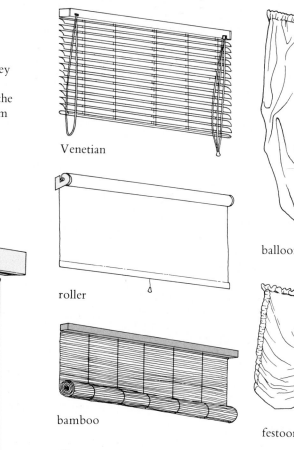

Venetian

roller

bamboo

vertical louvre

pinoleum or matchstick

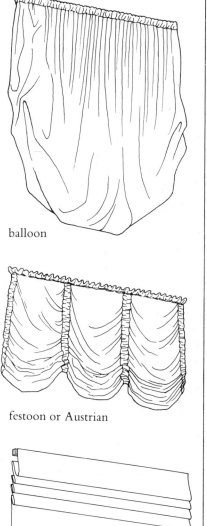

balloon

festoon or Austrian

Roman

Create an illusion

It is quite easy to change the look and apparent proportion of windows by the sort of window treatment you give them. These are some of the tricks you can use to deceive – and please – the eye.

To make a window look taller Fix the curtain track or rod 15–20 cm (6–8 in) above the top of the frame. This is most effective at night when the curtains are down over the track. If you have a deep pelmet fixed about 20 cm (8 in) above the frame, the windows will always look taller during the day as well.

To make a narrow window look wider Choose a wider track or rod than the window frame so that curtains hang either side of the frame instead of overlapping any part of the window. This will also let in more light.

To make an over-tall window look shorter This is not often necessary, but if it is, put up a deep shaped pelmet or gathered valance, which will distract the eye from the expanse of glass.

To make a wide window look narrower Let curtains meet in the middle and loop them back at the sides with tie-backs or cords or deep ribbon.

To make a small high window look larger You could raise the height of the floor below by making a platform. If this is too complicated, hang café curtains on a pole which is wider than the frame.

To make the most of an arched frame Try to fix a curved track, pelmet or valance to follow the contours of the window. If this is not possible, put up a pole or track high enough and wide enough to allow curtains to clear the frame during the day.

To do without net curtains If a window faces on the street so that you need privacy but don't like the look of net curtains think of using a roller blind which pulls up from the bottom, rather than down from the top. This way you will get both light and privacy.

To make a narrow window wider hang curtains well to either side

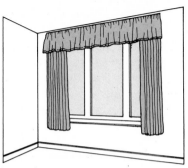

To make a window look taller fix track well above the frame

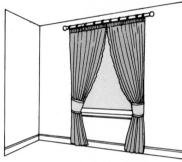

Make a wide window narrower by making curtains meet

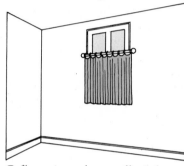

Café curtains make a small window bigger

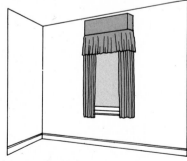

Deep pelmets shorten a too-tall window

Up-pulling roller blinds are a good alternative to net curtaining

Choosing curtains

To get the best value and effect from your curtains it's important to bear certain points in mind: be generous with the amount of material – it's fatal to skim; line them and if possible interline – they'll hang better and keep out unwanted light and draughts; get the length right – they should either reach the floor or the sill, nothing in between. (Short curtains are best kept for tiny cottage or attic windows.) Then go for the sort of curtain treatment that will be in keeping with the general style you are aiming for in the room.

The romantic, country look For this you might want rather heavy formal tied-back curtains in lace, muslin or net. Or you might decide on billowing floating lace curtains, or fresh broderie Anglaise over a more substantial holland roller blind.

Pelmets of all sorts seem to be making a come-back; deep gently-gathered fabric pelmets or valances, which might be edged or bordered, over tied-back curtains in a flowery print can look charming. A real pelmet is usually fabric-covered board or buckram, or a smooth stretch of fabric; soft, gathered tops are known as valances.

Creamy-white gathered curtains are here tied back over plain white roller blinds in a monochromatic room where the emphasis is on texture.

GETTING THE FRAMEWORK RIGHT

Top: White Austrian blinds under white curtains frame a sea view.

Above: Short chintz curtains look right in a cottage room.

Right: An attractive window seat.

The cottage look Sill-length curtains have an immediate cottage feel. They could be frilled along the leading (inner) edges and tied back with ribbons perhaps, or used in conjunction with either a gathered café curtain, or a café curtain on a pole for slightly more importance. If windows are very tiny, and the rooms rather dark, as happens frequently in old cottages, it might be better to hang a blind just above the architrave so that no light is shut out or wasted during the day. Alternatively, you could do away with any sort of curtain or blind and use the window like a picture frame to encapsulate the view. With equal simplicity you could just have a vase of flowers, a plant, a single stem in a glass, or some sort of pretty object on the sill and leave it at that.

The tailored look If you use curtains in spare, tailored, rather masculine rooms they could be in tweed or corduroy or woven wool hanging from a wooden or brass pole. But these sort of rooms might look best with roller or Roman blinds which could be edged or given a double or inset border. Crisp vertical blinds would also be in keeping, or wooden or Venetian blinds in an aluminium finish for real slickness.

Saving money – saving time

Custom-made curtains and blinds can be expensive because you are paying for labour, expertise and fabric. Ready-made on the other hand, are about half the price, come in a huge choice of colours, designs and styles, unlined, lined and sometimes thermal-lined and can be bought, taken home and hung up within a day. The only problem is that they come in standard sizes and while this is not a problem with the width it does often affect the length. This can sometimes be overcome by adding a deep border in a contrast or co-ordinating fabric and making it look intended by adding tie-backs in the same material.

Obviously, you get what you want and save money by making curtains and blinds yourself and there are now numerous books to tell you how to do it, but you can save time by improvising as well. Bedspreads, particularly Indian bedspreads and sheets can make excellent window coverings. All you have to do is turn over the tops to make a pocket for a rod or track, possibly add tie-backs – and hey-presto – you have instant curtains. Use the same material or bedspread on the bed for an instantly co-ordinated effect.

You do not even have to turn over the top come to that. Rods with clip-on café rings, like shower curtains, could do away with all sewing and give extra length – useful if the spreads are not quite long enough to reach the skirting board.

Shutters and screens

You are not, of course, limited to curtains, blinds or shades; there are other alternatives. Shutters and screens can make excellent window coverings and give an interesting architectural look to a room. Shutter panels can be bought louvred, in solid or open framework panels, and, in America, louvres, vertical and vaned shutters can be adjustable or stationary as you like. Open framework panels are also useful because you can insert shirred fabric, decorative glass or grill work of some kind into them. Solid panel shutters can be covered in fabric or wallpaper, painted or stencilled. If a room is rather small and otherwise broken up, solid shutters covered in the same finish as the walls will give much more unity to the space.

The Japanese Shoji screen with its black lacquered framework and translucent panels is another decorative way of letting in light without sacrificing your privacy. They are fairly widely available and can be made up by a good carpenter or handyman using, say, cheesecloth or lightweight sheets as the infill, and are especially useful for windows with a dreary outlook.

Hinged reversible screens which can be covered in different fabrics or finishes and reversed according to season or mood (try one side mirror, another side a colour to go with either soft furnishings, carpet or

walls) will make even an undistinguished short window look long, graceful and a decorative feature in its own right. Use them like shutters with a couple of panels on each side of the window which will meet in the middle when shut.

Shoji screens form a bed alcove as well as partitioning off the room in general in a Japanese designed room. An interesting contrast of textures and scale is made by the much coarser vertical lines of the bamboo window covering. The room seems calm and serene and when you look carefully at the various features in it you will notice that every surface has a different texture, and that, far from conflicting with each other, they, like the subdued colours, all blend into one mellow, harmonious whole.

269

The importance of lighting

As in all but the most functional rooms, bedroom lighting should be as good to look at as it is to see by. And in bedrooms it is particularly important that both general background lighting and specific lights for working or making-up are as warm and welcoming and restful as possible.

There are three main areas in which light should be concentrated: the head of the bed, the dressing area, and the dressing-table. It is also useful to have ancillary areas of light in wardrobes, on any side tables, beside any armchairs, and perhaps concealed behind plants or in corners in the form of uplights.

Plan ahead

Whether you are planning a room from scratch or just trying to improve it, try to have outlets or points positioned where the bed is to go, near the dressing-table, and the main room light in such a position that anyone dressing could have a clear undistorted vision in the looking glass. If you are planning on having wall-mounted lights over the bed, get them wired in before the walls are decorated. It is a good idea to

Left: Ceiling-mounted downlights are draped with flame-proofed lace to form decorative backings to these twin beds as well as to provide good reading light in bed.

Different shades of opinion: Period lamps like the art nouveau lamp, top left, and the converted brass oil lamp, top centre, are as important for the atmosphere they provide as they are functional. The third table lamp, top right, is modern but, like the other two, is decorative as well as useful. Each has been used as the focal point of a charming still life carefully echoing the surrounding objects as well as illuminating them. On the right, lighting is provided by the wall light as well as the more flexible swan-necked floor lamp, which provides good reading light both in bed and for working at the chest-cum-desk.

271

install dual operating controls at the same time; that is, one switch by the bed and a second one by door. It is always useful to get points put into corners of a room because it allows flexibility with uplights, floor lamps, and any other appliance that you might wish to use, like hair dryers, vacuum cleaners, a fan or extra heater.

Light for reading

Bedside table lamps should be high enough to shine on a book, but not so high as to disturb anyone else. Swing arm wall lamps placed just above the bedhead and slightly to the side are good, especially if they have dimmer switches to allow one partner to read without disturbing the other. Incidentally, in this respect there are now tiny extra lamps to keep on a bedside table which are adequate for reading or making notes in the middle of the night. Adjustable spots (again on a dimmer) or small angled lights are another solution. Table lamps should have the sort of shades that cast light downwards, rather than up.

If there are any armchairs or chaises in the room where you can relax and read, the best solution is to have either a table lamp on a small side table, or a floor standing lamp of some sort, like a brass pharmacy light, which you can move around to suit your particular needs and which does not look out of place.

Light for dressing

Light for dressing is usually the general or ambient light in a room. If the ceiling can take recessed downlights so much the better. They will give better and softer overall illumination. If you cannot do this and have to use a ceiling point try using a Japanese paper shade, or a pretty pendant which will diffuse the light rather than emit an over bright glare. If there is no ceiling point, or you prefer not to have a central light you can either use table lamps switched from the door, or wall-mounted uplights which will bounce light off the ceiling and give a soft overall light – especially beautiful and flattering if the ceiling is white or a pale cream or pinkish blush.

In general, fluorescent bulbs of any sort are to be avoided in bedrooms, although they get better and better all the time; incandescent light is still better for clothes and make-up. However, if a room is very dark it does not hurt to conceal fluorescent tubes under valances or pelmets just over the window to give extra concealed light from the point where you would most expect it. You can have light thrown up to the ceiling and you can have light falling down onto curtains or blinds.

Light for make-up

If you have a dressing-table in the bedroom it is very important to have the sort of light fittings that will throw light onto your face. If you can have both top and side light so much the better. Strip lights on top of a mirror are not nearly so good as a down light fixed just above the dressing table area boosted by lights either side. The sort of strip that people have on top of a mirror is not really very effective, but of course it is perfectly possible to get a domestic version of the theatrical mirrors with lights all round that actresses have in their dressing rooms. Although not particularly beautiful, they could hardly give you a clearer picture of yourself. If you can, use them in conjunction with a dimmer switch, unless your face can stand up to the sort of brutal frankness that they provide when turned full beam.

Top left: Four draped pendant lights hung at varying heights give a pleasant, general light to this room as well as highlighting the collection of postcards and the desk.

Bottom left: Theatrical make-up bulbs are set into the sides of the mirror at this dramatic dressing table. Note how the expanse of mirror ties in beautifully with the glass knobs and the transparent perspex stool.

Right: A covered baffle hides fluorescent general light in this room; articulated reading lamps are poised at just the right height.

Since we are always being told that we spend a third of our lives asleep, or at least in bed, it is extraordinary how neglectful we are about actually choosing and buying a bed. People spend days fussing about what make of car to buy, its performance, potential and looks, whilst a bed, in which they are probably going to pass many more hours, rarely gets more than a perfunctory look and prod. Not that a bed is a life investment, for even the best mattress won't last for ever, but given a good choice, you should at least get a decade or so of comfortable use from it – and with care, several more years after that.

If you have had the same bed for years you should definitely take a good hard look at the mattress. Is the surface lumpy? Are the edges sagging? Are there any ridges and hollows? Can you feel the springs when you press it with your hands? If the answer is yes to even one of these questions, you should start looking for a new mattress forthwith.

The mattress matters

There are four different kinds of mattresses to choose from: foam, interior sprung or inner spring, water-filled and air-filled.

The foam variety is made from latex rubber or polyurethane which is manufactured in large slabs and cut to size. Latex rubber ones are the most expensive, but because of their high cost are scarce. High-resilience polyurethane mattresses, or mattresses with embedded thermoplastic beads give good support and last well and are usually dense and quite heavy. A lightweight foam mattress, therefore, is not usually of good quality and will not last long.

Interior sprung or inner spring mattresses are made of coiled springs sandwiched between insulating materials and usually come in two varieties: those with pocketed springs and those with open springs. Pocketed springs are individual units, coiled, compressed and sewn into calico pockets, unaffected by the compression of neighbouring springs and so particularly good for double beds with two partners of widely differing weights.

A nicely rustic four-poster made from branches in an equally rustic room, left, is set off by lace-trimmed linen. Equally imposing, right, triple mirrored arches edged in black make a dramatic bedhead.

Choosing a bed

The sort of bed you choose depends on several factors: whether you sleep alone or with a partner, your size – and your partner's size, the style and size of your bedroom.

Bed sizes Basically, single or twin beds are 90 cm (3 ft) wide by 195 cm (6 ft 3 in) to 230 cm (6 ft 8 in) long, although they can be bought in a narrower size for very small rooms. A small double measures 135 cm (4 ft 6 in) wide by 195 cm (6 ft 3 in) long, and a standard double 153 cm (5 ft) wide by 200 cm (6 ft 6 in) long. A lot of people like to buy bedlinen in the States so it's useful to know American sizes include Queen size which is 168 cm (5 ft 6 in) wide by 230 cm (6 ft 8 in) long; and King size which is 198 cm (6 ft 4 in) wide by 230 cm (6 ft 8 in) long. There is also in America a longer single bed measuring 230 cm (6 ft 8 in) and a Californian King size which is 183 cm (6 ft) by 213 cm (7 ft). You might see some English beds described as King or Queen size but these sizes are not standard over here. Remember that the length of a bed is just as important as the width; it should always be 15 cm (6 in) longer than the person sleeping in it.

small double
4 ft 6 in
6 ft 3 in

standard double
5 ft
6 ft 6 in

queen size
5 ft 6 in
6 ft 8 in

king size
6 ft 4 in
6 ft 8 in

Open springs are cheaper and consist of a network of hour glass springs. The more springs there are in both types of mattress the better, and the thicker the wire the better, the number of coil convolutions the better. The best mattresses therefore, generally have coils made of low-gauge wire with six turns – lesser qualities have thinner wire and fewer turns. The springs should be covered with an insulator – to prevent the mattress cushioning from working down into the coils – and this is generally made from tough fibre padding, wire, or netting, or a combination of the three. The cushioning is usually made from polyurethane foam combined with cotton felt and other fibres, and the thicker this cushioning the higher the quality.

When you buy a mattress you should buy a partnering box spring base at the same time, it will reinforce the mattress' support and cost approximately the same amount of money. They too, have coil counts, or they may have metal grids bent in a squared zig-zag shape, or, the least expensive, be a combination of wood and foam. The foam should be at least 5 cm (2 in) thick to give any sort of adequate support.

Water-filled mattresses come in two different kinds: a sort of bladder filled with water, or a hybrid 'flotation' system which sounds, and is,

more complicated. The first type is designed to be inserted into heavy-duty framing resting on a pedestal base. The second or hybrid has a water-filled bladder which is surrounded by a foam shell, covered with conventional heavy duty ticking to look just like a normal sprung or inner spring mattress. The matching foundation is specially designed to support the water's weight. In fact, this second variety is lighter than the first because it uses less water and is shallower than the ordinary bladder type. It is also 'waveless', that is to say, special baffles reduce side to side and up and down movements of the water, and in some makes an added chemical partially solidifies the water to reduce motion.

If you are seduced into choosing a water bed, do make absolutely sure that it has a vinyl liner to contain all the water in case, dreaded thought, the mattress gets punctured. You can also get special water bed heaters which not only make the whole thing more luxurious but prevent condensation.

Air-filled mattresses are the latest thing. These are are based on the same principle as the collapsible mattresses used for swimming pools, beaches and camping. The centre of the mattress is another heavy duty vinyl sack or bladder, which is enclosed in a foam shell with a

cushioned zip-on cover like the hybrid water bed described above. Some of these air beds can be filled by means of a vacuum cleaner or even a hair dryer while others are available with a compressor unit and electric controls. Some larger mattresses have dual air chambers with dual controls to allow for differing tastes in firmness.

Does it pass the test?
The only way to tell if a mattress is right for your particular shape and weight is to try it out. Take off your shoes and lie down on it for at least ten minutes. Almost any mattress is going to feel comfortable at first but give it time and don't mind the sales people. They have got to make a sale, you have got to be satisfied. Stretch, turn over, make the sort of movements you would make in bed. A good mattress should feel firm and resilient, give support to your shoulders and hips and make your back feel thoroughly relaxed.

When you are satisfied that it feels comfortable, check the sides. They should be reinforced to prevent sagging when you sit on the edge of the bed. Sit on it and see. It should

This chrome-framed bed with its leaf design comforter/quilt and bed linen looks coolly elegant in a mirrored setting. The curved perspex table and chrome floor lamps are exactly right for this sophisticated modern room.

277

CHOOSING BEDS AND BEDLINEN

give a little, then spring back to shape when you get up. See if there is a cut away model on display which will show the insides. You have every right to ask to see one and the salesman should be able to explain it to you. Check the manufacturer's label which should give you complete details of construction and care. The most expensive mattresses are like the iron fist in a velvet glove, with a firm, heavy-coiled sprung core under a deeply soft top, thus providing both firm support and luxurious softness. If you and your partner prefer different degrees of firmness you can always buy different mattresses and get them linked with a zipper. Check too, about guarantees or warranties. Good quality mattresses will generally be guaranteed against defects of workmanship for some 15 years, lesser qualities for less. Good water beds, however, generally have a six to ten year limit and the heaters for three to five.

And so to the bed
Quite apart from the importance of the mattress and base there is the question of the look of the bed itself. Today you can choose from a huge range of styles from antique and reproductions of antique four-posters to specially-constructed frames with electronic controls to raise the foot and head of the bed to the occupier's fancy, or beds with

integral tv, stereo, clock, book-shelves, massage unit, lighting controls, the whole works.

If you are short of space you can get beds that fold right up into a wall of neat-looking storage units, or that are part of a series of slick modular units, or beds with lift-up divan bases and drawers inserted either at the side or at the end. Or there are the more straightforward sofa beds.

If you are nostalgically-minded there are shops full of originals and copies of Victorian, Edwardian and Colonial beds in mahogany, oak, brass or painted iron depending on the type you prefer. If you like a romantic look there are all sorts of elaborations that can be produced with fabric.

Bedheads
If comfort is of paramount importance to you, this will obviously affect the kind of bedhead you choose. Padded and upholstered bedheads should be attached to the bed frame and covered in some sort of easily sponged and cleaned fabric, or at least a cover that can be removed for cleaning, and it should either match or co-ordinate with the bedcovers or curtains. You could also cover a couple of squares or rectangles of foam and attach them to a wooden or brass pole behind the bed. Zip-on covers can be quickly zipped off again for ease of cleaning.

If aesthetics and looks are more important to you than comfort there is almost no limit to what you can use at the head of a bed. Bookshelves, screens, old gates, rugs, tapestries, huge posters, pin boards, windows, storage boxes, old mirrors can all be used to great effect. Use upended pillows and masses of cushions on the bed itself and you can get your comfort as well.

Dressing up the bed
There could hardly be a better choice of bed linen than there is now. Manufacturers are offering every conceivable permutation of colours,

Above: Milky-white crocheted bedspread and lacy cushions look good against the severe cane bedhead.

Top right: This brass knobbed, black painted Edwardian bed with side wings demands and gets romantic-looking lace curtains and valance.

Bottom right: Mini-flower printed duvet, pillows and curtains are teamed with co-ordinating paper and calm grey-blues and apricots in this peaceful little room.

Far right: Broderie Anglaise on a charming late Victorian bedstead.

Making a choice

The superabundance of beautiful new bedlinen and the current delight in decoration for its own sake make it all very easy to achieve romantic looking bedrooms. And the choice of co-ordinating fabrics and wall-coverings now available is so wide and so good that it is quite difficult to put a foot wrong. Bedlinen itself is so pretty these days it's a shame not to display it and let it become part of the general scheme. In this room a soft blue-grey carpet and a love-in-the-mist wallpaper with its own gentle border provide the framework for a splendid wood four-poster, so well dressed it practically becomes a room within a room. Bed curtains and valance are made in a flowered cotton to match the border and are lined with swirled pink cotton. This same pink is used as a top cloth over the flowered undercloth on the table and, together with a similar blue fabric, for cushions. Sheets are pale blue with white *broderie Anglaise* pillow slips, and the whole bed is covered by a blue and white quilt. The stripy rag rug on the floor picks up the various colours and the blue chair by the wicker laundry basket repeats the blue and white of the stored linen on the shelves. Finishing touches are supplied by a pair of brass floor lamps, judiciously placed uplights, and a collection of baskets as well as plants.

Sheets as show-offs

Since sheets are both highly decorative and the cheapest way to get a large amount of fabric together for comparatively little, it stands to reason that they can come into their own in more ways than one in a bedroom. Sheeting is also more convenient to use than unfinished furnishing fabric – ideal for the non-sewer.

Use sheets –

Instead of conventional material for a four-poster or half-tester.

To make festoon blinds or balloon shades or pull-up curtains and match them up with the bed treatment (on the bed itself, swagged across the top of a four-poster . . .)

For graceful tablecloths on round tables beside the bed, topping them with a contrast sheet or 'ace or broderie Anglaise.

To cover armchairs and/or a sofa or chaise longue in the bedroom.

To cover a dressing table.

To make pillow or cushion covers.

As wallcoverings, hanging them direct from a rod running all around the room.

Hang sheets at the bed's corner from curtain track on the ceiling

Use contrasting sheeting to cover bedside tables

Tie a sheet around an armchair for instant re-upholstery

designs, co-ordinating sets of sheets, valances, bed skirts or ruffles, pillow cases, bedspreads, duvet covers, comforter and blanket covers and pillow shams. These last three are innovations from America which has long been the instigator of every sort of bed fashion and comfort. Pillow shams go on top of pillow cases so that the pillows can be propped on top of the matching comforter (an elegant slimmed-down eiderdown-like version of the duvet) or blanket cover (like a thin sheet-weight bedspread). And pillows come in every shape and size to be piled in luxurious confusion or profusion at the head of the bed.

Duvets, comforters or blankets?

The look of your bed will depend a lot on whether you have a duvet, comforter or blankets and bedspread. Points in favour of duvets – they're warm, light, about a quarter the weight of blankets, and they do away with bedmaking. Duvet covers are changeable, washable, highly decorative and can be matched with pillows, valances and curtains. Comforters are thinner and neater than duvets, often come with their own matching valances and pillow cases and are coming, deservedly, more and more into favour. On the other hand, many people like to feel the weight of blankets and to be warmly tucked in. It's also easier to throw an extra blanket on or off,

whereas you're stuck with a duvet, which can be too hot in summer. Comforters are more useful for year round use although duvets are now available for summer use, designed on the same principle but lighter. Duvet and comforter fillings can either be natural or man-made. Down gives warmth with minimum weight and in order of quality and cost you can choose from eiderdown (very expensive), goosedown and duck down, down and feather (51 per cent down) and feather and down. The more feathers the heavier and cheaper the quilt. These natural fillings are comfortable and settle warmly around the sleeper. They should be sent to a specialist cleaner. Duvets and comforters filled with man-made synthetic fibre or mixtures like polyester with feathers and down are more moderately priced and usually machine washable – so good for children – though not as warm as a natural quilt. The categories of warmth of duvets are known as tog ratings (tog is a measurement of heat insulation). Low is 7.5 tog, high is 10.5. The one you choose will depend on how warm your bedroom is and how much you feel the cold.

Marvellous uses for fabric

Since there's no ignoring the bed, go to the other extreme and make it the most spectacular object in the room. And you can do this with fabric, achieving the most extravagant, elaborate and beautiful effects with hangings, drapes, bed curtains and canopies. If it's illusions of grandeur you're after, fabric, imaginatively used, will get you there.

● A modern four-poster in wood, brass or steel can have billowing side curtains in a light flimsy fabric like cheesecloth, voile, batiste or gingham, or be neat and tailored with straight folds of heavier fabric – tweed, corduroy or flannel.

● Attach a ply canopy or tester to the ceiling over the bed or have it cantilevered from the wall behind and cover it with fabric. Use it as a support for four sets of tied-back curtains. Alternatively, fix ceiling-mounted track around the top of the bed and hang with curtains and a valance. Curtains can be hung from small pieces of track mounted on the ceiling above all four bed corners.

● A half-tester or canopy can be attached to the ceiling just above the pillow area or cantilevered from the back wall about 1.80 m (6 ft) or so up, covered with fabric and hung with back and side curtains.

● A straight panel of fabric can be hung behind the bed, or a length of fabric can be looped over a central dowel or bracket fixed, say, 150-cm (5 ft) above the bed and then over a pair of brackets.

Using fabric to effect. In the room top left, wooden curtain rods are attached to the ceiling and hung with a valance and curtains of ribbon-edged voile to form a full tester. A very original treatment, top centre; multi-coloured ribbons are suspended in front of a panel of striped cotton hung from a brass pole. Thin blue, red and yellow lines on the bedspread repeat the ribbon colours. Crisp pink cotton is used to edge, line, and cover this white and brass four-poster, top right. The ends of the bed in the blue room, bottom left, have been upholstered in the curtain and quilt fabric, while left, voile curtains billow round bed and window.

Bedroom storage has to take care of most if not all of our personal possessions so it must be an essential and well planned part of its design. Somehow there has to be found space for all or some of the following: clothes, shoes, underclothes, hats, make-up, jewellery, personal papers, books, files, shoe-cleaning equipment, sporting equipment, bags, briefcases, luggage, accessories of every description, hobbies and the extraordinary amount of other impedimenta that inevitably ends up in the bedroom.

In an ideal world there would be a whole wall of storage behind not too conspicuous cupboard or closet doors where there would be slots for most of these things. They would all have their allotted place, would all remain tidy, and there would be space in the room for a large but elegant pedestal or bureau desk to take all papers, and shelves to take all books and other paraphernalia.

Alas, it is not an ideal world and there is seldom ideal space in a room to plan out the kind and amount of storage you would like. All the same, if you really set your mind to it and consider all the possibilities you can usually work small miracles. And even if it is impossible to give any sort of blueprint on storage that will suit everyone, there are certain common sense methods for organizing whatever space you do have at your disposal.

How to fit it in

First and foremost, whether storage is to be custom-built, bought ready-made or somehow improvised, it must be fitted into the room as neatly as possible. Otherwise the most elegant of furnishings can be spoilt by the undisciplined welter of belongings. If you are planning a room from scratch you should take a long, detached view of storage possibilities right from the start. Take particular note of your room's proportions and architectural details. In an old building, bedrooms with high ceilings and nice mouldings might be best served with a free-standing cupboard or wardrobe. Large old pieces can often

Exposed red and white storage units at one end of this bedroom-study, left, hold stereo equipment and tv, while space-enhancing mirrored doors are used to conceal a wall of wardrobe, right, in a well-planned bedroom. Note useful two-tiered rods.

Hiding it all away

This bedroom is as much sitting room as sleeping space and so well planned is the storage that by day there is hardly a trace of the bedroom's necessities. Pine louvered cupboards built all round the room contain drawers, shelves and a dressing table area as well as hanging space, and tie in neatly with the natural louvered shutters on the window. Drawers under the sofa beds keep bedlinen and duvets hidden away out of sight and the two upholstered stools with their lift-up lids cope with anything else that has to be concealed when the sitting room is in use. For the rest, the walls are done in an interestingly textured creamy basketweave covering, the cotton of the sofa beds is a slightly mottled apricot and both colours blend happily with the soft terracotta wool of the carpet. Plain blue and white striped cushions look good against the apricot covers and so does the patchwork quilt; the blue is picked up again in odd accessories. Tall green plants either side of the window add balance and freshness to the whole.

PLANNING EFFECTIVE STORAGE

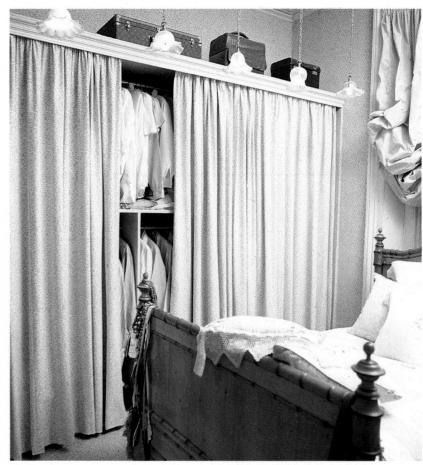

In a small room where any sort of conventional wardrobe space could look obtrusive, soft storage might well be the answer—that is to say, clothes covered or concealed by curtains rather than more rigid doors. In the room above, well-planned storage is arranged behind curtains which match the wallpaper. They are suspended behind a piece of moulding which repeats the cornice above. The top gap—which could have been unsightly—is filled with handsome old luggage while a series of old milky glass light shades suspended from brass chains hanging in front form a kind of unusual and decorative visual screen, an imaginative solution.

be bought gratifyingly cheaply, and can often be re-organized inside to take an extraordinary number of possessions.

If you definitely decide on built-in storage (or built-in *looking* storage because most storage units are modular and can be made to look custom fitted) and you have convenient recesses or a spare wall or corner, try to ensure that the cupboards reach ceiling height and that any mouldings or base boards or skirtings that are covered are re-introduced and matched along the fronts. Few things spoil the proportion of a room so much as an unsightly gap between the top of a wardrobe and the ceiling quite apart from the fact that it is an unnecessary waste of space and a dust trap. If the cupboard is then very high you can put away your least used objects up there and reach them when necessary with a small pair of steps.

To be really unobtrusive any sort of cupboard fronts should be made to seem part of the walls and brought in with the same decorative treatment whether painted, wallpapered or covered. Wallpaper or covering should either be wrapped around the doors or brought to the edge and covered with thin beading to prevent frayed or torn or worn edging. If you give the wallpaper a coat or two of matt or eggshell polyurethane this will make it much tougher. Alternatively, wardrobe

doors can be mirrored. This can be an excellent solution especially in a small or darkish room where it will serve to expand both space and light.

If you want cupboards to look like objects in their own right they should still, if possible, incorporate some detail or feeling from the rest of the room whether it is in colour or trim or general proportion. If you decide on louvred doors, try to buy half rather than full louvres to prevent too much dust entering the slits. Panelled doors can be painted to match the room door or doors, or inset with a colour or paper or fabric that matches the walls.

How to conjure up space

Sometimes you can look at a room and feel that there is simply no place at all to put a cupboard. But look again. A wall that has one or two doors in it, for example, could have cupboards built *around* the door or doors so that you seem to walk through deep closets to the room, landing or corridor beyond. This is often a very effective way of getting good storage space without seeming to encroach on valuable room space. The same thing could be done around a window or windows, especially if you can incorporate a dressing-table and drawers as well.

Occasionally in a smallish room you can build cupboards around the bedspace with the top cupboards continuing over the bed to form a

All about storage

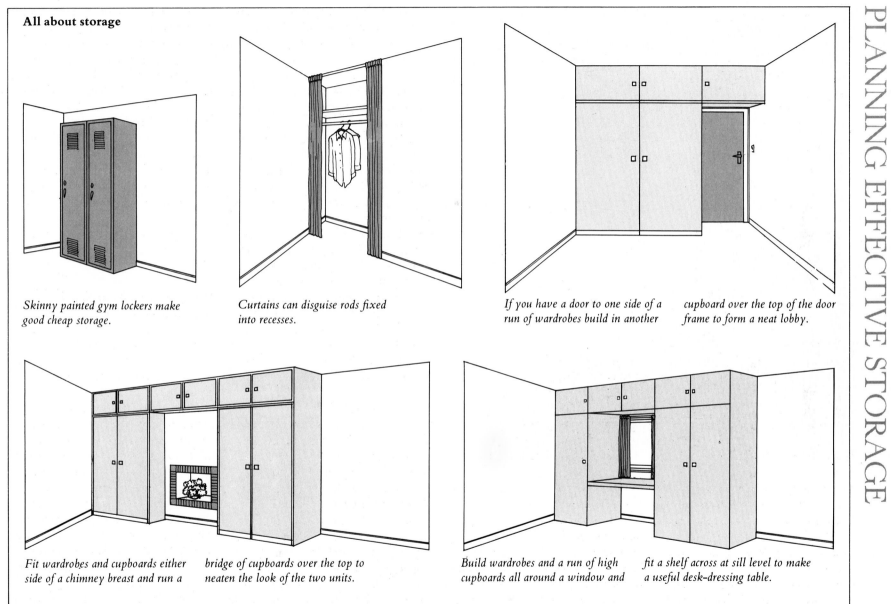

Skinny painted gym lockers make good cheap storage.

Curtains can disguise rods fixed into recesses.

If you have a door to one side of a run of wardrobes build in another cupboard over the top of the door frame to form a neat lobby.

Fit wardrobes and cupboards either side of a chimney breast and run a bridge of cupboards over the top to neaten the look of the two units.

Build wardrobes and a run of high cupboards all around a window and fit a shelf across at sill level to make a useful desk-dressing table.

sort of recess. Sometimes it is even possible to fit small shelves into the sides of the cupboards to hold books, and other bedside clutter. Lights can be fitted across the underside of the top cupboards or on the side walls so that everything looks and is beautifully and neatly integrated.

If there are two windows, the space between the windows might be used either for a cupboard or shelves, or the space might just be big enough to take the bed, leaving the rest of the wall space clear for storage.

Again, you might put a bed up against the window (as long as it is well draught-proofed) which will put more room space at your disposal for storage purposes.

In a very small room, it might be best to put up cupboards in the corridor outside rather than curtail sleeping and dressing space still further.

Or a bed can be set up on a neat platform of carpeted drawers, or right up on top of low cupboards. In any event, if there is space under a bed for extra storage drawers so much the better.

Other space-saving tricks are folding doors on top and bottom sliding tracks which will take up the minimum of space when they are opened; cupboards with curtained fronts rather than doors; cloakroom racks concealed by curtains or screens as a temporary measure.

Organization and method

Whether you are building new storage or trying to re-organize the storage you have or that already exists in a new room there are certain helpful pointers to using the space to its — and your — best advantage.

For example, clothes racks are often fitted unnecessarily high so that the space below is not properly utilised. A reasonable height is 1.5 m (5 ft) from the bottom of the cupboard leaving the top part free for generous shelving space. Alternatively, you can have two banks of rods for short clothes like shirts, jackets and skirts in one wardrobe, or part of a wardrobe, and longer hanging space in another. If there are few drawers in a room but many shelves, wire or cane baskets are a good idea for keeping underclothes, shirts, sweaters, tights, socks and similar items tidy. Tie racks can be fixed to the insides of doors, so can racks or hooks for belts. Stacking plastic drawers can be inserted into any suitable space for shirts and sweaters and are especially good in clear plastic so that you can see contents at a glance. It's a good idea to store shoes on shelves one above the other rather than in a heap at the bottom of a wardrobe. Or shoes can be stashed away in one of those hanging wardrobe bags or shoe tidies for extra efficiency.

If you're lucky enough to have a whole wall of storage or a walk-in

Top far left: Industrial shelving and wire baskets hold an amazing amount of clobber from luggage to linen, clothes and general paraphernalia. A desk top has been fitted in too.

Bottom far left: A useful storage wall has been built around a door for maximum use of space. Roller blind fronts repeat bedspread colours.

Left: Brilliantly coloured and devised Hi-Tech system lets it all hang out in a decorative way.

Above: Decorative storage can be made from almost anything if you care to put your mind to it.

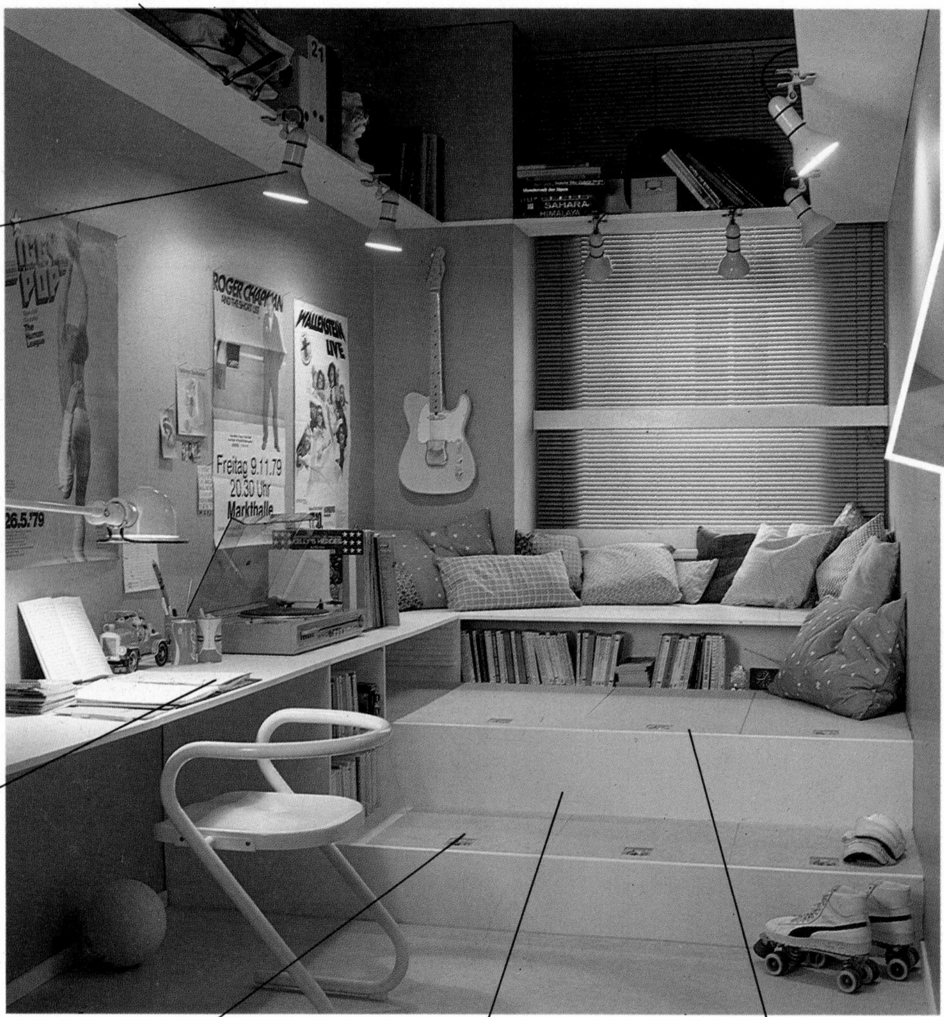

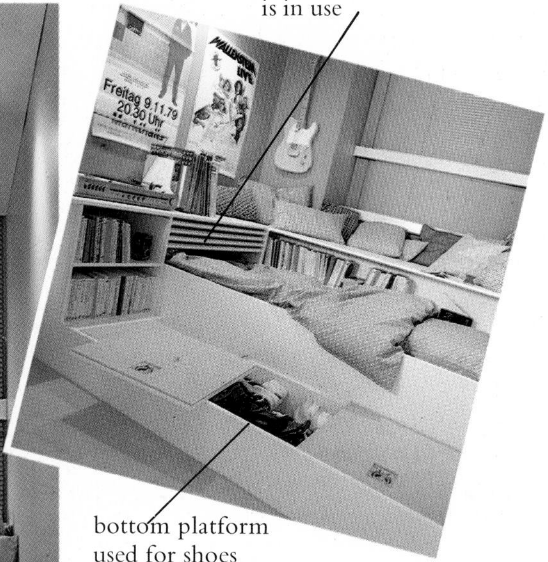

dead space used for storage of infrequently used objects

locker tops slide into special grooves when bed is in use

lights clipped to shelves

bottom platform used for shoes

desk top continues into seating and bookshelves

linen stored under bed during day

steps provide seating by day

seating unit converts to bed at night

Built-in storage on a very intensive scale in this cleverly planned study-bedroom. The stepped-up seating platforms open up for storage lockers (see above) and even better, for a mattress and duvet. Note in detail picture how locker tops slide into runners by bookshelves when the bed is in use. More storage has been built across the window and under the ceiling, for possessions that are not often used, so that virtually every possible space is used to advantage.

cupboard, drawer or shelf space will be part of this. Otherwise you might have room for a chest or chests of drawers or a dresser. If a dressing-table is not included in a storage wall (or in the bathroom) a separate one could be used as a desk/dressing-table with drawers for papers as well as cosmetics. Another space-saving idea is to leave sufficient knee-hole space between two or three chests of drawers or 70 cm (28 in) high filing cabinets, and run a separate top over them; this gives you a writing and dressing-table surface as well.

And don't forget that most valuable area of storage space – under the bed. Drawers here can take lots of spare bedding or clothes.

Building-in the basin
If you have room for a wash basin in the bedroom, this will certainly relieve pressure on a family bathroom, and if you can incorporate it into a cupboard which can then act as a dressing-table area as well, you will have solved several problems very neatly indeed. Build the basin into a small vanity unit with a vinyl or tiled top and try to include a drawer unit, a towel rail, some hooks, electric points for razor, toothbrush and hair dryer, and, of course, a well lit mirror (one with lights all round, like a theatrical mirror would be ideal). If there isn't room for such a cupboard, a screen would make an admirable substitute.

How to improvise
If you're short of space or money or both, there are various ways to improvise quite adequate storage. A piece of wood with hooks to take hangers will serve very well as a temporary measure. Always add hooks to the backs of doors too, to take coats, dressing gowns and the odd overflow of clothes.

Cloakroom racks can be bought comparatively cheaply and can look quite decorative if they're tidily hung with clothes and left like that, or concealed by a screen or curtains. Old gym lockers can be painted and used for shirts and underclothes. Recesses either side of a chimney can be used very effectively for temporary storage by mounting dowelling or broom handles across them from which to hang clothes.

Old lace curtains hung from a brass rod repeat the feeling of the bedspread as well as concealing rather more utilitarian storage. Wood shelves can be varied to hold everything from luggage to linen. Wire filing baskets are slotted in for smaller items and the same system is stretched to form full length hanging space as well. The whole concept is as effective as it is simple.

293

ROOMS THAT GROW WITH THE CHILD

Children's rooms – whether they are combined sleeping-cum-playrooms (which are the norm), or just bedrooms (which are a luxury), have to be capable of growing up with the child. When you are first planning the room try to keep in mind the subtle modifications you can make over the years so that with the minimum of background change – and thus expense – cribs can give way to cots, cots to beds, and toy cupboards to wardrobes and storage for adolescent paraphernalia.

This does not mean that you cannot go to town on the decoration; on the contrary, you can have great fun with this room and be as bold, as fantastic, as indulgent as you like with accessories, fabrics, storage boxes and so on. But rather that the background or framework of the room should be as simple, sturdy and classic as possible. In this way you can afford to change certain parts of it, like window treatments, bed sizes and storage without structural or expensive alterations to walls, floors and other basics.

From nursery to bed-sit

With thought and ingenuity it's possible to make the same space

work for years. Recently, for instance, I evolved a child's room which was designed to last in just such a way from infancy to late teenage. This is how I did it:

Stage 1 – Infancy The walls were painted white, and vinyl-coated cork tiles laid down on the floor for quietness and practicality. A large washable rug went on top. Machine-washable broderie Anglaise was used to pretty up the cradle and Venetian blinds were put up at the window. A white melamine trolley held the plastic bath, nappies, soft towels, aprons talcum powder, gripe water, pins tissues, cotton wool and a plastic bucket. A pair of white-painted chests of drawers with a kneehole space between and white laminate top over the two provided a useful surface for changing the baby. A full-size wardrobe or closet with a stack of shelves on one side and a double row of

Platform-based beds, left, set at right angles and massed with cushions make maximum use of space. This cot, top right, will easily give way to a bed with no change of scheme. The deep border, cut-out figures and painted piano, right, all look fun.

hanging rods on the other was built in and completed the storage. At this stage the shelves were for holding soft toys and so on and the lowest rod could go on being used for clothes that needed to be hung up and continue to do this for quite some time. Final touches were a rocking chair, a few pictures and wall lights on a dimmer switch so that there would be no safety hazards once the child started to crawl and also so that the lights could be dimmed right down for minimum disturbance and maximum reassurance at night. These lights were placed near the changing area and near the cradle. A cork pin-board was added behind the laminate-topped chests of drawers for pinning up weight charts, diet sheets and so on.

Stage 2 – Toddlers and pre-school At this point the cradle was put aside and a cot introduced. This had to be both safe and sturdy which meant making sure that the slats were not more than 6 mm ($2\frac{3}{8}$ in) apart, that the rails were an adequate height for protection even when the drop side was lowered, that the drop sides themselves were the sort that could not be released by a child and that the mattress was a perfect fit with no dangerous gaps left.

The blind was left where it was as it helped to delay the start of the day, made day-time resting easier and meant that daylight could

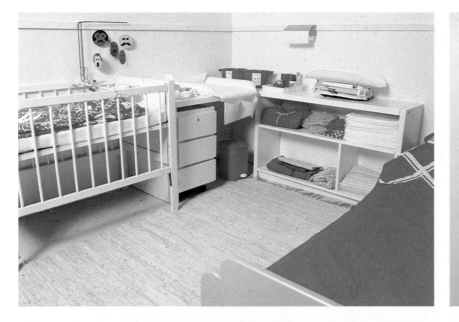

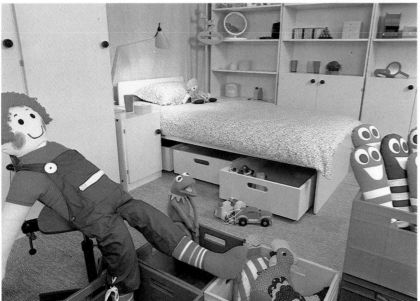

Opposite: Maximum use is made of a barn-like ceiling with contrast colour, stencilled border and Christmas lights strung along the beams.

Top left: The tops of these white units make excellent changing/weighing space that will convert later.

Top right: Diagonally-laid vinyl stripes repeat colours in Austrian blinds in this sleeping/play space.

Bottom far left: Modular units match bed with its capacious drawers and give excellent variable storage.

Left: Fun tower gives work/play/bed space.

297

Left: White-painted scaffolding makes an attractive bed-cum-climbing tower in a tongue-and-groove, pine-lined attic space. Candy coloured stripes and spots add to the cheerfulness.

Above: Red and white checked paper, yellow painted floor and furniture, grid shelving and red Venetian blinds are used together to make an arresting study/bedroom for a teenager.

be adjusted when necessary. An old wooden chest catered for the overflow of toys. All of the baby's accessories, like nappies etc, which were no longer needed were taken away but the trolley was left as a useful place for storing games. Some reasonably close-together vertical wooden bars, clamped into a frame were screwed into the sides of the window so that there would be no possibility of adventurous explorations onto the outside sill when the window was opened. Nor could the bars be used for climbing since they were vertical and too close together to provide any sort of head trap.

The cork pin-board was now used for pinning-up first drawings and paintings, and the walls were still able to be kept fairly pristine in spite of the ravages of dirty little hands and scribbles because white was so easy to touch up. Still, just to encourage drawings in the right place, I added a large blackboard and secured it against the wall from the floor for easy access. Bookshelves were put in.

Stage 3 – Early school days The cot went out and was replaced by a couple of modular bunk beds. These were useful in a variety of ways since they were the kind that could be dismantled and turned into two ordinary beds and also had an extra large drawer underneath for even more toy and games storage. Even

though this room was for one child, bunk beds were a good investment as they meant that there was always room for a friend to stay overnight and they provided a play area at different levels. It was safe to take down the window bars. A couple of chairs and an angled desk light were added so the laminated top over the chests of drawers could now be used as a desk for homework as well as for painting, model-making and so on. The pin-board went on being practical and the shelves in the wardrobe were now used for sweaters and shirts instead of toys, while the top rod in the wardrobe was beginning to come into its own. The trolley became useful for jigsaw puzzles and other games and the walls were adorned with more and more posters, drawings and other memorabilia with just enough space left for a mirror.

Stage 4 – Secondary school The bunk beds came down and turned into two couch-like beds placed at right angles, with tailored covers, cushions and an extra drawer under what was the top bunk. The major purchases at this stage were a new rug and blinds to go with new bed-covers (these could be home-made), and a low plastic table to go between the beds with a bedside lamp. The trolley became an excellent base for the tv whenever it was brought in but there was no longer any need at

299

From nursery to bed-sit

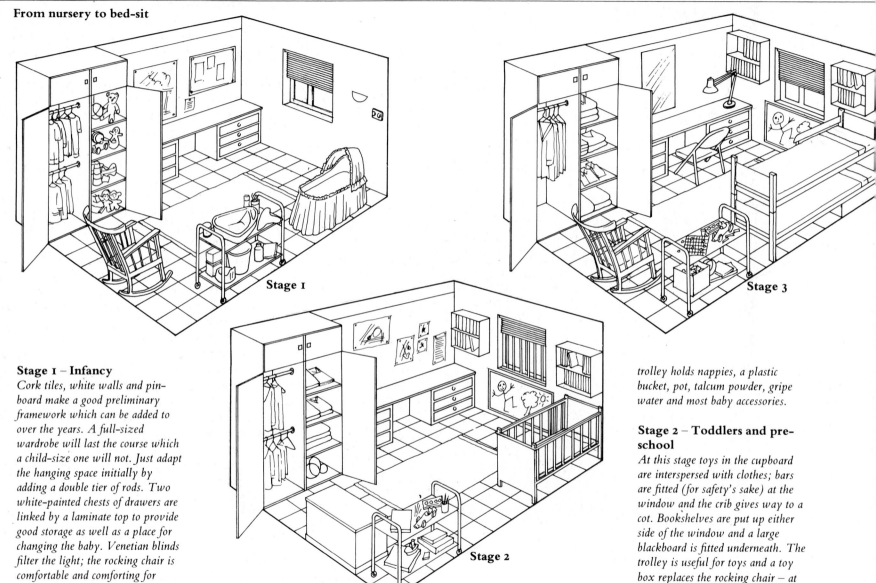

Stage 1

Stage 2

Stage 3

Stage 1 – Infancy

Cork tiles, white walls and pin-board make a good preliminary framework which can be added to over the years. A full-sized wardrobe will last the course which a child-size one will not. Just adapt the hanging space initially by adding a double tier of rods. Two white-painted chests of drawers are linked by a laminate top to provide good storage as well as a place for changing the baby. Venetian blinds filter the light; the rocking chair is comfortable and comforting for nursing and cuddling, and the trolley holds nappies, a plastic bucket, pot, talcum powder, gripe water and most baby accessories.

Stage 2 – Toddlers and pre-school

At this stage toys in the cupboard are interspersed with clothes; bars are fitted (for safety's sake) at the window and the crib gives way to a cot. Bookshelves are put up either side of the window and a large blackboard is fitted underneath. The trolley is useful for toys and a toy box replaces the rocking chair – at least temporarily.

Stage 3 – Early school days

The child is now old enough to need a single wardrobe rod and the rocking chair comes back. The trolley is still used for toys and games but the cot is replaced by bunk beds. The chest fitment now becomes a desk/dressing table with the addition of a mirror, desk lamp, and folding chair.

Stage 4 – Secondary school

Now the old Venetian blind has been changed for a smarter fabric roller blind and the bunk beds have been dismantled to form two sofa beds at right angles to each other to

Stage 5

Stage 4

allow greater floor space. New additions are a small side table and lamp between the beds, posters, ornaments, a mass of different coloured cushions, a smart new rug – and that faithful trolley becomes a TV stand.

Stage 5 – Late teenage

At this stage the cork tiles give way to a wall to wall carpet. The pin-board is replaced by a panel of mirror and the roller blind, dirtied very quickly by early teen extravagances, is replaced by a pretty more feminine affair.

this stage for the blackboard.

The rather sculptural ladder for the bunk beds could be painted yellow and hung on the wall like a piece of sculpture along with the pop star posters and so forth, and the pin-board began to be used for school timetables, reminders and other more useful notices.

Stage 5 – Late teenage Since this particular bedroom was a girl's, I now wall-papered the walls and put carpet to the floor for a softer, more feminine look. The pin-board was taken down and replaced with more pictures and prints. Bookshelves, wardrobe, chests of drawers all stayed the same except for a coat of paint and I changed the bedcovers and cushions. By adding a table mirror the laminated shelf became a dressing-table as well as desk. The trolley was repainted and remained a tv stand. (If there had been room it would have been a good idea to add a small armchair at this stage. Similarly the toy chest could be stencilled and used for storage.) The room by now had assumed a totally different and pretty bedroom-like character but it had by no means been a costly metamorphosis, just a very gradual one and affordable at every stage.

Bed and playspace combined

If the room is to be used as much for playing as for sleeping – and most are

301

– it is obvious that every inch counts. Let's start with the bed. Once a child is past the toddling stage there are all sorts of space-saving beds which can either be used for playing and climbing over (bunks) as well as providing extra storage underneath, or can be folded up into the wall to take up the minimum of floor. Other ideas are modular beds with backs which can be used as sleeping-seating areas as well as to define space; sleep/play 'tower' structures which can also encompass storage and seating and, of course, truckle beds where one bed slides under another.

When there is more than one child it is essential to try and make some sort of private territory for each one, even if it is only visual. You can divide the room with screens or a two-sided storage unit or a low wall or even a ceiling-hung Venetian or louvred blind. If the space is fairly small, keep background colours neutral and identify each child's equipment (toy boxes, stools, chests of drawers) with a different primary colour to provide vivacity and accent and immediate recognition.

Far left: Red painted tubular steel bunk beds can be curtained off by a large blind.

Top and bottom left: More tubular steel used for beds and shelves gives work exercise and sleeping space as well as bright and useful storage.

Making it safe

Vertical bars at the window, cots that conform to proper standards, out-of-reach wall lights to prevent accidents with trailing wires and free-standing lamps – these are some of the most important safety factors to be considered during the very early stages. From here on children are more active, mobile and curious and the hazards increase. Sensible parents can reduce the possibilities of accidents by dealing with the following danger points:

See that electrical points or outlets are flush with the wall and not placed down near skirting or baseboards or within crawling reach. Keep any electric appliances well out of reach and see that cords or wires are as short as possible.

Have non-slip floors, carpet if possible – or as non-slip as possible. If they also deaden sound, especially if the room is on an upper floor, so much the better.

Make sure that fireplaces, stoves and fires of any kind – open, gas, electric – are well guarded with a childproof fireguard all the time.

Put a safety gate on the stairs and see that it is kept shut at all times as a matter of course.

See that lights are on a dimmer switch and can be dimmed right down to act as night-lights. They are also useful if you have a second baby which needs to be attended to in the night without disturbing the older child. If a dimmer switch is impractical for some reason install a low-powered night-light, and if a child remains afraid of the dark buy small illuminated plugs that fit into wall outlets and give a comforting glow for little cost.

Make or buy vertical kiddi-bars – no more than 12.5 cm (5 in) apart

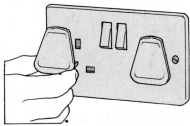

Fit covers over electrical sockets or outlets as a precaution

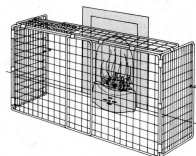

Buy a strong, child-proof fireguard which you can attach to the wall around any fire you use

Use an approved safety gate to fit at the top or bottom of stairs when you are busy elsewhere in the house. They are equally effective fitted in doorways

Put it away

Keeping things tidy in children's rooms unless the occupants are naturally tidy is like trying to dig a hole in wet sand. However, there are enough good storage units around at the moment to encourage a modicum of neatness. They don't have to be worthy or expensive; in fact, the more exciting, inventive and unusual they are, the more likely they are to be used. And brightly-coloured containers can add just the right touches of cheerfulness and fun to a sturdy basic room.

How to cope with the clutter

● Use old school or gym lockers and paint them in different shades of bright gloss paint, one for each child if you have several. They'll take clothes or, fitted out with shelves, can be used for books and papers as well. They can be bought fairly reasonably from institutional suppliers and you can often find them in junk yards and shops.

● String canvas bags and pouches on rope frames for the kind of 'soft storage' that is popular in America. Or copy this good home-made idea of a 3 m (10 ft) ladder raised on wood strips with the struts used to support home-made canvas bags in bright colours like red and blue.

● Nail strips of wood 25 mm by 75 mm (1 in by 3 in) to the wall to form 60 mm (2 ft squares). Fill the insides with cork tiles, pegboard, blackboard and shelves and you have both practical off-the-floor storage and a wall that's full of interest.

● Use a window wall to make an entire run of shelf and cupboard storage. Use 50 mm by 100 mm (2 in by 4 in) uprights, build them around the window, fill with shelves at different heights and support them on a row of edge-to-edge lockers or chests. The top of the lockers will provide a good play surface, the narrower shelves will hold books and toys and the lockers will house a multitude of possessions.

● Fill in an unoccupied top bunk to make a marvellous out-of-sight dumping ground. Frame the sides and top by putting up painted strips of wood measuring 25 mm by 100 mm (1 in by 4 in) and fill in the gap above the bottom bunk with vividly coloured roller blinds or bamboo blinds to match whatever you have at the window.

Run a series of boxes with lift-up lids all down one wall and cover the top with long slabs of cotton – or vinyl-covered foam to make seating as well as storage units. Add bright and patterned cushions for extra comfort and accent colours.

Let them choose

Adolescents should be able to decide their own room schemes as far as it is practical – and affordable. At the very least they could be offered a number of choices so that they feel the final say-so has been theirs. Obviously they will need a bed and, if possible, a spare bed for a friend; a work-table-cum-dressing-table; at least one chair; storage space; a long mirror and good lighting for working, dressing and atmosphere. Uplights and/or spotlights with coloured filters will add the sort of disco glamour that's often required at that age, but for the rest they can hang up fabrics on walls, paint murals, make dados, and generally inject their own character into the space without doing too much harm. In fact, fabric on walls and carpet covered by rugs are to be encouraged as good sound-deadening devices for the stereo.

Top left: Large-scale green and yellow filing trays cope neatly with a multitude of toys and clutter in a bright parrot-coloured room and encourage children to tidy up.

Right: A simple green unit with a small-scale side piece and toning diagonally striped blind makes an excellent and eye-catching work/play space in this well-equipped room.

Far right: A tiny space tucked under the eaves in a top floor flat has been cleverly turned into a two-bedded room/play area. A series of green and white cubes provide seating and storage. The diagonally striped carpet makes the space seem twice as big as it really is. Clever painting completes the grand illusion.

Rented bedrooms and bedsitters can be very dreary. The problem is how to cheer them up without investing too much that you'd only have to leave behind. Many landlords will not allow their tenants to repaint, knock nails into walls or change curtain fittings. Don't worry – there are ways around such difficulties.

● Cover dirty or worn patches on carpet with a large rug or rugs. You can choose from a great variety in every colour and at every price level and you simply take them with you when you move on elsewhere.

● Brighten up windows either by looping the old curtains back with cord tiebacks and adding rattan or matchsticks blinds which you attach to two hooks screwed into the window frames (fill in the holes afterwards and paint over them). Or take the curtains down altogether and just have blinds – it's neater. Put the curtains back before you leave. A third idea is to take the curtains down and put up ready-made curtains of your own, using the same fixings. Or tie the old curtains back and hang some plant baskets in front of the window to introduce some living colour and freshness to the room. Windows can get very cold so select plants like ivies, that can withstand sudden changes of temperature.

Stand big plants in generous cane baskets wherever there is a space or corner. Stick an uplight behind them for instant night-time glamour. You can take both plants and lights away with you. Add a large basket full of plants to a space beside a chair; mass plants on the window sill, and droop ivy and similar trailing plants with tendrils from bookshelves or the top of ugly wardrobes.

Hide a really ugly piece of furniture with a screen. Either buy one or just buy a frame and fill it with shirred fabric of your choice.

● Dress up the bed with pretty or stunning bedlinen – it's so well designed these days that it deserves to be shown off and can provide a real bright spot in an otherwise dull room. Pile a mass of cushions in colourful heaps on bed or chairs.

Paper butterflies, a toning rug and bedspread, and healthy plants make a charming room, left, for little cost; while, right, a cheerful miscellany of fabrics and rugs has instant impact.

When less is more

To live successfully in a one-roomed flat or bed-sitting room you have to be disciplined. It stands to reason then, that if the room itself looks disciplined and is well-planned from the start you are more than half-way to making a success of what, for many people, is an unnaturally restricted environment. In a small space less is definitely more. Once you have decided on your furnishing necessities (supposing you have the choice) and come to terms with the space you have to play with, you should think up a limited colour scheme – confining yourself to only one or two colours will greatly help to both smarten and expand the space available. In this case I chose grey and white cheered with touches of red. To give as much living space as possible I decided to invest in a wallful of units to include wardrobe, bar, cupboards, drawers and a bed, which neatly folds away behind wardrobe-type doors during the day). I fitted white shutters to the window, added a chrome-and-glass desk which can also double as a dining table and fixed an outsize hook on the side of the wardrobe to take more see-through plia folding chairs. Two armchairs covered in grey flannel completed the furniture together with a wicker storage basket with separate lid to turn it into a side table. Grey flannel walls, grey and white sheets, grey quilt bedcover, and the red in the carpet, cushions and rug, and obligatory plant and floor lamp finish it off.

BRIGHT IDEAS FOR RENTED BED-SITS

● Disguise walls that cannot be re-painted or papered. Fix stretch wire all around the perimeter of the room just below the ceiling or better still, if you are frightened of leaving any marks from fixings, buy those ex-tendable rods which will just click into place. Hem some wall length fabric at top and bottom – use inexpensive cotton, or butter muslin – thread it on to the pole or wire and either let it hang to the floor or catch it again on to similar rods or wires just above the skirting boards.

● Make your own colourful back-drops by hanging those long rolls of coloured paper that photographers use. You can get them from photo-graphic supply stores. All you have to do is run them through the extendable rods mentioned above and let them drop to the floor. Result: instant wall colour change at the flick of a wrist.

● If disguise is out of the question, try distraction instead; some in-ventive colourful feature that costs little but will immediately attract notice, divert attention from other-unsightly bits of the room and also be a delight in itself. Kites, for example, like the paper dragonflies in the picture in the top left hand corner of the opposite page, will instantly provide a centre of focus. Their bright colours can be picked up in piles of cushions.

What's on screen

Screens disguise eyesores, increase the feeling of space by adding perspective, are marvellous for dumping things behind or for concealing a rack of clothes, and are generally decorative in their own right. Either make one yourself, if you are handy, and paint it, lacquer it, decorate it, stencil it, cover it with fabric or simply fill in a hinged screen with shirred fabric. An alternative is to stretch translucent textured paper or net onto a hinged frame for an oriental look. If you can't make one, find a second-hand one and re-paint or re-cover it.

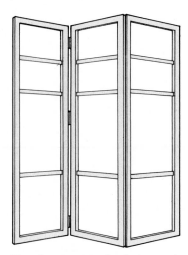

Translucent paper looks oriental

Attach gathered fabric to a hinged frame

Hinged louvered doors make a screen

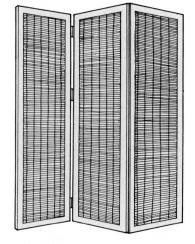

Glue split bamboo to a second-hand screen

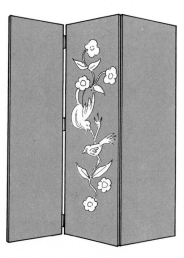

Repaint, stencil or decorate an old one

Top left: Stunning printed cushions and paper butterflies allied to pink and lavender blue immediately add character to a simple room.

Top right: Green and white checks and a mini-print make a pretty fresh little room enhanced by green paint and plants.

Right: Colourful ceramic birds and flowers surround a small Victorian fireplace and grate to give it a good deal of extra charm.

Far right: Colourful inexpensive curtains, bedspread and rug give personality and warmth to a spartan white-washed room.

I was going to say the bathroom has come a long way from the uncomfortable cold space it often was. But in fact Egyptian bathrooms, Roman bathrooms, ancient Greek bathrooms were immensely sumptuous affairs with good plumbing and a great deal of luxury. That there was a gap of so many centuries before we really began again to treat the bathroom as the healing, cleansing, refreshing place it should be is almost incomprehensible, but there it is. Once again we are taking enormous interest in the room as a room to enjoy and not just a place to house those indispensable items, the bath, washbasin, shower and WC.

Bathrooms need some deep thought of course, especially if you have the opportunity of planning one from scratch. Young childless couples, elderly couples, families with babies or teenage children, those with spare, Spartan inclinations and those who love comfort and glamour all have their differing needs. But basically the problem can always be defined and isolated by your answers to the following three questions: How much money have you to spend? How much space have you got to play with? Do you want a luxurious bathroom or a practical, hygienic splashing place?

Practical bathrooms that come in from the cold

If you live in a modern house or block you will generally have efficient new plumbing even if the actual bathroom or rooms are given very little space, and nondescript space at that. If your bathroom is one of these and has a shower over the bath you might think of tiling it all over. Although it will be more expensive initially than painting or wallpapering you won't need any more maintenance for years to come. Forget about tiles being cold and clinical; these days the repertoire of beautiful colours and patterns is enormous and you can always soften any hard lines with large fluffy towels in luxurious shades, with interesting window treatment and a stunning carpet. If you do want to save money

Boldly striped cotton is used to form a decorative canopy over the bath area in an interesting bath-exercise room, left. The same fabric is neatly pinned back by the shower. Stripes again, right, are used to good effect to give character to a wood-lined room.

by using mostly white or cream tiles you can insert a border of patterned tiles to run underneath the ceiling, down corners and around the bath. This will inject colour, relieve the monotony and take away any arctic feeling.

If you live in an older house or block you might trade elderly fittings and antiquated plumbing for more space. Although changing the plumbing around is a major expense – if indeed it is possible at all, you can at least change the fixtures for contemporary versions which will work a whole lot better.

For example, you might think of looking for water-saving WCs or showers which will conserve your hot water supply. If changing the fixtures seems impossibly expensive (and don't forget – you can often find second-hand baths, basins and WCs in good condition for half the price because they have been thrown out in favour of later models or different colours) think of changing the taps and shower fittings: this comparatively minor change will instantly give a more stylish look.

New baths for old

If the plumbing works well but the fixtures are jaded, chipped and stained do not automatically think of throwing them out. Baths, basins and even WCs can be renovated and resurfaced by professional firms (listed in trade directory). Or

Far left: Border tiles are used to create a panelled effect in this elegant, restrained bathroom. The polished wood bath panel looks good against the mole grey carpet.

Above: A tiled partition wall divides lavatory and shower stalls in a neat blue and white room. Floor tiles have been used to form a defining border below the ceiling.

Left: A bath has been cleverly inserted here into what might have seemed an impossible space. Mirrored walls and cleverly designed storage make the most of the remaining area.

Styles for tiles

Plain white tiles are usually the least expensive type to buy. Make them look more distinguished by laying them on the diagonal, colouring the grouting with added pigment, adding border tiles to the leading edges or just below the top run, or making a checker board effect.

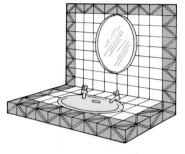

Use border tiles, or ordinary decorative tiles, for a decorative edge

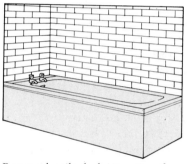

Rectangular tiles look interesting if you lay them like stepped bricks

Lay square tiles diagonally and they will make the area seem much bigger

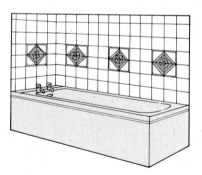

Cheer up an expanse of plain tiles by dropping in the odd decorative block

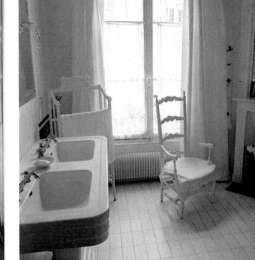

Far left: A completely mirrored wall gives a light and airy feeling to the bathroom of this tree-surrounded country house. The polished wood cabinet for the basin and the arched mirror superimposed on the larger slab of mirror look especially effective with the stripped and polished floors, the beamed ceiling and the abundance of plants which serve to link inside with outdoors.

Top: Tawny faux marble cornices, skirting boards and splashback blend well with the fabric used for the elaborate festoon blinds. They also provide an effective counterpoint to the art- and photograph-covered walls.

Bottom centre: The border on the graceful long white curtains is carefully matched to the tiled bath surround in another elegant and personal room. An old painted chair, wood framed prints and nice old hanging shelves are handsome additions.

Bottom left: Modern lozenge-shaped floor tiles look good with the classic twin basins on their sturdy porcelain pedestals, the long curtains, the fireplace with its flowers and mirrored overmantel and the painted, towel rail and chair. Although mostly white the room looks very far from clinical.

you can resurface them yourself with epoxy paint if you are handy and, above all, patient. You must first take the time to prime the original surface to ensure a really smooth slick finish when you spray or roll on the epoxy, and you must wait the requisite time (usually a day or two) before you can safely use the fixtures again.

Outsides of old baths can also be painted with a design, or stencilled to look especially interesting. It's often a good idea to have the sides built-out a little and panelled with wood so that they look both generous and contained, especially if the sides are deep enough to sit on or to put things on. Old basins too, with their sad underpinnings of twisted pipes, can also be enclosed with wood to gain respectability and provide storage space at the same time.

Plants in the bathroom

An instant facelift for an existing bathroom can be achieved by the addition of plants. Their vivid colours, plant pots and often sculptural leaf shapes can all be used to great effect for little outlay in either time or money. Moreover, the warm humid conditions are often particularly suited to certain varieties of houseplant. But remember that they need good light as well as bright direct, though not necessarily hot, sunshine. Few plants thrive in deep shade or gloomy places. Air con-

ditioning will de-hydrate them and if your bathroom has fan ventilation this will cause draughts which plants dislike. Some require constant humidity and should be stood in plastic trays on a layer of constantly moist gravel or pebbles. If your bathroom is kept at a low temperature – around 5°C (40°F) – your choice of plants will be more limited, but *aspidistra, hedera canariensis, rhoicissus rhomboidea, sansevieria* and *ficus pumila* are sturdy enough and should be satisfactory. Bowls of mixed plants are a good choice for a small bathroom; they take up little room but give a variety of colours and textures. Don't overwater these and remember that containers without drainage holes should have a thin layer of gravel in the bottom. Some plants, like ferns, hate drying out and some, like aspidistras, dislike dust and need to be sponged occasionally. All plants should be turned to let the light get at all sides. To avoid disappointment, only buy plants that come with good instruction labels telling you how to care for them and what sort of temperatures and conditions they prefer.

Not only but also

If it's big enough there's no reason why it shouldn't serve not one but two useful purposes. You could consider making a bathroom-dressing room, a bathroom-exercise room, a bathroom-study, or you

might add a bathroom end to a bedroom, simply screening it off. If there is room for clothes storage, either in the room, or in a lobby just outside, you can add a hanging cupboard or closet, bring in a chest of drawers, install a long mirror or a mirrored wall, insert a comfortable chair, maybe a rocking chair or an old wicker chair, put down a carpet and you will have an interesting dressing-room – especially if there is space to add a dressing-table and chair or stool as well.

Keep-fit enthusiasts might find the bathroom a good place for an exercise bicycle, a rowing or jogging machine or whatever. If all this gym equipment doesn't look particularly beautiful it could be screened off with a screen, a hardboard partition or tall plants.

One of the most interesting bathrooms I have seen was a bathroom-study with the desk and chair partitioned off from the bath area by a towel rail acting as a low divider. Shower, WC and bidet each had their separate alcoves on another wall, and the far wall was covered in floor to ceiling bookshelves with a comfortable leather chair, reading light and small side table in front of them. Even if there is no space, or more to the point, no funds to provide all this, you might still be able to provide a work table, chair, telephone and wall-fixed work light in an odd corner, or alcove.

A rose-tinted bathroom

The bathroom is, or should be, a warm, cheering place, so a nice rosy glow, as in this scheme, could be very suitable. Walls are covered in a highly practical old rose vinyl which looks like corduroy, all the wood is mahogany stained, and the rose is picked up again in the carpet, which is rather darker than the walls. The bath is placed along one side wall, slightly raised on a platform and enclosed by two sets of shelves, one of which forms a separate recess for the WC. The wall behind the bath and shower is covered in rosy brown and pinky beige checked tiles which amalgamate the other colours in the room, and towels are shades of light and dark rose. More towelling is used for the cushions on the cane chair and as a shower curtain lined with plastic and hung on a polyurethane-coated mahogany pole. Other details: brass bracket lamps either side of the mahogany mirror, the mahogany clock on the end wall, the collection of healthy plant life, and, on the bath step, the generous basket full of sponges and soaps.

porthole-like
wall lamp

red/white/blue
umbrella (for showers?)

all trims
painted blue

Everything has a highly nautical air in this blue, white and red bathroom. Well, perhaps not everything. There are two amusing exceptions: the Shakespearean bust to the side of the basin, and the baskets more pretty than shipshape. For the rest, the room is very spruce with its blue outlined trim, red door, pipes, lavatory cistern and radiator, nautical towels and its porthole-like wall lamps. The bath is set interestingly at an angle and divided from the red-edged deckchair end of the room by the radiator. Note the life-belt.

no window
treatment but
life belt as
decoration

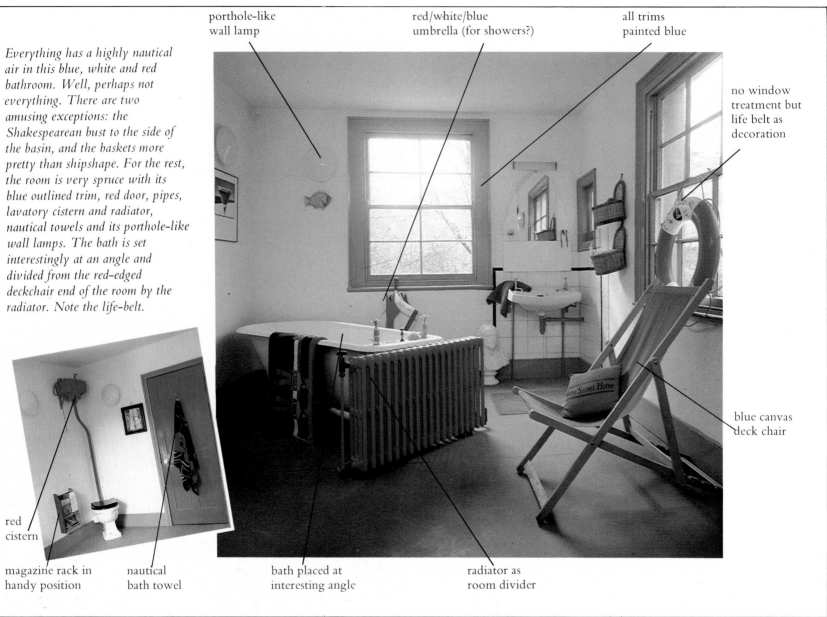

blue canvas
deck chair

red
cistern

magazine rack in
handy position

nautical
bath towel

bath placed at
interesting angle

radiator as
room divider

Incidentally, the new cordless telephones are perfect for calls in the bath and if this is where you have your inspirations, a battery operated recorder could be at hand.

Comfort on a shoe-string

My own feeling is that bathrooms should be comfortable, civilized, rather decorative, and certainly personal rooms – an ambition one can achieve more cheaply in this area than in any other part of the house bar the cloakroom or powder room. For with care, one can usually manage to achieve an air of luxury for a comparatively small sum, using expensive fabrics, tiles, and wall coverings that can be afforded here because they are only needed in small quantities. Conversely, you can of course spend a fortune, and still end up with an unsatisfactory and uninteresting space, since bathroom personality depends much more on colour, mood and accessories than on actual equipment.

Problem areas

If you inherit an existing, boring little space with fixtures that cannot be moved or changed it isn't the end of the world but it does call for positive action. There are literally dozens of cosmetic changes you can put into effect without spending a fortune. Here are some instant face-lifts that will give any jaded bathroom a new lease of life.

● *Large expanse of tiles in a colour you hate* Paint over them with eggshell yacht paint followed by a coat of gloss paint for a lustre finish, or with epoxy paint. Give the walls a good clean first to get rid of all lingering traces of dirt and grease and then apply a coat of primer. Alternatively you can tile over the top, either with new tiles or with sheets of ceramic tiles or mosaic with flexible grouting already in place.

● *Shabby walls* Put up plastic-laminated surfaces which can go over almost anything. Or panel the walls with wood, or cover them with tongue-and-groove wood coated with polyurethane.

● *Unexciting walls* Cover them with a wallpaper which might be far too expensive to use in a larger space; or with fabric or felt above a run of tiles, or at least a run of transparent perspex or plexiglass or glass around bath or basin.

● *Uninteresting room* Paint the walls a dark rich colour and use them as a background for prints, drawings,

Right: Black-painted tiles, black carpet, smart black and white border, and black and white towels make a very dramatic space out of this small room. Gilt-edged prints and the red brass-trimmed blind add elegance; the plaster cast feet and the plaster bust of Nefertiti provide the right extra balance of white as well as humour.

THE BATHROOM IS A ROOM TOO

Left This small bathroom was made to look extremely pretty at very low cost by painting every surface white, curtaining off the bath with white lace-curtains and adding plenty of plants.

Above: Fabric curtains are used to conceal the storage area below the set-in basin in this graceful bathroom.

Right: Mirrored ceiling, side walls and bath panel give interesting illusions of grandeur to this actually very small room with its burnt-poker-wood finish.

photographs, collections of this and that, memorabilia, whatever you fancy, in order to add lots of interest and impact.

● *Dull dark room* Paint everything white from top to bottom, white tile or sheet vinyl the floor (white carpet would get dirty too quickly but you could put down easily washable cotton rug) and mass every available space, including the window embrasure with plants. This will make even the dreariest little room look fresh and airy.

● *Cramped space* Don't forget the power of mirror. Panels will open the most confined space even if you only mirror the back of a door.

● *Ugly windows* Pretty them up by covering horrible obscured glass with a permanent blind in flimsy fabric or put up café curtains—in two tiers if necessary, one for privacy, the other to let in the light.

● *Tired old towels* Jazz up old white towels you cannot afford to change by adding a border of contrasting colour, say pink, or green, or use both colours, all round the edges. This will also restore the chic to towels with frayed and dog-eared edges from too much washing.

● *Unsightly plumbing* Hide unsightly pipes below washbasins with a cupboard or closet which will also be useful for extra storage. If you cannot build such a cupboard, shirr fabric on a rod, gathering tape, or stretch wire and fix it around the basin. Hide other pipes by boxing them in if you can. The resulting ledge can be used to stand things on. Alternatively you can make a feature of them with bright paint.

● *Bath that's seen better days* Cover bath panels with carpet to match the one on the floor. Or tile them. Or paste them with vinyl paper or wallpaper protected with at least two coats of polyurethane (test the paper first to make sure that it does not run. If it does, you could try covering it with a protective film of clear plastic). If there is not a bath panel to cover, you can always make one by boxing in the bath with plywood, leaving a deep shelf all around which can either be tiled or covered in plastic laminate and used to hold objects, bottles and jars. This will also give the effect of having a luxurious built-in bath.

● An extension of the above idea is to frame both bath and basin with mahogany panelling to give a semblance of Edwardian opulence. Get a carpenter to fit neatly panelled wood sides (or do it yourself, fixing the real thing if you can afford it or staining the wood mahogany and polishing and lacquering it if you cannot).

● *No atmosphere* Create it. Add a small set of shelves for books (best covered in clear plastic in case of splashes) or objects, or collectables,

Left: Mahogany-stained wood was used to make the vanity unit and panelled doors and bath panel as well as to frame the mirror. Doors are filled in with alternate panes of mirror and obscured glass for reflection, extra light and privacy. Rose and cream mini-print wallpaper was given a coat of clear eggshell varnish for extra toughness and goes well with the blue and off-white Brussels Weave Carpet.

Above: You can, of course, recess basins into almost any sort of unit, including a pine chest of drawers as here. The drawers provide instant storage facilities.

or small plants or an interesting mixture. Bring in a cane table and a cane or wicker chair and spray them white or leave them natural, and cover a cushion or two with towelling to match the towels you are using. Have a small table drawn up near the WC with piles of magazines. Keep a bottle of mineral water near the bath together with a glass.

● *Lacks luxury* Pile a glass dish or brandy balloon with pretty soaps in an appropriate colour. Decant bath salts and oils into beautiful glass jars or carafes. Let it *smell* expensive – perfume, oil, talc. Even if you just manage to buy some really luxurious deep-pile towels in a beautiful colour or a few china or brightly coloured plastic accessories, you'll be amazed at the difference such small touches make.

Family bathrooms can still look good

With the best will in the world it is almost impossible to keep a family bathroom looking tidy and elegant. All too often, towels are dropped in a soggy heap, bath toys are left lying around or stranded like sea flotsam in dry baths. Shelves are filled with a litter of ancient toothbrushes and half-finished tubes of toothpaste. Shower curtains have gone mouldy at the bottom and bath edges are thick with mostly-finished bottles, jars and tubes. It is a sorry sight. What can you do about it?

How to foresee – and forestall – eyesores

Abandon all thoughts of using wallpaper or wallcovering in a room used by a multi-generational family; it will get splashed and start to look forlorn in no time. Much better to tile all over or use plastic laminate or even paint such an area.

Fit in as much storage as possible; children and teenagers are invariably untidy. See that there are places where bath toys can be stashed away when not in use, where cleaning things can be within easy reach but out of sight and where unsightly clobber can be hidden away.

Fit a glass partition rather than a shower curtain which can get shabby or at least disarranged all too quickly.

Have separate and distinctive tooth mugs, face flannels and towels in co-ordinated colours for each member of the family – they won't look a mess, or get muddled.

Try to double the amount of heated towel rail space or have a long radiator with a rod going all the length of one wall. This way towels will at least dry quickly.

Put up hooks everywhere: on the back of the door; by the bath (for face cloths); by the basin or basins for hand towels.

Try to have double medicine cabinets, or a whole wall of cabinets like a kitchen. In fact, kitchen cabinets might be a very good idea if you have the wall space. Some manufacturers make cabinets that will go in any room.

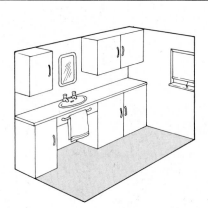

Kitchen units maximise storage space

Perspex screens are tidier than curtains and don't rot

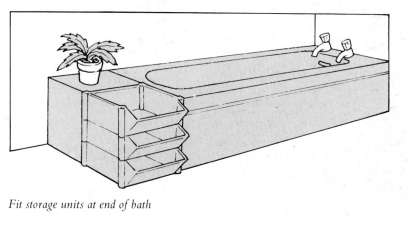

Fit storage units at end of bath

325

Whether you are re-modelling a bathroom or starting one from scratch there is a huge range of equipment available from the most luxurious to the purely functional.

Don't just go out and buy a bath without arming yourself first with as much information as possible. These days there are oval baths, octagonal baths, corner baths, curved baths, copies of old baths on claw feet . . . you name it . . . the choice is tremendous, not to say bewildering. So do your homework, research the market and shop around to see what's available. Remember too, that for those who are able to afford the money and the space there are now steam baths, whirlpool massage baths, shower massagers, hot tubs, jacuzzis and baths big enough for two, any of which will add to the sybaritic possibilities of your bathroom.

Basically, the more conventional baths are 1700 mm (5 ft 6 in) long by 700 mm (2 ft 3 in) wide but you can buy many other shapes including lengths from 1475 mm (4 ft 11 in) to 1800 mm (5 ft 11 in–6 ft) in widths from 700 mm (2 ft 3 in) to 8000 mm (2 ft 7$\frac{1}{2}$ in). If space is very tight you can find corner baths or sitting rather than lying baths which measure about 1375 mm (4 ft 7 in) by 710 mm (2 ft 4 in) or 120 mm (4 ft) square; or extra deep baths or shower trays which can be used for both showering and bathing. It's important to take note of these measurements when planning a space where every inch may count. Before ordering decide exactly where you want your fixtures placed; this will determine the size of the space you have to play with and the type of bath you can fit in and still have room to manoeuvre.

More often than not, baths are fitted against a wall, tight up to a corner, but if both your space and your plumbing runs and waste pipes can stand it, you could plan for one to be centred along a wall or even in the middle of the floor. If you centre a bath in the middle of a long wall you can build a floor to ceiling partition at either end which will make it look built-in. This will allow a WC and bidet to be placed one side and a

Garden trellis on walls, left, is a sure-fire way to open up a room and get an instant summer look. Here it is used with a geranium print and marbled bath. In the room on the right walls covered with mirror panels make all the difference to this cramped space.

basin on the other. Add shower curtains from a track inset into the ceiling or fixed tight up to the ceiling, tie them back on either side and you immediately get a gracious look. You can achieve much the same look of a curtained-off aperture if the bath is fitted tight into one end of a small room.

Whatever the size and colour of the bath you choose, do try to get one with handles either side. You might be limber enough now but a bath is a long-term investment and you have to reckon on growing older and stiffer with the years. Also, handles are essential for small children and elderly people or people with back problems.

Baths: which material?

Acrylics The cheapest and most common material for baths is acrylic, which can be moulded easily to incorporate seats, soap dishes, bathrests and so on. Water stays hotter in acrylic than metal baths and they are fairly resistant to knocks and chips although they can get scratches. The best way to cope with these when they happen is to make sure the surface is quite dry and to rub the scratch down with metal polish and rinse off thoroughly.

Acrylics burn easily, so avoid cigarettes in the bathroom. They can also be damaged by nail varnish, varnish remover and some dry cleaning liquids.

It is important to install them exactly to manufacturer's instructions or they may not remain rigid.

Glass fibre These baths are made of layers of glass fibre bonded together with polyester resin. They are much stronger and more rigid than the acrylic variety and come in a range of colours, including metallic and pearlized finishes.

Pressed steel These are fairly light and rigid baths with a smooth vitreous enamel coating and good wearing properties.

Cast iron This is the traditional and the classic, but expensive material for baths and still holds its own mainly because it has an excellent, fairly stain-proof and easy-to-clean finish or porcelain enamel fused onto the metal at very high temperature.

Bath surrounds

Unless your bath is in the centre of the room you absolutely must have a splash-resistant surround which is usually of tiles or plastic laminate. Some people choose to fix a sheet of clear or milky perspex, plexiglass or lucite over paint or wallpaper, but I have found that water can all too easily seep down the back. Whatever the material, the surround should be at least 500 mm (1 ft 8 in) high and come up to the ceiling if your bath

The green and white bathroom above has been made to look much more interesting with its centrally-placed bath flanked by bamboo chests, useful and decorative. The bath itself has also been made to look more substantial with its green tiled surround, which is quite wide enough to make a convenient seating ledge. Slim Venetian blinds at the window add to the neat architectural look as well as giving a pleasant filtered light.

Planning your space

When planning a new bathroom from scratch, you will have to consider whether to include the WC in the main area or install it separately elsewhere. There are points in favour of each arrangement and you should decide which is best suited to your needs.

Bear in mind that each fitting must have enough surrounding space for it to be used comfortably and easily. Allow 1100 × 700 mm (43 × 28 in) alongside baths and 2200 mm (86 in) headroom. Wash-basins should have 200 mm (8 in) on either side and 700 mm (28 in) in front. WCs and bidets need 200 mm (8 in) either side and 600 mm (24 in) in front. For showers enclosed on three sides allow 900 × 700 mm (35 × 28 in) alongside and for enclosed showers 900 × 400 mm (35 × 16 in).

It may seem as if you need an enormous amount of space to accommodate these appliances. But as only one or two of them are likely to be used at the same time, the activity areas can easily overlap.

These layouts for different-shaped bathrooms indicate the *optimum* space around fittings

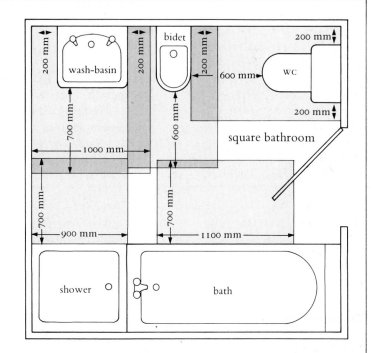

square bathroom

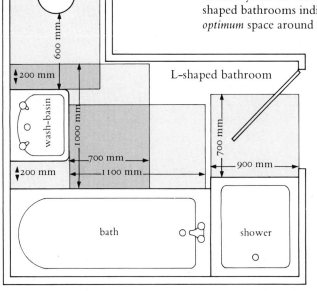

L-shaped bathroom

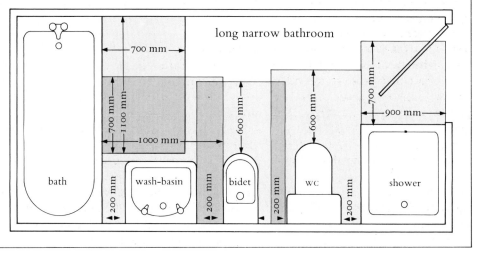

long narrow bathroom

includes a shower. The gap between bath and wall – and there will always be a slight one – should be well sealed with a ceramic tile trim, a sealing strip or a non-hardening mastic, otherwise water can trickle down and cause rot.

If you want to square off the bath you can either box it in yourself, using boarding, which you can stain, tile, carpet or laminate. If you are not handy, get a carpenter to do it, or buy ready-made front and back panels. Remember to have one re-movable panel so that pipes and waste can be inspected and repaired.

Save with a shower
Quite apart from being refreshing and invigorating, showers save water because they use about one-fifth of the amount needed for a bath. And they save energy, espe-cially if you connect them to an instantaneous electric water heater which heats only the water actually used. Another advantage to a shower is that since it only takes up about one square metre (1 sq yd) of floor space it can be installed in all sorts of odd corners providing that there is a water supply and drainage near to hand and the sort of instan-taneous electric heater which takes water from the mains. Otherwise the water cistern should be at least a metre (3 ft) higher than the shower head or there will not be enough pressure for the shower to work.

If you have a shower built in you will need a mixer valve and spray attachment with a thermostatic valve and a ceramic, steel or acrylic shower tray. Install them in a corner or an alcove, cover the walls with tiles and fit a glass door, glass screens or curtains according to what is appropriate to the position and your pocket. It is also very easy to put in a shower above a bath tub, again screening it off with a glass panel if that is possible with your bath design, or shower curtains. Or you can buy special shower cubicles which range tremendously in price.

Basins
You can buy free-standing pedestal wash basins, wall hung basins, basins partially supported by front legs, or basins that can be sunk into counter tops or vanity units. Like baths, they are available in porcelain enamel over cast iron, acrylic, glass fibre or in the popular vitreous china. They can be oval, round, square, rec-tangular, corner-shaped or shell-shaped and range in size from the small 300 mm (1 ft) widths to around 750 mm (2 ft 6 in) or more. They come in the same range of colours as baths or they can be decorated in some way. It is often sensible in a family bathroom to have two basins set side by side in a counter or vanity unit which can be made from plywood or other wood, then either stained, polished and

lacquered or covered with tiles or with plastic laminate. More lavish counters can be made from marble or slate or stone.

Choose your taps and hardware at the same time as you order your bath. Again, there is an enormous choice to suit all tastes and pockets. The cheapest place to have taps installed is at the end of the bath and above the waste. You can choose between a pop-up waste (controlled by a lever or handle of some sort) or a plug and chain. But you can, of course, buy baths without tap holes to use with wall-mounted taps, or with separate function taps – the spout at one place, the controls in another.

WCs
WCs are generally wall-hung or the pedestal variety and can come as low as 230 mm (9 in) from the ground or considerably higher and in a variety of widths. Wooden seats are popular again, or you can buy seats to match the lavatory colour.

Bidets
If there is room, bidets should de-finitely be included in bathroom fixtures. They should be as near the WC as possible and, generally take up about 350 mm (1 ft 2 in). Again, you can buy them in the same colours as baths and WCs or in white. If possible, choose one with a built-in douche spray.

Top right: Bath, WC and washbasin look very much built-in in this substantial terracotta tiled and mirrored room. Note how an access door has been concealed under the basin.

Far right: Shiny black paint and a white vinyl floor give a literally smart-as-paint background to the interestingly moulded bases of bidet and basin. Their curved lines are echoed by the Michelin man perched above the rounded laundry basket, by the round mirror and light, rounded plastic storage unit and the picture of lights above the bath whose colours look more intense against the black and white scheme.

Centre: The deep round porthole mirror above the basin here has convex glass to expand the view. The thoughtfully-placed shower is ideal for hair washing.

Near right: Tongue-and-groove wood lines all the walls in a nice uncluttered room. The smooth surfaces conceal generous storage space as well as providing support for a shower stall. The cork-and-vinyl floor looks equally handsome as well as being warmly practical.

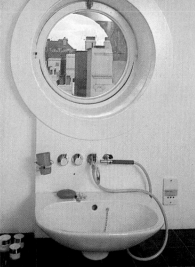

Working out

This is a bathroom for the fitness freak: half bathroom and half home gym. Functional, with its exercise bicycle and wooden bars, yet sumptuous with those same parallel bars stretched across panels of mirror, and undeniably comfortable – the deep tiled bath and shower recess, the twin basins, pine-boarded walls and sense of space make sure of that. If fitness is important to you, and you have the space and the money, such a room would be a wonderfully luxurious asset to your well-being. Colours are kept to a minimum and confined to towels and the odd accessory like the plants in their terracotta pots. Lights are spaced all around the room just under the ceiling and the room is further defined by the neat walkway of white tiles all around the wood block floor. There is a panel of mirror by the bath and, together with the others behind the parallel bars, it provides lots of extra light and sparkle as well as reflection. The whole area with its clean lines, its whiteness and its wood, has an air of wholesomeness and health totally in keeping with its twin functions. And it manages to be a remarkably handsome room as well as thoroughly practical.

Cupboards either side of the bath form a good-looking alcove in a peachy rag-rubbed room. The splashback has been lined with thin marble tiles and these combined with the specially cut arched mirrors over the bath and basin (seen in detail in inset) give a rather Thirties charm. This impression is reinforced by the shape of the wall light, the woven basket chair and festoon blinds. More useful storage space has been incorporated under the washbasin so that clutter is hidden.

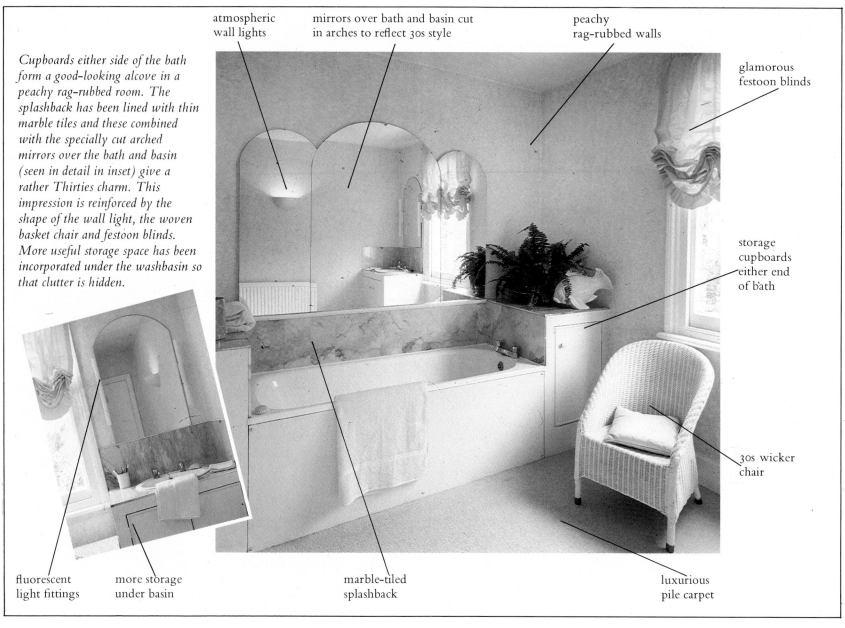

atmospheric
wall lights

mirrors over bath and basin cut
in arches to reflect 30s style

peachy
rag-rubbed walls

glamorous
festoon blinds

storage
cupboards
either end
of bath

30s wicker
chair

fluorescent
light fittings

more storage
under basin

marble-tiled
splashback

luxurious
pile carpet

Neat and tidy storage

Bathroom storage is generally a real headache – especially storage in a family bathroom. Medicines and medicaments, powders, soaps, toothpastes and toothbrushes, razors, personal electric equipment, shampoos, bath oils and salts, tissues, cotton wool, cleaning accessories, bath toys, toilet paper, towels and wash cloths all have to be accommodated somewhere, somehow, since they cannot all crowd the counter top and bath surrounds. The conventional medicine cabinet is hardly big enough and yet there seems no other space in the standard box-shaped bathroom. Where do you go from here? For a start, if you have not already got a built-in basin or vanity unit what about that area? It's a good space for a cupboard which will also cover any previously exposed pipes. You can always curtain-off a basin and hide a multitude of stuff behind the fabric; it isn't very difficult to fix a skirt to the basin itself. You should allow double the measurement of the basin in material. Turn over the fabric at the top and run a gathering string through it. Cut some 'gripper tape' to length and glue it to the bottom of the basin. Sew exactly the same amount of tape onto the gathered skirt and clamp it to the tape on the basin. Or buy some stretch wire, run it through the top hem of the fabric and attach it to the wall either side of the basin.

Tiny bathrooms

When space is at a premium such desperate situations call for desperate measures. See if there's room for shelves or cupboards in all sorts of unexpected places. What about above the window or door or toilet or at the end of the bath? You only need narrow shelves on the whole so the smallest alcove could be used up and given a door too, if you like. If space is very tight think about fixing shelves on the backs of cupboard doors.

Corners are always possible either for an old corner cupboard, for floor-standing étagères in wood or cane, or for narrow cabinets set at right angles. Always fix a couple of hooks to the back of doors and have plenty of towel hanging space: at least one heated towel rail if there is room or a long pole over a radiator as well as hooks or rods near the basin for hand towels.

Right: Eighteen inches or so of wall depth have been stolen here to turn into a handsome mirror-lined alcove surrounded by a whole range of top and bottom storage cupboards. The other side of the room (reflected in the mirror) has been similarly treated with open shelves for towels as well as a full length linen cupboard. The neutral print wallpaper on walls, doors and ceiling harmonizes with the cream-painted dado and bath panel and is offset by the towels.

335

In this elegant room, top left, shiny pink and white paint, and a white tiled floor are set off by glamorous-looking wall sconces, neat white shutters and, best of all, a chaise-longue. The tiny cloakroom, above, is prettied up with a heart-printed vinyl wallpaper and scalloped pelmets for blind and light. The deliberately uneven wood panelling used to line the walls, bottom left, has a pleasantly rustic effect as well as being practical. Green carpet and towels make a good contrast.

Floor and wall treatments

Obviously in a bathroom you have to think first and foremost about surfaces that are resistant to steam and water. Ceramic tiles are clearly very practical for both surfaces: with a high glaze for walls and a skid-proof surface for floors. But you could also use quarry tiles, earthenware tiles like Mexican and Portuguese, and glass bricks or mosaic. I once saw a small bathroom entirely covered – ceiling as well – with mirrored mosaic tiles and the effect was stupendous.

Cheapest of course, is paint which is best in an eggshell or high gloss finish. Wallpaper looks good, but must be applied above a good run of tiles around bath and basin, or else covered in clear perspex or plexiglass or glass around the damp prone areas. Vinyl and vinyl-coated papers are practical. Another good idea is to paint over any bathroom wallpaper with a clear eggshell glaze like polyurethane. This will preserve the paper for a far longer time.

You can apply laminated panels of hardboard with a baked-on plastic coating in a large range of colours and finishes including a realistic marble. A wide choice of panels is available which can be applied straight to the walls as well as to counter tops, and then there is the real McCoy – marble itself – which now comes in 12 mm ($\frac{1}{2}$ in) thick veneers for floors, walls and other surfaces. If you don't mind the occasional steaming-up, mirror-lined walls look very glamorous and will also expand the space. Wood panelling or tongue-and-groove boarding with a coating of polyurethane looks warm and interesting, as do nice wood floors.

Vinyl-coated cork is a popular choice for floors and so are vinyl tiles, resilient sheet flooring and the new fibre carpets and carpet tiles which are more practical than wool in a wettish environment. Cotton tumble twist comes in a large range of colours and lifts up easily to shake, clean or put in the washing machine. If areas around bath and basin are very well protected and occupants are reasonably docile in the bath and shower, wallcoverings like felt or wool, cotton, hessian or burlap can look warm and smart. So too could lengths of towelling stapled to the wall with the cut edges covered in a braid or beading.

Right: Glossy rubber stud flooring, which is fairly inexpensive, lines the floor and walls of this platformed sunken bath area. Other walls are laid with plain white tiles and the lower half of the room is carpeted. This contrast of textures, colour and finish is heightened by the slim white slats of the blinds, (which also serve to separate off the bath area from the rest of the room), the plants, baskets and figured lights.

Window dressing

Bathroom windows are generally small so can lend themselves to quite lavish treatments that might not be affordable on larger windows. If you are not overlooked you can use tied-back curtains or festoon or Austrian blinds in muslins, laces, light cottons or broderie Anglaise for a particularly pretty look. If you want to disguise ugly bobbly bathroom glass which you cannot replace, try using café curtains, or translucent net, or white holland blinds. Matchstick or bamboo blinds can look good, so can Venetian and wooden louvred blinds. Shutters, especially the adjustable variety look very fresh and rural. Again, if you are not overlooked, you could try leaving the windows bare and just standing plants or a row of glasses on the window sill. Another idea is to fill the window frame with narrow glass shelves on which you can mass

Left: Sweeping lace curtains frame both bath and window in a nicely unusual country bathroom with its old-fashioned claw-foot bath and china jardinière. Bountiful plants provide almost as much green inside as can be seen through the window. The romantic window treatment has the added effect of literally framing the thoroughly pleasing view outside. The gentle feel is helped by the Edwardian light shade and warm cork floor tiles which blend with the wood.

plants or coloured glasses or blue and white jugs or what you will.

If you do have a big or biggish window, treat it like a living room or bedroom and use a blind with tied-back dress curtains. And if you do have an otherwise slickly-tiled bathroom, the way you dress the window will make all the difference between an impersonal space and an interesting one.

Choosing accessories

There can hardly have been a better time than now for buying pretty bathroom accessories, so there's no excuse for not being able to titivate the plainest little space even if – as in rented accommodation – you cannot change equipment, walls or layout. Take towels – they can be worth their weight in gold. Look for the sort of colours that will make an unfortunate shade in equipment or tiles look much more integrated, or buy towels to match or contrast with a predominant colour on walls or floor.

Buy matching porcelain tooth-mugs and soap dishes, tissue holders and cotton wool jars, cache pots and paper holders. To update a very plain cold space look for those large primary coloured hooks and rails, mugs and holders, or find accessories in pine or brass or clear perspex or plexiglass. These sort of vivid, eye-catching accents can make a dull bathroom seem lively and friendly.

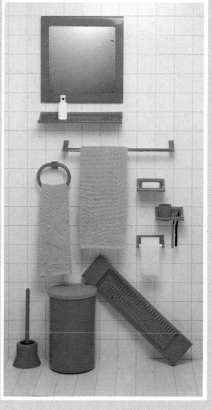

Colourful accents in the bathroom. Red is the current hot favourite for bathroom accessories; see the basin, top left, and the assembled collection, above. More red in many-ranged towel rail, bottom left, with its tap-printed towels and red-edged head rest. And red again, bottom right, between the slightly sci-fi lights. Yellow, top right, cheers up an all-white bathroom.

EQUIPMENT AND LAYOUT

Heat and light

Warmth is important

One of the most important ingredients for comfort in a bathroom is getting it the right temperature: cosily warm in winter and cool enough in summer. If you can possibly have a heated towel rail you should do so, but beware of one that is run solely off the central heating system. This is fine when the heating is chugging away, but what about when it is not? To make sure of warm dry towels at all times try to get one run off the hot water system itself, or have a supplementary electrically-heated rail, or just an electric rack. If your hot water tank is placed in a cupboard in the bathroom this will also help to keep the room warm as well as making an extra drying place for towels. If you do not have a radiator of some sort, extra warmth can be provided by a wall-mounted fan or an infra red heater mounted above the door or above the mirror.

If you have to have an electric water heater in the bathroom it is worth knowing that you can buy it in the form of a cabinet with a mirror front which looks neater than the old tank-shaped variety.

Avoiding condensation

Condensation which can be such a nuisance in bathrooms, steaming up the mirrors and windows, can usually be avoided to a great extent by steady warmth and adequate ventilation. If you do not want to open a window in winter, you can install an extractor fan on the wall or in the window itself. And the sort of extractor fan that is obligatory in all internal bathrooms will automatically keep a room free from fogging. Mirrors with built-in lights which warm the glass will also eliminate condensation.

The best sort of lighting

If your room is very small, the best solution for general light is a central ceiling fixture, for this, like the kitchen, or utility room, is the one place in the home where you don't particularly want mood lighting.

Lights either side of the mirror or all around as for theatrical dressing rooms are best for make-up and shaving, or just above if only for shaving. You can buy mirrors with strips of bulbs all around or at the top, or you can buy separate strips to superimpose yourself.

If you have a large room, perhaps a bath-dressing-room, bath-study, you can conceal strip lights behind curtains or window treatments of whatever sort, recess spots into the ceiling (if you have a reasonable recess) to pin-point particular objects or plants, or install waterproof downlights and control the whole system with a dimmer switch for glamour. If you have an internal

bathroom, you might also consider some of the luminous ceilings available, or try putting light up behind a floating false ceiling – which is also a good idea for any small dark bathroom, with or without windows.

Safety factors

It is absolutely essential that you do not use any electric appliances near water. Radiant electric fires must be placed high up on a wall and switched on or off by a cord; lights should preferably be controlled either by switches outside the room or by further cords. Wet hands that come into contact with switches result in tragedy. Never iron in the bathroom and don't dry your hair with an electric hair dryer there or use any other electric appliance.

Above: Warm, wood-lined walls and bath panel never suffer from the effects of condensation. Two ideas worth noting are the bath set at an angle from the corner and the continuous towel rail running all round the room above the radiator so that lots of towels can dry at once. Matting on the floor allied to the wood adds to the sporty training-room feeling.

Right: Recessed ceiling lights and theatrical bulbs above the dressing-table (reflected in mirror) give excellent overall and make-up/shaving light in this attractive and spacious looking bathroom. Heat is provided by a wall-mounted radiator which also serves to warm the towels.

GLOSSARY

Accent colours Contrast colours used to spice up room schemes.

Accent lighting Decorative lighting which is used to draw attention to chosen objects, and to create moods and highlights.

Acoustic tiles Ceiling tiles which absorb sound. They are made from pre-finished slotted insulation board or from polystyrene or fibreglass.

Architrave A moulded or decorated band, usually of wood, framing a panel or an opening such as a door or window.

Armoire A tall, heavy storage cabinet with two doors.

Austrian blind Ruched blind which is also known in England as a festoon blind or pull-up curtain. It has rows of vertical shirring and can be raised and lowered by cords threaded through rings which are attached to the back of the shade at regular intervals.

Baffle A narrow screen or partition placed so as to hinder or control the passage of light or sound.

Balance Arrangement of objects around an imaginary central point to achieve a pleasing result. Balance can either be symmetrical (where objects on one side of the 'point' are mirrored by those on the other) or asymmetrical (in which case they are not).

Baldachin A draped canopy like those used over pulpits and altars.

Balloon blind A shade or blind with deep inverted pleats which create a billowing balloon-like effect. Like an Austrian blind, it is pulled up and down by cords threaded through rings attached to the back.

Banquette A long, upholstered seat, frequently built-in along one side of a wall.

Bas relief A sculpture or carving whose design projects a little from the surface.

Batiste A fine fabric like cambric.

Bevel A process whereby surface edges are cut to a slant eg. on glass, wood or worktops.

Buckram A stiffened linen cloth.

Burlap A coarse sacking material also known as hessian.

Butcher block A continuous run of thick wood, or a wooden block with legs, such as butchers use in butchers' shops. Both are useful for chopping and preparing meat and vegetables.

Butt-edged Two edges which meet but do not overlap.

Café curtain A short curtain hung from a rod going half way across a window, as in French cafés. It is sometimes hung in a double tier, and is a useful treatment for windows that open inwards or face the street.

Cane Slender, flexible, woody stems, split into narrow strands and woven into chair backs, seats etc.

Cantilever A projection from the wall.

Casement window A window that opens on vertical hinges.

Ceramic tiles Fired clay tiles with a very hard-wearing glaze. There is a large range of colours, patterns, textures and sizes.

Chintz A cotton printed in several colours on a light or white background.

Console table A small rectangular table, longer than it is wide, usually set against the wall.

Cornice A decorative, horizontal band of plaster, metal or wood used to surmount a wall or to conceal curtain fixtures.

Corona A crown-shaped projection above the bed from which drapery is hung.

Cosmetic decoration Purely decorative as opposed to structural alteration, which improves appearance.

Coving A curved moulding connecting the ceiling and wall.

Dado The lower part of a wall where separated by a rail known as the dado rail.

Deck paint A strong, dense paint used on boats. Tough and hard-wearing.

Dhurrie (Also durry; dhurry) an Indian cotton carpet.

Dimmer switch A knob (or rheostat) or panel that is used to control brightness of light. It saves energy as well as giving a flexible range of lighting levels.

Dormer A vertical window set into a sloping roof.

Downlights Fittings which can be mounted on, or recessed into a ceiling to cast pools of light onto the surface below. Most are fitted with an anti-glare device, and the direction of light can be controlled with a baffle (q.v.).

Dragging A paint technique which gives a subtle effect to a large wall surface. Paint is applied in a thin wash in vertical strokes with an almost dry brush in a contrasting shade to the base coat.

Eclectic To choose from various sources; not following any one system, but selecting from and using the best components of several styles.

Ephemera A collection of objects, not necessarily valuable, such as old posters and theatre programmes.

Ergonomics The study of work patterns and conditions, in order to achieve maximum efficiency.

Etagère A set of open shelves supported by columns or corner posts.

Faux bois An artificial wood effect on a surface achieved by painting or graining.

Festoon blind Similar to an Austrian blind but rather more elaborate.

Framing projector A light fitting whose beam can be shaped accurately so that a given surface, such as a painting or table top, can be lit exactly.

Galley kitchen Small and narrow, like the kitchen in a ship or boat.

Grasscloth A fine soft fabric made from the fibres of the inner bark of an eastern plant.

Grouting Filling up or finishing joints between tiles with a thin mortar.

Half-tester A small canopy or tester (q.v.) over a bed, covering only the pillow end.

Hessian A coarsely woven cloth.

Hi-tech Contemporary style adapting industrial components for domestic use.

Hob The surface on which pans are heated. It is sometimes separate from the oven, and set into a worktop.

Hourglass curtains Curtain stretched between two rods (fixed at top and bottom of the window) and tied in the middle to show a triangle of window pane at either side.

Lacquer A durable varnish which is applied in layers and then polished to a mirror-like finish.

Laminate A very strong, multilayered material.

Louvres A series of overlapping slats which filter or exclude light while allowing ventilation. Fitted in frames they are used for doors, screens and shutters.

Making good To repair as new.

Marbling A paint technique which gives a veined, marble-like appearance to a surface.

Matchstick (or pinoleum) blind A blind made with fine wooden sticks which are stitched together.

Matt finish A completely flat finish, with no shine or lustre.

Mexican tiles Ceramic tiles whose colours and patterns are inspired by traditional Mexican designs.

Moiré The wavy design on silk, or other fabrics, which gives a watered appearance.

Monochromatic scheme Design using one basic colour as its theme, in a variety of shades and textures.

Ottoman A long, low upholstered seat with no back; alternatively, a circular seat divided into four, with a central back.

Parquet A form of wooden flooring where the grain of one square runs at right angles to that in the adjacent square.

Parson's table A square or rectangular table with wide, straight legs.

Pedestal table A table supported by a central, single post.

Pediment A triangular part crowning the top of a building or piece of furniture.

Pegboard A board perforated with holes from which pegs can be attached. Can be used in the kitchen for hanging utensils.

Pelmet or valance A decorative, horizontal band of fabric usually attached to the top of the window frame or just above, to hide rods and provide added interest.

Pendant lighting Lights which hang from the ceiling.

Peninsular unit A unit that juts out into a room and can be approached from three sides.

Pharmacy lamp A lamp with a flexible neck, suitable for both reading and conversation.

Pillow shams Covers for pillows to match bed covering, when pillows are propped on top of the bed.

Pin-board A board, usually made from cork, on which papers or pictures can be attached with pins.

Pinhole lighting A spotlight fitting through which a narrow beam of light is projected, the beam spreading widely downwards.

Quarry tiles Fired tiles made from unrefined clays which provide very durable flooring. They are impervious to grease and liquids, and come in a range of muted colours.

Ragging on Print effect using paint-soaked rag. See page 58.

Rag-rolling Decorative technique of creating patterns with a rag on wet painted surface. See page 58.

Refectory table A long narrow dining table.

Reveal (embrasure) The sides of a window between the frame and the outer surface of the wall.

Rise-and-fall fitting Used to adjust the height of a pendant lamp, especially when it hangs over a dining table.

Roman blind One that draws up into neat horizontal folds by means of cords threaded through rings attached at regular intervals to the back of the fabric. You can either use rings alone, or on heavier fabrics, you can attach light battens to keep the folds crisp. Ideal for a smooth, tailored effect.

Sash curtains A piece of fabric or curtain panel with rod pockets at top and bottom. Ordinary brass or tension rods are then threaded through and mounted at top and bottom of the window to stretch the curtain between them.

Shoji screen A traditional Japanese screen, made with translucent paper.

Sponge stippling Speckled effect for wall painting, using a paint-soaked sponge. See page 59.

Spotlight A light that directs a strong, controlled beam on to an object or place. Can be fixed or adjustable.

Stencil A decorative design which is cut out of waxed paper or acetate, then reproduced onto a surface below with paint using a stencil brush or spray can.

Stucco Smooth plaster decoration for interior walls.

Swag and tail Elaborate pelmet-like treatment for curtains. The fabric is caught near each end so that the middle part, or swag, falls in a graceful curve, and the ends hang in tails.

Swirling Method of painting top coat allowing undercoat to show through. See page 59.

Tester A wood or fabric canopy, covering the whole bed area.

Tongue and groove panelling Wood panelling, where the boards are interlocked along the edges.

Track lighting A length of track along which a number of light fittings can be positioned and supplied by one electri-cal outlet. It can be mounted on any wall or ceiling surface, or recessed.

Trompe l'oeil Anything which deceives the eye.

Truckle bed A low bed on castors or wheels for rolling under another bed.

Uplights Accent lights which are placed on the floor. They can be concealed behind sofas and plants to give dramatic effects.

Valance See pelmet. Also term for the decorative length of fabric covering the sides of a bed.

Vanity unit A storage unit which encloses a wash-basin.

Veneer The thin layer of wood laminated on top of another.

Venetian blind A pull-up blind made with horizontal slats that can be adjusted to let in or exclude light.

Wallwashers Angled downlights (q.v.) which bathe the wall surface in light.

Wash stand A piece of furniture which holds the basin.

Webbing A strong, woven band of tape usually used for upholstery.

Wicker (wicker-work) Slender, pliant twigs, plaited or woven to make chairs or baskets.

Window terms See page 71.

Work triangle An imaginary line linking the three main work areas around the sink, cooker and fridge.

Yacht paint A tough, hard-wearing paint, also known as deck paint, used on boats or to paint wood floors.

Yacht varnish A boat varnish which gives a very resilient finish.

INDEX

ACKNOWLEDGMENTS

The author and publisher would particularly like to thank the following people and companies for their contribution to this book

for their invaluable help and research work: Virginia Bredin, Pamela Gough

for technical advice: David Champion, Colour Counsellors Ltd, Deborah Evans, Shirley Heron, Aileen Levene

for allowing us to photograph their homes: Glynn & Carrie Boyd Harte, Felicity Bozanquet, Virginia Bredin, Fenella Brown, Anthony Collett, Francesca Fennymore, Charlotte Fraser, Oliver Gallagher, Catherine & Jonathan Giles, Felicity Green, Jenny Hall, Jane & Caradoc King, Dieter Klein, Sandy Kom Losy, Ann Lloyd, Daniel & Lily Morocco, Richard Reynolds, Judith & Graeme Robertson, Jancis Robinson, Chris Serle & Anna Southall

for supplying merchandise for the room sets: Judy Afia's Carpet Shop, Amtico, Bernstein & Banleys Ltd, Brintons Carpets Ltd, Coexistence Ltd, Cole & Son Ltd, Colour Counsellors Ltd, The Conran Shop, Coriam Ltd, Davis Douglas Carpets, Descamps Ltd, Designers Guild, Domus Decor Ltd, Mary Fox Linton Ltd, Gaskell Broadloom Carpets Ltd, Liberty, Marks & Spencer plc, Osborne & Little Ltd, Paris Ceramics, Rye Tiles, Sekers Fabrics Ltd, Helen Sheane Wallcoverings Ltd, Tidmarsh & Son Ltd, Tile Mart, Tintawn Ltd, Tissunique Ltd, Waldorf Carpets, World's End Tiles & Flooring Ltd

for supplying props for special photography: Albany Linens, And So To Bed, Le Cadeau, Covent Garden General Stores, Debenhams plc, Descamps Ltd, Designers Guild, Mary Fox Linton, Heals, ICTC, Lunn Antiques, Marks & Spencer plc, The Neal Street Shops Ltd, The Poster Shop, Sanderson Ltd, Tissunique, Today Interiors, Warner, Christopher Wray's Lighting Emporium

Special photography

Jon Bouchier 11 centre and right, 27 below right, 36 above left and right, 46 below left, 48, 56 below right, 59 below right, 72 above right, 79 below left, 84 above right and below right, 91 below right, 124 (designer Jonathan Giles), 129, 137 left and right (designer Judith Robertson), 140 (designer Dieter Klein), 160 below left, 166 left and right (designer Lenny), 180, 188, 190, 200 (designer Jonathan Giles), 202 left and right, 228, 232 above left, 236 above left (designer Dieter Klein), 238 left, 243,

245 centre and above right (designer Lenny), 254 centre and above right (designer Anthony Collett), 263, 267 (designer Anthony Collett), 278, 311 above left and below right (designer Fenella Brown), 314 (designer Dieter Klein), 316 above right, 320 left and right, 321 (designer Lenny), 334 left and right (designer Jane King), 341.

Jessica Strang 6, 17 below left, 23 above left, 31 left, 37 left, 51 above left, 70 below, 71, 72 below right, 79 above, 81, 87 below left, 90 below right, 136 above right, 201 centre, 211 left and right (designer Boyd Harte), 220, 232 above right, 236 below left, 250, 251 right, 335.

The publishers would like to thank the following organizations and individuals for their kind permission to reproduce the photographs in this book: Acme Wardrobes 285 right; Allmilmö Kitchens 145 right, 165, 169 right, 192; Alno Kitchens 160 below centre, 167 above left and right and below left; B & Q DIY Supercentres 141; Berger Paints Ltd 26 left, 58 above right and below right, 59 above right; Jon Bouchier/EWA 47 below centre and right, 75 right, 136 below right, 222, 242 above right, 322 right, 331 below left; Michael Boys/Susan Griggs Agency Ltd 27 above right, 39 below right, 41 below right, 46 above left, 49 right, 50 below right, 62, 89 above right, 95 above left and right, 108 below left, 161 above left, 209 above, 214 left, 217 right, 253 right, 255 below, 259, 262 above, 264 right, 270, 291 right, 297 below right, 304, 315 below, 181; Camera Press 45 above left, 55 above left, 57, 95 below, 103, 160 above right, 168, 184 left, 197 right, 227, 233, 283 below centre, 292 left and right, 297 above left, 298, 302 left, 311 above left, 313 right, 315 above, 339 above right; Steve Colby/EWA 56 above right, 160 above left, 204; Cover Plus Paints 4, 125, 331 right; Crayonne 339 above left and centre; David Cripps/EWA 76 above right, 256 below centre; David Crockett/EWA 70 above centre, 87 above left, 232 below left, 238 above right, 293 above right, 305 right; Crown Paints Ltd 91 above left; Crown Wallcoverings 283 above centre; Michael Datoli 42, 269, 277; Designers Guild 60, 78, 271 above right, 283 below left, 288, 294; Dulux Paints 51 above centre, 206 above centre; Michael Dunne 8, 13, 18, 26 above right, 27 below left, 28, 31 right, 34 left, 38, 55 above right, 94, 109, 116, 121, 122 left, 136 above left, 138 above right, 142, 143 above left, 147 left, 149, 159, 177 right, 184 right, 191

right, 193 right, 196, 199 above right, 210 above right, 203 right, 208 right, 214 right, 216, 221, 224, 225 below centre, 230, 239, 240, 244 left, 252, 255 above centre, 256 above centre and above right, 257 left, 264 left, 268 above, 279 above left and right, 290 above, 297 above right, 306, 322 left, 324 left, 326, 336 above centre, 338; Du Pont (UK) Ltd 138 below, 187 right; Elizabeth Eaton; Richard Einzig 76 left, 96, 99 above right; Leonardo Ferrante 24 left, 30 above right, 295 below right; © Peter M Fine 1983 45 below left, 68 above centre, 199 above left, 336 below left; Formica Ltd 284; Christine Hanscombe 2, 20, 51 above right, 88, 130, 242 above, 268 centre left; Nelson Hargreaves 178, 225 above centre left; Clive Helm/EWA 29 right, 47 above left, 110, 122 right, 138 centre, 143 below left (designer Behrens), 153 right, 179 centre (designer Johnny Grey), 241 right (designer Jennifer Granville Dixon), 261, 327 right (designer Campbell Pelner); Graham Henderson/EWA 30 below right, 255 above right, 305 left (designer Nicolas Hills); Frank Herholdt 64, 107 right, 176; Frank Herholdt/EWA 87 above right, 206 below centre; John Hill 139, 207; International Wool Secretariat 55 below left; Ann Kelley/EWA 41 below left; Ken Kirkwood 45 below centre, 72 above left, 133 right, 209 below, 249 left and right; Mary Fox Linton 17 right, 55 below centre, 295 above right; David Lloyd/EWA 46 below right; Neil Lorimer/EWA 113, 132, 155, 198 above left, 206 above right, 297 below left; Maison Marie Claire/G Mahe/M Mahe 104, 108 above left; Maison Marie Claire/von Schaewen 89 below right; William Mason 90 above right, 133 left; Mayfair Mix & Match Collection 279 below left; Chris Mead 231 right, 262 below, 274; Moben Kitchens 118, 144, 185 below right; Nairn Floors 186; National Magazine Company Ltd 68 above left; Michael Nicholson/EWA 1 (designer Maggi Heany), 9 right, 23 above right, 39 above right, 41 above right and below centre, 45 above centre and above left, 50 above right, 65 right, 70 above right, 76 below right, 77, 102, 106, 108 above right, 111 right, 114 above left, 115, 128 above right (designer Piero di Monzi), 195 (designer Leila Corbett), 205 right (designer Maggi Heany), 223 above left (designer Walker/Wright), 223 above right and below left (designer Virginia Bates), 244 right (designer Chester Jones), 251 left (designer Maggi Heany), 256 below right, 257 right, 268 below centre

(designer Coombe Manor Fabric), 271 below (designer Dorit Egli), 272 above (designer Tricia Guild), 275 right, 311 below right (designer Elizabeth Dickson), 323, 331 above left (designer Twyfords), 336 above left, 339 below right (designer Campbell Zogolovitch); Osborne & Little 225 above left; Max Pike's Bathroom Shop & Whirlpool Centre 339 below left; Spike Powell/EWA 21 right, 41 above left, 69; Malcolm Robertson 131 right, 185 above left; Jessica Strang 41 above centre (designer Barry Weaver), 46 above centre and 84 below centre (designer Lorraine Johnson), 99 below left (designer Valentina Boffa), 105 right (designer Liz Farrow), 119 right, 136 below left (designer Ken Grange), 153 below left (designer Antonia Graham), 170 above right, 179 right, 203 left, 208 left, 215, 271 above left, 290 below, 293 (designer Britta Morse), 302 above right and below right (designer J Strang), 307 right (designer Antonia Graham), 316 below centre (designer Ann Mollo), 324 right, 331 below centre, 340 (designer Lou & Mei-Lou Klein); Tim Street-Porter/EWA 34 above right, 40, 47 below left, 51 below left and centre, 74, 86, 114 right, 128 below (designer Joan Sachs), 156, 185 below left, 225 below right, 226 left, 272 below (designer Rosen), 273 (designer Frank Gehry), 296; Sunway Blinds Ltd 187 left, 199 below right, 328; Syndication International 80, 99 above right and above centre, 283 above left, 337; Friedhelm Thomas/EWA 112, 193 left; Transworld Feature Syndicate 17 above left, 23 below centre, 37 above right (Elyse Lewin), 97 right, 107 left (Elyse Lewin), 108 above right and centre, 153 above left, 154, 157 right, 198 below (Elyse Lewin), 225 below left, 291 left, 312, 316 left (Elyse Lewin), 316 below right; Jerry Tubby/EWA 120 (designer Igor Cicin Sain), 164 above, 185 above right (designer Isabel Czarska); Elizabeth Whiting Associates 198 above right; Winchmore Kitchens 158, 161 below left, 164 below left and centre, 167 below right, 170 below right; Wrighton Kitchens 170 left, 171, 174, 175, 218; Zenith Windows Ltd 299.

Black and white line illustrations by Stuart Perry. Colour illustrations by Ross Wardle/Tudor Art Studios and other black and white illustrations by Greg Jones/Tudor Art Studios.